Visual Learning, Thinking, and Communication

**ACADEMIC PRESS
SERIES IN COGNITION AND PERCEPTION**

SERIES EDITORS:
**Edward C. Carterette
Morton P. Friedman**
*Department of Psychology
University of California, Los Angeles
Los Angeles, California*

Visual Learning, Thinking, and Communication

Edited by

BIKKAR S. RANDHAWA

Department of Educational Psychology
University of Saskatchewan
Saskatoon, Saskatchewan, Canada

WILLIAM E. COFFMAN

Division of Educational Psychology,
Measurement, and Statistics
University of Iowa
Iowa City, Iowa

ACADEMIC PRESS   New York   San Francisco   London   1978
A Subsidiary of Harcourt Brace Jovanovich, Publishers

ACADEMIC PRESS, INC.
111 Fifth Avenue, New York, New York 10003

United Kingdom Edition published by
ACADEMIC PRESS, INC. (LONDON) LTD.
24/28 Oval Road, London NW1 7DX

Library of Congress Cataloging in Publication Data

Conference on Visual Learning, Thinking, and
     Communication, University of Iowa, 1976.
     Visual learning, thinking, and communication.

     (Cognition and perception)
     "Cosponsored by the Iowa Measurement Research
Foundation and the Visual Scholars' Program."
     Includes bibliographies.
     1. Cognition——Congresses. 2. Interpersonal
communication——Congresses. 3. Visual perception
——Congresses. 4. Visualization——Congresses.
I. Randhawa, Bikkar S. II. Coffman, William
Eugene, Date   III. Iowa Measurement Research
Foundation. IV. Iowa. University. Visual
Scholars' Program. V. Title. VI. Series.
BF311.C62 1976   153.4'2   77–11220
ISBN 0–12–579450–9

Contents

Contents

List of Contributors

Numbers in parentheses indicate the pages on which the authors' contributions begin.

SAMUEL L. BECKER (39), Department of Speech and Dramatic Art, University of Iowa, Iowa City, Iowa

GORDON W. HEWES (1), Department of Anthropology, University of Colorado, Boulder, Colorado

ROBERT H. McKIM (61), Mechanical Engineering Department, Stanford University, Stanford, California

THOMAS MULHOLLAND (77), Veterans Administration Hospital, 200 Springs Road, Bedford, Massachusetts

ALLAN PAIVIO (113), Department of Psychology, University of Western Ontario, London, Ontario, Canada

BIKKAR S. RANDHAWA (191), Department of Educational Psychology, University of Saskatchewan, Saskatoon, Saskatchewan, Canada

ROGER N. SHEPARD (133), Department of Psychology, Stanford University, Stanford, California

IRVING E. SIGEL (93), Educational Testing Service, Princeton, New Jersey

ROGER WILLIAMS WESCOTT (21), Anthropology Department, Drew University, Madison, New Jersey

Preface

Historically, emphasis on verbal processes has been influential in determining directions of research on cognitive processes and of educational practice. However, stress on verbal determinism has led to extreme interpretations of data and to misdirected theoretical formulations. One such formulation proposed that "the human permanent memory system is mainly a verbal memory system. Incoming information, if it is to be effectively stored, is recorded as verbal information before it is placed in the storage system [Travers, 1970, p. 148]." This would suggest that visual information, too, must be in verbal form as it is recorded in the memory system. Such a view is no longer consistent with the evidence.

The current revolution in visual communication and the pervasiveness of visuals in learning, thinking, and communication have begun to change research directions and theoretical formulations and to influence educational practices. Still, many theoretical ambiguities exist and no coherent set of practical guidelines can be provided to educational practitioners.

In preparing the present volume, with these ideas in mind, each contributor was specifically charged to review his own work and that of colleagues in his particular area of interest as it related to the role of the visual and figural in learning, thinking, and communication; to make specific recommendations for future research and applications; and to suggest the nature of an interdisciplinary academic program of study and research in the area. We think each contributor did an excellent job in carrying out the charge and providing a genuinely interdisciplinary treatise.

In their respective chapters Gordon W. Hewes and Roger Williams Wescott survey evolutionary development of the visual system and its relationship with the other sensory systems. From this evolutionary perspective, they have shown the primacy of the visual system in learning, thinking, and communication. In particular, the influence of the visual in the structure and form of various languages is demonstrated in a thought-provoking manner.

Samuel L. Becker's chapter deals with problems in research in communication and offers a perspective in terms of a dynamic model of communication, the communication mosaic. He conceptualizes the communication mosaic as consisting of sources of information (message), information increments provided by the various sources of a message, elapsed time, and other related message sets, and supports the conceptualization by extensive citations of related interdisciplinary research.

A description of the Imaginarium, a physical environment and an educational program designed to assist participants in the rediscovery of the powers of their sensory imagination, is the focus of Robert H. McKim's chapter. After a very brief theoretical background to this development, the chapter details the physical facility (including a sketch), outlines the objectives and methods of the educational programs, and gives selected excerpts from four 1-hour programs designed to facilitate effective visual thinking.

Thomas Mulholland's contribution is a rationale and a method for an experimental study of visual attention using records of alpha suppression in the occipital EEG. This interesting strategy, though speculative, grows out of a solid research base. This proposal for the study of visual attention promises to provide answers to numerous yet unanswered questions related to visual communication.

In his chapter Irving E. Sigel discusses the development of pictorial comprehension from two basic premises: first, that the comprehension of the external world evolves through an active engagement and subsequent construction of the external into mental representation, and second, that the cognitive system functions as both a filter and a moderator of behavior. Sigel proposes that picture comprehension is analogous to reading the printed word and that the principal mechanism involved in each case is the process of transformation.

Allan Paivio's chapter is about the psychological study of visual knowledge as a theoretical and applied problem. The chapter first provides a theoretical and methodological orientation that stresses the relevance of verbal processes in research on visual knowledge. Then it examines research designed to explore the characteristics of visual knowledge. Finally, it summarizes studies on the exploitation of visual knowledge in such applied endeavors as learning, problem solving, and creativity.

Chapter 8 by Roger N. Shepard is concerned with the use of mental imagery in creative thinking. In the first section of the chapter he reviews the cases of a number of highly original and significant creations of the human mind and argues that these creations derived rather directly from nonverbal internal representations or images of spatial and visual character, and that they represent through externalization the corresponding subjective and private images. Shepard then considers attempts that some artists, scientists, and others have made to externalize their own mental images by means of drawing, painting, or related techniques. Throughout this chapter, applied and theoretical issues are interwoven.

In the concluding chapter of this volume, Bikkar S. Randhawa considers visual learning, thinking, and communication as an interrelated trinity, requiring a unified approach to research questions related to any of them. As an overview chapter, it considers the theoretical consistencies in the other chapters and ponders their potential for stimulating educational and instructional applications. It also outlines some emerging issues and suggests specific guidelines for research and practice.

The Iowa Measurement Research Foundation and the University of Iowa Visual Scholars' Program cosponsored a conference on the topics of this book, held October 1–2, 1976, and preceded by a planning conference held March 1–2, 1976 that enabled the contributors to share their ideas with one another and with the University of Iowa faculty and students associated with the Visual Scholars' Program. Out of this planning conference emerged a framework for a more effective integration of the final papers and guidelines for rewriting, reorganizing, and the metamorphosis from the conference presentations to the chapters of this book.

As is indicated in Randhawa's overview chapter, prepared following the conference, we believe the materials presented in this volume will motivate further discussion leading to productive theory building and research endeavors in a wide variety of settings. The volume should also be suitable for advanced graduate students in education, psychology, and communication sciences with interest in visual learning, thinking, and communication. In particular, those contemplating the establishment of interdisciplinary training and research programs will find this volume a valuable source of ideas.

ACKNOWLEDGMENTS

We are indeed grateful to many people who assisted us in the preparation of this book, and especially to Kay Byrd for her assistance in the planning and coordination of the Conference and to Jackie Shadle for her able handling of all the typing involved. We are thankful to the Iowa Measurement Research Foundation for financial support for the Invitational Conference and for the special costs of producing the color plates; and to the Eastman Kodak Company for the grant that has supported the establishment of the University of Iowa Visual Scholars' Program, which provided all the support for the March Planning Conference and which cosponsored the October Conference.

REFERENCE

Travers, R. M. W. *Man's information system.* Scranton, Pennsylvania: Chandler, 1970.

Visual Learning, Thinking, and Communication

1

Visual Learning, Thinking, and Communication in Human Biosocial Evolution

GORDON W. HEWES
University of Colorado
Boulder, Colorado

SENSORY EVOLUTION AND DIFFERENTIATION

The forest niches of our primate ancestors are a key to understanding why we remain primarily visual in our thinking, and why human language, although chiefly auditory and vocal, is still largely a system for encoding information presented to us in the visual channel. In the millions of years during which primates evolved as acrobatic tree-dwellers, visual control of their motor activity became very precise, and vision, and hearing, and touch took precedence in their sensory hierarchy over the sense of smell. Fortunately, the primates that returned to the ground retained the skills acquired in the tree tops (Campbell, 1966).

Responsiveness to light is, of course, a very widespread attribute of animal behavior, and eyes capable of using incoming light to detect significant conditions or happenings in the environment have evolved in several separate phyla. Perhaps the most remarkable convergent ocular evolution has occurred in the vertebrates and the cephalopod mollusks. The story of the evolution of vertebrate vision—including its intimate relation to the brain, (of which in fact the eyes can be regarded as a part)—has been traced in great detail, and we need not review that entire topic here.

1

Visual Learning, Thinking,
and Communication

H. Jerison (1973) has provided an excellent account of vertebrate brain evolution from the lampreys and sharks onward, stressing the increasing capacity of the brain to integrate sensory stimuli to form increasingly comprehensive models of the external world.

The reptilian ancestors of the mammals and birds have generally efficient diurnal vision, based on rods, sufficient for detecting movements of prey or predators. But perhaps somewhat like the visual system of the frog, their systems involve mostly retinal (i.e., peripheral) data processing. The birds, who were relatively late offshoots of dinosaurian reptiles, invaded the diurnal niches of the reptiles when most of the reptilian class died out at the end of the Mesozoic and went on to perfect their auditory capacities far beyond anything found in reptilians. Although the evidence is not yet absolutely conclusive, the early mammals followed a very different path, starting out mainly as nocturnal creatures for whom enhanced hearing and olfaction were the critical sensory channels. However, when various mammalian orders reentered the diurnal niches, their vision was highly encephalized, permitting longer storage of visual information and visual space constancy (Jerison, 1973).

Although the sense of smell has declined in importance in the primate order, the olfactory bulbs have not so much absolutely decreased in size as they have been overtaken by the parts of the brain concerned with the other senses. Even man, whose sense of smell seems rudimentary compared to that, say, of a dog, may be able to make more cross-modal linkages with the odors he does sense than many creatures for whom olfaction is the primary sense. However, some degree of olfactory recession is apparent in the higher primates, all of whom lack the *rhinarium*—the area of specialized snout skin, normally moist, which evidently helps to fix vagrant odors wafted to the noses of most mammals. Significantly, the prosimians (lemurs, galagos, and tarsiers) engage in scent marking of their territories in the manner of dogs and many other carnivores (Buettner-Janusch, 1966). In the monkeys and apes, the role of olfaction is diminished (though not extinguished) even with respect to sexual signaling, and visual signs—most strikingly in macaques, baboons, and the chimpanzee—take the place of olfactory cues. Man, acknowledging primate insufficiencies in this department, has learned to employ other species—notably dogs, where scent detection becomes important.

The primates have by no means lost *touch* with the world; the palmar and plantar surfaces, but especially the former, are especially rich in tactile end-organs, and are represented on the cortex in accordingly disproportionate fashion. The human skill in making and using hand-tools is very dependent on this tactile sensitivity, although visual and kinaesthetic feedback are also requisite.

Mammalian vision generally is monochromatic and nonstereoscopic, befitting an animal stock that spent a long time operating in darkness or at dusk. Color vision emerged chiefly or exclusively in the primates (including the prosimians) as something of adaptive value to daylight-active tree-dwellers and fruit or leaf eaters. For the early mammals, and for most mammals still, space and time are mainly integrated through smell and hearing—with audition accounting for the limited time-sequencing exhibited by most mammalian species. About 60–70 million years ago, however, with the rise of the primates, visual information about distant objects and events again became important. Jerison (1973) thinks that the re-emergence of distance sensing in mammals followed the neural paradigm already developed for auditory data processing. Peculiar difficulties attended the primate mastery of the arboreal visual world—notably the very contrasty or, as Jerison calls it, *mottled* character of the usual visual field, with spots of bright sky or sunlight, and varied shades of green (mostly) against the gloom of the undergrowth and ground below. This was rendered even more confusing by wind-produced movement of these patches of light and dark and the branch-shaking activity of the animals themselves as they climbed or leaped about.

Nocturnal mammals (including the nocturnal primates) have a preponderance of rod receptors, but diurnal primates also have masses of cones. The rods are efficient receivers of low-intensity light, but collectively deliver fuzzy images, whereas the cones operate at high light intensities and produce sharp pictures (Kaufman, 1974). Whereas dogs and cats, for example, have about 150,000 fibers in each optic nerve, man and diurnal primates possess a million or so in each optic nerve. Moreover, the retina has the famous macula lutea or yellow spot, almost wholly lacking in rods. In man, apes, and monkeys, the macula lutea has a specialized area, the fovea centralis, consisting of a single layer of cones, without blood vessels, which is the point of maximum visual acuity (Young, 1971).

In the lower vertebrates, there is a total decussation of the optic nerve fibers, such that each side of the brain receives only input from the contralateral eye; in many and higher primates, on the contrary, nearly 50% of the optic nerve fibers cross over in the optic chiasma, so that each hemisphere receives visual information from both eyes simultaneously. Moreover, the eyes have moved forward in the higher primates, affording considerable overlap of the two visual fields (this also occurs in the cats, to be sure), providing, thanks to the slight parallax difference, the convenient illusion that enables us to perceive visual depth beyond that afforded by the lenses alone. Almost all prosimians are binocular and presumably have stereoscopic vision, as do the higher primates, including man. Three-dimensional environmental models can be based on not only depth of focus and the perspective reduction of familiar objects at a distance, and on the parallax effect of moving the head and eyes with respect to the scene, but by other senses, such as hearing. Smell is a rather imprecise indicator of depth or distance, except when a breeze is blowing, or a scent trail can be traced by moving the body toward or along it. Aquatic mammals appear to form three-dimensional spatial maps by echo location, and bats do much the same in the twilight air. Man and the primates generally can determine the direction of sounds in a not too precise fashion, using the distance between the two ears, but the precision varies with the frequency—a fact that has been made use of with respect to general alarm calls.

The color vision of primates presumably is a clear reflection of arboreal life. The emergence of highly colorful flowering plants was under way when the early mammals began their separate evolutionary career, and it is no coincidence that birds, fruits, and flowers, along with many highly colorful insects, and even some amphibia and reptiles occur along with prosimians and monkeys in tropical forest environments. Among mammals, the primates include some of the most highly colorful animals, both in pelt coloration and skin pigmentation—the latter being especially prominent in connection with sexual attributes among Old World monkeys. Facial mask patterns are highly diversified among higher primates, often at the subspecific level.

The structure of the primate skull has been strongly affected by the emergence of primate visual capacities, with the forward positioning of the orbits, and the presence of either a complete orbital bony ring, or in the higher primates, a complete bony cup or socket, quite unlike the much less bonily protected eyes of other mammals. Many Old World monkeys and the apes (aside from the orang-utan), along with the early hominids, also have prominent bony browridges, to complete the fortress-like protection of the eyes. The browridge also serves as part of the complex system of facial expressions, a social-signaling device practically limited to the higher primates. Very little of the white (or sclera) of the eyeball can be seen in most nonhuman primates (and it is often not very white, for that matter), but man has come to exhibit a significant portion of the sclera on each side of the iris, permitting others to determine with considerable accuracy the direction of the glance. That human beings, at least, attend first to the eyes of others, has been abundantly shown in eye-movement experiments.

Of course, not all of the evolutionary changes were limited to the eyes or the optic nerve; the visual cortex became larger, and the nerve tracts from it to other parts of the cortex became increasingly prominent, especially into the temporal lobes. Most of the expansion of the visual cortex in primates has occurred in the midline area. Thus, it does not show up obviously in the usual illustrations of the cerebral hemisphere seen from the side.

Primates locate their food visually, checking it by close inspection and sniffing. The wide range of foods utilized by most primates at least partly reflects their ability to find trees or other vegetation containing edible fruit, nuts, leaves, shoots, and so on within forests usually of great species diversity, and to benefit from visual and auditory information about the feeding activity of other animals—especially birds.

Most primates are highly sociable or gregarious, and they tend to remain in fairly close visual and vocal contact with their fellow troupe members. Within most primate social groups, the behavior of others is constantly monitored by attending to body postures and movements, stares or glances, and, in the anthropoid apes, facial expression. There is solid evidence from several species of monkeys and from apes that individuals are recognized and dealt with on the basis of long-time familiarity with their idiosyncrasies. In particular, mothers and siblings are known as individuals on a life-long basis among macaques and baboons, and the great apes. This recognition is primarily visual. The self-concepts of anthropoid apes can be demonstrated in experiments with mirrors (apparently this is limited to apes and man, and does not extend to monkeys). Obviously, in all the behaviors related to social displays and individual (including self-) recognition, the decisive stimuli are visual rather than vocal or olfactory.

Of all the primates, man possesses the most intricate facial musculature, seemingly evolved mainly to enhance visual transmission of emotional states, intentions, and response to the actions of others (Young, 1971). However, some nonhuman primates have developed specialized areas of depigmentation (such as the eyelids, which seem to direct attention toward the eyes). Quite widely among the primates, but not in the hominids, hypertrophy of the canine teeth, notably in males, serves more as a visual threat display than for actual biting, although such teeth can inflict deep and dangerous wounds.

There are few predators for arboreal primates, chiefly certain tree snakes, and a few species of large raptorial birds (mainly dangerous for the very young primate). Effective predator avoidance thus becomes mainly a matter of accurate visual monitoring. Terrestrial primates encounter more problems from hunting canids and felids and from crocodiles as well as terrestrial snakes. In any case, vision remains the best defense.

While the visual system of primates became less and less preprogrammed, hearing seems to have remained more stimulus-bound or stereotyped, which the evolution of species-specific call-systems did not much modify. In this respect, many species of birds exhibit greater stimulus-freedom, including the ability to mimic or learn the songs of other species, including human speech.

Despite the limitations mentioned, the primates have, over the past 60 million years, developed (so far as we can tell) the most complete systems for comprehending the world around them of any animal group. This is true even if we leave man out of the picture. The higher primates, at least, appear to perceive the environment much as we do—resolvable into discrete objects capable of differential manipulation and possessing constant attributes. Nonprimates of a few mammalian lines approach this—dogs, for all their sensory-world differences from us, perhaps most of all (which is why they became such useful companions and community hangers-on). Thanks above all to the superior visual data-processing and integrating capacities of the higher primate ancestors of the hominids, the way was paved for the emergence of conceptual thinking. Much to nearly everyone's surprise, experiments within the last decade with present-day higher primates—chimpanzees, gorilla, and two orang-utans—have caused nearly all of this particular phylogenetic gap to disappear. Under suitable conditions, the great apes can, it seems, acquire rudimentary language behavior from us and exhibit the beginnings of conceptual thinking.

LANGUAGE, VISION, AND COMMUNICATION

With the recent revival of serious scientific interest in language origins, stimulated significantly by the chimpanzee language-acquisition studies, the possible visual rather than auditory origins of human language have received new consideration (Hewes, 1973). In the eighteenth and nineteenth centuries, many theories about language origins suggested that a phase of gestural (i.e., visual) signing preceded speech—or initially carried more of the burden of language communication than vocal noises (Hewes, 1973, 1975, 1977). The ape language studies certainly reinforce such ideas. In any event, it is easy to show that everyday language still tends to be accompanied by much gesture, and not only in a few overly dramatic individuals or societies. Whenever speech fails to communicate, as in encounters between speakers of unrelated languages, gesture takes over immediately and easily. The arguments about glottogenesis would take up too much of this presentation, but interested persons are invited to refer to the author's papers on this topic.

Among the many items connected with languages, personal names come to mind as frequent instances of the use of visible attributes (especially in nicknames). It is interesting to note that nicknames among the profoundly deaf are commonly of this sort.

It would be belaboring the obvious to explain at length how the advent of language contributed to the growth of human conceptual thinking. In connection with this presentation, it is perhaps enough to observe that a very large part of the labeling that characterizes all languages involves visible attributes. The vast majority of lexical items in any natural language can be most readily explicated pictorially (with the obvious exceptions of types of smells or sounds, in which their sources are not associated with a picturable object, such as rotten eggs, a bell, or a drum). Experimental and clinical work with young children, mental retardates, and victims of brain damage, all show that visual presentations can circumvent striking deficiencies in lexicon and syntax. To mention only one line of such work, the use of Blissymbolics, which enable severely handicapped children to "read," illustrates the power of semipictorial codes over the more arbitrary speech or alphabetic codes (Bliss, 1965; Blissymbolics Communication Foundation, 1977). There have been several successful applications of manual sign language—which is, in general, more iconic visually than speech or writing—to severely retarded children's training programs both in the United States and in the United Kingdom.

MENTAL MAPPING AND NAMES

Several investigators have been concerned in recent years with mental maps," both of actual geographic areas, and of more abstract phenomena (Downs & Stea, 1973; Gould & White, 1974). The ability to form dependable, accurate mental maps of terrain must have been important for the survival of ground-dwelling primates, and especially of the hominids who seem to have ranged over fairly wide areas when they began to hunt on a regular basis. Not all of the necessary information going into an effective mental map has to be visual: odors, sounds, feedback from body-orientation and locomotion, appreciation of the effects of time on the appearance of things (e.g., different times of the day), must be worked in as well. It is possible to study mental maps of individuals and the average mental maps of social or cultural groups. The growing literature on this topic is certainly germane to that of visual learning, thinking, and communication.

Until about 30 or 40 thousand years ago, man lived in mainly natural environments little affected by his own activities, save at campsites or where fires he started had gotten out of hand. Artifacts were few, clothing and ornament minimal or lacking altogether. Even so, there were some natural sources for imaginal creativity. There were striking cloud forms, brilliant sunsets, odd effects of light or shadow, along with unusually shaped rocks and other landforms capable of suggesting other objects. (I am reminded of a mountain pass in Colorado, presumably named "Rabbit Ears" by the Indians. It could well have been first so named 10,000 or more years ago by the earliest people to enter the area.) Other animals may occasionally respond to such environmental items, but lacking language, their experiences remain internalized. For a very long time the natural landscapes have been given names by human beings, especially on the basis of their visual attributes, and such names enter into the mental and also social mapping of the human world.

Metaphorical extensions of meaning, especially based on visual similarities or parallels, are found in the lexicons of all natural languages. Thus, among plant names we have such forms as larkspur, foxglove, lady slipper, bell-flower, snapdragon, crowfoot, goosefoot, milkweed, kidney bean, toadstool, and so on. Although these examples are from English, one could readily compile such lists in many other languages. Names of body parts applied to land forms and many other entities, are equally commonplace: foothills, mouth of a river, vein of ore, mouth of a bottle, tooth of a saw, wagon tongue, hair line, and so on. True, many of these have functional as well as formal resemblances.

Turning to more abstract terms, we find a great many examples in which easily visualized actions—ordinarily performed with the hands or other body parts—are employed to convey meanings on entirely different semantic levels: extract, understand, restrain, involve, implicate, overturn, and so forth. These often can also be appreciated kinaesthetically; the point is that most actions we can understand by thinking how our fingers, hands, arms, and legs might perform an action, are also simultaneously appreciable in the visual mode (but not in the acoustic or olfactory mode!). There are special terms that do arise from other sensory channel metaphors, such as disgust, putrid, airy, temperate, heated, and so on, but I am suggesting they are considerably less frequent. What is remarkable about all such extensions of meaning, however, is that language experimenters working with nonhuman primates report that just such metaphors have been independently created by apes.

Well back in Paleolithic times, man had become a very unusual kind of mammalian hunter or predator, relying only marginally on his sense of smell, unlike all of the other successful mammalian flesheaters. Carnivorous birds are mainly visually guided, although some carrion-eaters such as vultures do employ smell in addition to sight. Effective hunting in extensive ranges very much involves mental-mapping skill, and is probably greatly aided by language labeling of landmarks and ability to integrate time and distance information. One feature of hunting behavior in humans is apparently unique in the world of predators—the reading of tracks— hoofprints and the like not only to identify prey that may be out of sight, but to read the direction, speed, or gait of their movement often long after they have passed by (Murie, 1975; Ennion & Tinbergen, 1967). Skills of the same order are involved in the effective human exploitation of wild plant food resources, although they entail other aspects of the general mental-mapping process, such as knowledge of where particular plants are available for harvesting at a given time of year. The resemblance of these skills to that of reading written messages is to be stressed.

TOOLMAKING AND VISUAL PROCESSING

Toolmaking and tool-using, so characteristic of mankind, also depend heavily on high-level visual processing, from the search for and selection of suitable raw materials to often quite complex procedures for fashioning or employing implements. It has sometimes been claimed that spoken language is essential for even Lower Paleolithic toolmaking and tool-using, but this seems doubtful. Much practical knowledge of tool manufacture and use depends on watching others at work on or with tools or weapons. Such observation of tool-use has been reported for chimpanzees in the wild by Goodall (1971). Indeed, the opposite is probably the case: A verbal description of how to make or use a tool is unlikely to succeed if the learner cannot *visualize* the steps or techniques in the process. Even when we come to deal with nonspatial abstractions, understanding usually seems to come down to our being able to reduce or transform such abstractions into spatial–visual models (cf. Huggins & Entwisle, 1974). Mathematicians have told us that most of their productive thinking is essentially in the visual mode (Chernoff, 1976). That the congenitally blind often learn to handle high-level verbal abstractions as well as sighted individuals might only be because language has been created over vast numbers of generations by sighted people, and visual relationships are most easily translatable into kinaesthetic or tactile ones, with acoustic, thermal, olfactory, or gustatory dimensions usually subordinate.

VISUAL LITERACY

We may now turn to the question of "visual literacy," at least from an anthropological perspective. Since the majority of the world's peoples, in all cultures, possess normal vision and are exposed to the world of visible phenomena in which there are worldwide consistencies it might be argued that visual literacy is simply the general human condition. If so, the notion of visual literacy is superfluous, whereas literacy with respect to being able to read and write is significant. However, there is perhaps a sense in which we can think of visual literacy as at least a continuum from very restricted competence, even where vision is normal, to high competence. I think it reasonable to say that not all cultures offer their members equally rich visual information, and that not all segments of the cultures that do so may be equally informed. To begin with, ethnologists know that some so-called primitive cultures have fairly elaborate visual arts, whereas others seem strikingly deficient. There are, or have been in modern times, some groups with practically nothing describable as visual art in such forms as ornament and body decoration—to say nothing of representational or realistic forms. The range of man-made visual experience in the world's cultures is very great. Beyond that, it is uncontestable that geographic environments differ enormously in the naturally occurring visual forms they provide to their inhabitants. For example, dwellers in parts of the Arctic or in some extreme deserts have very restricted opportunities to respond to many kinds of visual forms; neither plant nor animal life may be especially colorful, and soils, rocks, and even the skies may present limited stimuli. Other natural terrestrial environments (and offshore ones accessible even without highly developed technology) offer fantastic visual forms and colors—birds, fishes, flowers, etc., with splendid colors and varied shapes, along with landforms that carry one's attention far above the horizon. We do not really know just what effects, if any, generously endowed or very restricted landscapes may have on the visual thinking and imagery of people around the world. The question should be pursued.

Even with rather simple technology, human beings can create visual worlds from their artifacts and structures, from their costumes or body decoration, and by producing pictures, carvings, and so on in a wide variety of commonly available media. Access to a wide range of pigments is, to be sure, more of a problem, and rich palettes of permanent colors have only been achieved by cultures able to draw upon long-distance trade in some rather scarce substances. In the modern world of chemical dyestuffs and pigments, we tend to forget how complicated it was even for Renaissance artists to assemble a workable set of paints, or what networks of trade underlay the multicolored rugs of Central Asian weavers. But the technical equipment to produce visual arts and crafts is only part of the issue—people had to find out how to draw, paint, weave, and so on. Until 1977, we could confidently assert that only modern *Homo sapiens,* during the last 30,000 years or so, had discovered how to draw and paint.

Apes provided with drawing or painting materials seemed limited [as Desmond Morris (1962) reported at length in his *Biology of Art* (cf. Alland, 1977)] to the production of scribbles or rather messy finger-paintings, without a glimmering of representation or of decorative design patterns. (Many such design patterns seem to have arisen from repetitive artifactual techniques, such as basket weaving). However, during the summer of 1976, the Gardners, famous for their earlier work with Washoe, reported that another young chimpanzee, Moja, had started to produce quasi-representational line drawings. Having made these quite uncharacteristic pictures, Moja proceeded to state, in ASL (American Sign Language of the Deaf) that they were, for example, a "bird," and a "strawberry." This unexpected achievement requires much further study and analysis, but we can no longer say with confidence that ape artists can only scribble. Language labeling presumably has something to do with this surprising chimpanzee performance. However, we can still say that, to the best of our knowledge, prior to 1976 no anthropoid ape had achieved representational drawing.

Man, on the other hand, started drawing or engraving lines toward the close of the Lower Paleolithic, when the most advanced hominid present was Neanderthal. In the Upper Paleolithic, graphic competence made a kind of quantum leap in which, in a few parts of the Old World, people began to depict various game animals with surprising realism, along with what appear to be geometric abstractions, only because they do not seem to resemble anything recognizable in nature. Leading up to these astonishing productions, which we call "Paleolithic Art" without knowing the contexts in which they were made, was a longish build-up of simpler tally-marks and scratchings recently subjected to close scrutiny by Alexander Marshack. There are reasons for assuming that late Paleolithic people decorated themselves with red ochre and other pigments, and definite evidence in the late Upper Paleolithic of shell necklaces and bone and stone pendants, and the like. On the analogy of recent or surviving non-literate people, we may assume that many perishable artifacts were probably also decorated—wood, hides, basketry material or matting, and dwelling surfaces. Lost to us, but also highly likely, were the visual effects of dance and ritual, in which participants produced distinctive visual effects with their bodies and with costumes and paraphernalia of perishable materials.

A glimpse of the possible extent of such visual art products and performances is provided in the early Neolithic of places like Çatal Hüyük (southern Anatolia), where, several thousand years ago, people achieved a level of presumably religious art quite comparable to that of recent Southwestern U.S. Pueblo Indians. Recent nonliterate cultures exemplified by many Melanesian groups—the Maori of New Zealand, or the Indians of the American Northwest Coast—illustrate the levels of visual complexity attainable without more than a Neolithic technology.

LANGUAGE AND ART:
THE DEVELOPMENT OF PRINTING

Starting about 5500 years ago in southern Iraq and in a few other places in the ensuing three millennia, the invention of writing joined graphic representation (all the early scripts were initially pictographic) with language codes, the implications of which we have so far not fully explored. As Wrolstead (1976) has ably observed in his "A Manifesto for Written Language," we have for too long accepted the simplistic dogma of certain linguists to the effect that writing made little or no difference to language or language users, and that scripts can be ignored or neglected except as convenient ways of recording speech sounds or as otherwise unrecoverable evidence about languages no longer spoken. That graphics can play a powerful role in language-related matters is obvious enough in the history of mathematics, and it is hard to imagine what the development of Chinese literature would have been like if the Chinese had adopted an alphabet back in the Chou Dynasty (cf. Gerr, S. 1944; Wieger, 1965). Multiplication of written inscriptions, as well as of other patterns goes far back—to the invention of seal stamps for impressing designs on clay, wax, textiles, and even the human skin, followed in the first millennium B.C. by the invention of coins. Curiously, the next seemingly easy step to printing of entire texts was long delayed, and when printing did appear it was initially in a religious context, for the propagation of Buddhism. Religion has had important influences on the visual arts in many cultures, occasionally ruling out entire media or kinds of subjects, as in the prohibitions on graven images in Judaism and Islam, the iconoclastic movement in the Byzantine church, the attacks on figural art by the Puritans, and the even more thorough suppression of visual arts (including the use of colorful materials) by the Quakers.

Many writers have dealt at length with the effects of printing, especially in Western civilization, though they seem less interested or perhaps simply less well informed on its impact in the Far East, where printing began. In focusing on the printed word, however, we may underrate the importance of printed pictures, maps, and other materials—from calendars to playing cards—in making possible enormously expanded distribution of formerly very costly hand-copied graphics. The illustrated herbals, textbooks of anatomy, astronomical charts and tables, and all sorts of works containing, for example, technical diagrams or plans on architecture, shipbuilding, and fortifications were an essential ingredient of the scientific and technological revolution of the past few centuries, as Ferguson makes clear (1977).

Not long before the wide dissemination of printed works in the fifteenth century, European artists worked out the principles of linear perspective, previously only crudely approximated East or West, which, whatever one's aesthetic response to Renaissance visual realism, was a forerunner and stimulus to the later invention of photography. Indeed, the camera obscura—a box with lens and ground-glass—was devised to simplify veridical representation of scenes involving complex problems of linear perspective, as in the numerous photographically accurate paintings of the buildings and canals of Venice by Canaletto in the eighteenth century. The seventeenth century saw the invention of the magic lantern, at a time when theatrical scenery was becoming more elaborate, and when the application of technology to fantastic visual effects for stage and pageantry was attaining levels never reached by the Romans and other ancient peoples. It should not be forgotten that a principal factor in the development of gunpowder and other special combustibles was fireworks—for their visual display effects—and that for a long time some of the most advanced techniques in hydraulic systems were used to produce elaborate fountain displays in royal gardens.

THE ART OF TIME

Man has noted the passage of time chiefly by visual markers or visible effects, and certain Paleolithic sets of engraved marks have been interpreted as tallies of lunations and the like. Impressed by the circular movement patterns of the sun, moon, and stars, people in widely separated cultures have conceptualized and represented large units of time in terms of rounds or cycles. For obvious physical and technical reasons, devices constructed for measuring time have been based on circles or parts of circles—from Stonehenge and sundials to mechanical clocks. We are by now so used to clock faces that we may not think of them as circular graphs. Bells and other acoustic devices have also been used in connection with time marking, and the metronome combines simultaneous visual and acoustic time-signals. But the familiar ticking sounds of mechanical clocks, while affording the listener another sensory channel for his awareness of the passage of time, may be regarded as a kind of incidental bonus, except where we are interested in very short time-intervals. The clock face has served as the prototype for all kinds of other instruments that display their information as dial-readings, even though digital displays have tended in recent years to replace some dial-display instruments (including clocks). Some useful information may be lost in such displays of numbers alone.

Starting with simple lenses for spectacles, telescopes and microscopes were developed in the seventeenth century, facilitating immense advances in astronomy and biology, which suggests that some scientific paradigm-shifts can be attributed to seemingly unrelated branches of technology and not just to powerful new systems of thinking. To these tremendously important extensions of man's visual apparatus and capacities for seeing both the very large and distant and the extremely small, spectroscopy was added, still another way of bending light-rays.

Another direction of visual representation lay in the use of Cartesian coordinates to depict motion through time and the use of other interrelated variables in a manner superior to numerical or verbal description. The full-fledged resort to curves to report scientific, economic, and social phenomena came in the nineteenth century. A Berkeley mathematician has observed that mathematical understanding does not arise from plodding checks of each step in a long equation, but "what is crucial is to see through the technicalities to grasp the underlying ideas and intuitions which often can be expressed concisely and even pictorially [Chernoff, 1976, p. 276]."

THE TECHNOLOGY OF VISUALIZATION

At the close of the eighteenth century and on into the nineteenth, technological advances related to greater visualization came in a veritable flood: lithography as a cheap and easy way to produce illustrations, replacing the much more tedious processes of engraving; color printing, which reached an early high level of excellence in Tokugawa Japan; blue printing; and the immensely popular art of portraiture in silhouette. Photography was, of course, the most important of these innovations. There were other inventions that contributed heavily to the visual revolution of the nineteenth century—the application of steam power to printing presses; the production of much cheaper, if more perishable, paper from wood pulp rather than rags; the aniline dye industry; and photoengraving processes. Illustrated papers, magazines, and children's books became much more abundant and inexpensive (Atwater, 1977). Photographic transparencies were projected in the magic lantern. In the late nineteenth century there was a craze for stereoscopic views and a series of inventions that produced the consumer interest in photographic peepshows, and eventually the motion picture. Similarly, commercial interests developed advertising arts, illuminated signs, and an immense outpouring of poster-art, in which some now highly regarded artists were willing to participate (e.g., Toulouse-Lautrec). The mid-nineteenth century saw the development of the postage stamp as a miniaturized graphic art industry, and of the postal card, which added new dimensions to tourism long before the general public began to carry cameras as a matter of course. Some now almost forgotten visual displays should be noted in passing—for example, the impressive dioramas, operated as commercial enterprises, now surviving in only a few places, but which, significantly, happened to have been the business of Monsieur Daguerre, before he became involved in photography. Out of the nineteenth-century infatuation with visual similitude there also came the creation of new kinds of museum exhibits, such as the animal habitat group, and the miniature diorama.

I have not begun to exhaust the inventory of devices, processes, and so on which so hugely enriched the visual world to which we are now so accustomed in the late twentieth century. It is worth considering the significance of the trend, beginning in the late seventeenth and early eighteenth centuries, of deliberate imitation of exotic art and architectural styles, almost without precedent in previous civilizations. To be sure, there had been the Orientalizing fad in Greek vase painting, and a certain amount of Egyptianism in Roman art, but none of these movements equaled the infatuation of Europeans with Chinese art in the eighteenth-century *chinoiserie,* nor the Arabesque fad, which led to the building of the Brighton Pavilion, to say nothing of the deliberate Classical and then Gothic revivals that swept Northern Europe. Now that we have ransacked all past civilizations and primitive cultures for their visual arts, we take it for granted that one may furnish a living-room with Yoruba wood-carvings, Navajo rugs, Japanese kakemono, and perhaps a Metropolitan Museum copy of a Greek or Cambodian sculptured head. Nor have I dwelt on the whole matter of the visual component of architecture, city-planning, and environmental design, including the layout of gardens—where visual aesthetic considerations are played against practical, functional, or even economic ones.

In view of all of this, what can we say about visual literacy or competence? What should people learn, beyond what they learn anyhow, about the enormously complex world of visual experience? Are there just a few principles we need to master—some visual aesthetic guidelines or psychological facts about visual perception—or is there much more to the question (cf. Arnheim, 1969)? Is visual scholarship such a large portion of human concern that we need do no more about it than what is already being done in all kinds of institutions, workshops, studios, and so on around the world? If there are deficiencies in visual literacy, how do we go about diagnosing them, or developing tests to indicate individual visual literacy quotients? Psychologists working in the cross-cultural area have already come up with some results, suggesting that people raised in different societies, or exposed to different kinds of formal education, vary in their responses to pictorial materials (Alland, 1977).

In connection with the notion of visual *literacy*, the implied parallel between "reading and writing literacy" (the normal meaning of the term) and competence with respect to visual information presents some difficulties. Reading and writing have a commutative relationship, a reciprocal connection, as do speaking and hearing. But for most ordinary human beings, visual inputs are not matched at all by comparable visible informational outputs. Unless we can draw or paint or otherwise *produce* something like what we take in, the relationship remains very one-sided indeed. Two photographers taking pictures of each other come close to the speaking–hearing, hearing–speaking situation, but there is still something unresolved about this matter.

In the mid-seventeenth century, the Czech philosopher–educator, Jan Komensky (or Johannes Comenius) wrote *Orbis Sensualium Pictis,* the first effort to provide for school children an inventory of picturable things in the whole world, together with their linguistic labels—originally in Latin and German. English and other translations followed (the first English version appeared in 1659). In his preface, Comenius wrote:

> We can neither act nor speak, unless we first rightly understand all the things which are to be done, and whereof, we are to speak. Now there is nothing in the understanding which was not before in the senses. And therefore to exercise the senses well about the right perceiving the differences of things, will be to lay the grounds for all wisdom, and all wise discourse, and all discrete actions in one's course of life.

Comenius obviously believed that pictured things conveyed more to children learning to read than simply other words. The general idea of a picture-dictionary persisted—it was, for example, a significant part of the great French Encyclopédie of the eighteenth century, which included a volume illustrating all kinds of arts and crafts in detailed engravings. The great encyclopedic works on Natural History of the eighteenth and nineteenth centuries carried on this pictorial tradition, as in Buffon's multi-volumed *Histoire Naturelle,* and in Audubon's well-known work on American birds. In this century, perhaps the most ambitious work along these lines has been the *Duden Picture-Dictionary* (*Bildwörterbuch*), issued in the 1930s, with illustrations of over 10,000 items accompanied by tables of their verbal labels (eventually issued in five languages). The great modern encyclopedias have likewise turned to much more lavish use of illustrations—in color to a large extent, as may be seen by comparing the very similar formats of the *Encyclopédie Larousse,* the new *Britannica,* and the *Encyclopaedia Japonica.* An analogous development has taken place in the world's great museums, which, on a scale never previously attempted, now offer not only excellent color-reproductions of the pictures and other items in their collections, but increasingly supply color transparencies for what would appear to be a huge market.

Files and archives of visual material are producible and made available as never before in history, with ramifications we do not seem yet to have measured or even surveyed. I do not mean to minimize the importance of sound archives, consisting mostly of recorded music and of human speech, likewise rendered possible by nineteenth- and twentieth-century technology. It should be noted, however, in thinking about our present-day knowledge of sound, that much of it has depended upon the transformation of sound records into *visual* outputs—into visible wave forms on various kinds of instruments, from the earliest needles passing over cylinders coated with carbon-black to modern oscillographs or sound spectroscopes. Even the study of vocal sounds has been made possible largely because of the relatively simple transformability of acoustic patterns into line graphics.

At the broadest level of generalization, and expanding on the idea expressed in the quotation from the mathematician Chernoff, a very large part of modern science has been made possible by methods for reducing data and relationships from almost all domains of the natural world to visible patterns—to graphics of one sort or another. In genetics, for example, the earliest breakthroughs came not only from being able to observe and draw the phenomena of mitosis and meiosis, but from the discovery that the new aniline dyes could be used to stain and make visible what therefore came to be called *chromosomes*. Later, in the Watson–Crick era, understanding of the structure of the critical DNA molecule came from analyses of X-ray crystallographic photographs, and then the actual construction of three-dimensional models of the elusive molecule. To an overwhelming extent, science has advanced by finding means to *visualize* relationships and events.

CONCLUSION

In coming to the end of this presentation, it is worth commenting on some recent assumptions about the intellectual and aesthetic effects of brain lateralization and the notion that some cultural systems overemphasize functions localized in only one cerebral hemisphere. Considerable experimental work has apparently validated at least a part of this: In most individuals, language and analytical functions are carried out mostly in the left hemisphere, whereas some kinds of nonverbal synthesis, along with musical data-processing are right-hemisphere activities. The implication that has been drawn from these clinical and laboratory findings is that, for example, Western civilization has overemphasized the left-hemisphere functions, to the virtual deprivation of the right, except for a fortunate few creative persons. Probably the entire matter has been prematurely oversimplified, but it may contain some kernels of truth. It may be that some kinds of educational systems have tended to stultify the nonverbal side of our minds; it may be that some of the distressing symptoms of this era in educational institutions and in the culture of the Western world as a whole arise from the massive new impact of the "post-Gutenberg" media— notably television, to which large segments of the present younger generation in several countries have now been exposed from infancy. In fact, we do not yet have reliable methods for detecting or measuring the effect of the new visual media. In any case, I do not think the would-be visual scholar can afford to neglect these problems. The crisis in reading and writing skills now recognized by alarmed academics may be based in part on the impact of modern technology, including the visual media technologies of the past century or so, but it is unlikely to be solved by abandoning the immensely efficient technique of putting language into visible forms, just as it is unlikely that the tremendous advantages of the nonverbal visual media will be laid aside.

REFERENCES

Alland, A., Jr. *The artistic animal.* Garden City, N.Y.: Anchor Books, Doubleday, 1977.
Arnheim, R. *Visual thinking.* Berkeley: Univ. of California Press, 1969.
Atwater, W. S. Visual, verbal/visual propositions: The effect of the photographic image on childrens' textbooks 1800–1950. Semiotic Society of America, 1977 Annual Meeting, Denver. Abstract, p. 21.
Bliss, C. K. *Semantography.* 2nd edition. Sydney, Australia: Semantography Publications, 1965.
Blissymbolics Communication Foundation. *Bulletin,* 1977, *2* (1,2).
Buettner-Janusch, J. *Origins of man.* New York: Wiley, 1966.
Campbell, B. *Human evolution: an introduction to man's adaptations.* Chicago: Aldine, 1966.
Chernoff, P. R. Letter to the Editor. *Science,* 1976, *193,* 276.
Comenius, J. A. *Orbis Sensualium pictus.* Nürnberg, 1658. (Reprint, Osnabrück, 1964).
Downs, R., & Stea, D. (Eds.). *Image and environment: Cognitive mapping and spatial behavior.* Chicago: Aldine, 1973.
Ennion, E. A. R., & Tinbergen, N. *Tracks.* Oxford: Clarendon; New York: Univ. Press, 1967.
Ferguson, E. S. The mind's eye: Nonverbal thought in technology. *Science,* 1977, *197,* 827.
Gardner, R. A., & Gardner, B. T. Comparative psychology and language acquisition.

In K. Salzinger and F. Denmark, (Eds.), *Psychology: The state of the art.* New York: New York Academy of Sciences, Annals.

Gerr, S. *Scientific and technical Japanese.* New York, 1944.

Goodall, J. *In the shadow of man.* Boston: Houghton, Mifflin, 1971.

Gould, P., & White, R. *Mental maps.* Harmondsworth: Penguin Books, 1974.

Hewes, G. W. Primate communication and the gestural origin of language. *Current Anthropology,* 1973, *14* (1/2), 5–24.

Hewes, G. W. *Language origins: A bibliography.* (2nd ed.). 2 vols. The Hague: Mouton, 1975.

Hewes, G. W. Language origin theories. In D. M. Rumbaugh (Ed.), *Language learning by a chimpanzee: The LANA project.* New York: Academic Press, 1977.

Huggins, W. H., & Entwisle, D. *Iconic communication: An annotated bibliography.* Baltimore: Johns Hopkins Press, 1974.

Jerison, H. H. *Evolution of the brain and intelligence.* New York: Academic Press, 1973.

Kaufman, L. *Sight and mind: An introduction to visual perception.* New York: Oxford Univ. Press, 1974.

Morris, D. *The biology of art: A study of the picture-making behavior of the great apes and its relationship to human art.* New York: Knopf, 1962.

Murie, O. J. *A field guide to animal tracks.* Boston: Houghton, Mifflin, 1975.

Wieger, L. *Chinese characters: Their origin, etymology, history, classification and signification.* New York: Dover, 1965.

Wrolstad, M. E. A manifesto for written language. *Visible Language,* 1976, *10,* 5–40.

Young, J. Z. *An introduction to the study of man.* New York: Oxford Univ. Press, 1971.

2

Visualizing Vision

ROGER WILLIAMS WESCOTT
Drew University
Madison, New Jersey

This chapter is an exploratory essay in the field I call *eidetics:* the study of vision and visual phenomena. I follow Marshall McLuhan in preferring "probes" to definitive statements in areas of study which, like eidetics, are still taking shape. I would not even presume to term this offering a re-search report, since, in my view, research is necessarily consequent to search; and the search—for me at least—has just begun.

With most of my colleagues in this volume, I share a fascination with vision and a fervent hope that we may, before long, attain visual sophisti-cation. But I cannot accept the sharp distinction that some scholars draw between visual and verbal phenomena, for it seems to me that two of the three forms that language commonly takes are visual: namely, writing and manual gesture-signing. (To meet the objection that manual signing is restricted to the deaf and the speechless, I call attention to the fact that nearly all of us, when encountering people with whose speech we are wholly unfamiliar, resort to gesture to make our basic needs known. Such gesticulation, no matter how crude, constitutes in effect a manual "pidgin," comparable to the spoken trade jargons still found in highly multilingual areas like Oceania.) Moreover, like my fellow anthropologist Gordon Hewes, I believe that there was a time, perhaps as recently as 35,000

Visual Learning, Thinking, and Communication

years ago, when all language was manual–visual and vocal auditory sig-naling served only to add emotive color to hand gestures.

THE EVOLUTION OF VISION

As an anthropologist, I am committed to the view that man's complex social and cultural behavior cannot be understood apart from the complex anatomy and physiology of the human organism that manifests it, so that any discussion of visual communication or education requires prior con-sideration of the biology of vision. Moreover, to understand the structure and function of the human eye, we must likewise know something of its evolution from prehuman visual systems.

Organic evolution may be viewed iin either of two ways—typologically, in which case it is the development of the entire biosphere that is being surveyed, or phylogenetically, in which case it is only the lineal ancestry of our own species that is surveyed. Beginning with a typological overview, we find the steps in the evolution of the human eye to have been these:

1. Light-sensitive skin, as among most protozoans from the early Ar-cheozoic Era, about 3 billion years ago
2. A flat eye-spot on the skin, as among some phytoflagellates from the late Archeozoic Era, about 2 billion years ago
3. An ocellus, or open concavity, as among acoelous flatworms from the Proterozoic Era, about 1 billion years ago
4. A pit eye, or closed lensless concavity, as among primitive cephalo-pods, such as the chambered nautilus, from the Ordovician Period of the Paleozoic Era, about 450 million years ago
5. A camera eye, or nonfocusing, lens-covered concavity, as among early arachnids, such as water-scorpions, from the Silurian Period of the Paleozoic Era, about 400 million years ago
6. A pupillary, or focusable, eye, as among early jawed fish from the Devonian Period of the Paleozoic Era, about 350 million years ago
7. A color-sensitive eye, as among advanced cephalopods, like squids, from the Jurassic Period of the Mesozoic Era, about 150 million years ago
8. A stereoscopic eye, providing triangulated depth perception, as among anthropoid primates, such as Old World monkeys, from the Miocene Epoch of the Cenozoic Era, about 30 million years ago

The phylogenetic sequence of ocular evolution, which, for our chordate ancestors, excludes parallel or convergent developments among arthro-pods and molluscs, such as bees and octopuses, is serially identical with the biospheric sequence just outlined. But, because vertebrates appeared about 100 million years later than the major invertebrate phyla, most of the pre-Tertiary dates for our own ancestors are substantially more recent than the ones just given.

Photoperiodism

Returning to the biosphere as a whole, we find that a majority of the Earth's organisms—including those which, like most, lack the highly developed eyes of insects, squids, and primates—exhibit photoperiodism, or a tendency to synchronize their activities with daily, monthly, or seasonal changes in the amount of light reaching them, directly or by reflection, from the sun. Common examples of photoperiodic behavior are the flowering of plants, the rutting of mammals, and the migrations of birds.

Among vertebrates, this protoperiodism may be controlled by the pineal gland, a small outgrowth of the epithalamic roof of the diencephalon, which links the forebrain with the midbrain. At any rate, paleontology makes it clear that among our earliest vertebrate ancestors, the Ordovician agnaths, or jawless fish, the now internalized pineal was external and constituted, in fact, a third eye situated at the top of the head and serving, probably, to alert those lowly mud-grubbers to any predatory activity in the water above them.

The neurophysiology of the human eye is particularly interesting. No fewer than 60% of all the sensory nerves that enter the human brain are optic nerves. For this very basic biological reason, I am unable to accept Marshall McLuhan's claim that the visual order of "the Gutenberg galaxy" is about to be replaced by the oral world of "the global village." Visual perceptual primacy seems to be built into the human organism, and nothing short of a genetic mutation is likely to alter that fact.

Foveality

Another interesting characteristic of the human eye, as of that of all our simian relatives, is foveality. Our vision is foveal in the sense that its acuity is dependent on a small pit at the back of the retina called the fovea, which allows us to form a much sharper image of things viewed than is possible for most other animals. The foveal image, however, is highly circumscribed; and the peripheral vision which permits perception of things that are out of focus is correspondingly weaker in us than in most other animals. It may be, then, that both the "narrow-mindedness" that intellectuals decry in popular stereotyping and the overspecialization that free-wheeling generalists decry in academia are predictable products of our ocular anatomy. What we see clearly we rarely see broadly, and vice versa.

Nonetheless, our central vision is unusually powerful, and few animals can equal it, still less surpass it. The minority of animals whose visual power exceeds our own are invariably fliers—either winged insects or birds. Bees, probably the visual leaders of the arthropod world, can perceive both polarized light and ultraviolet light, to both of which we are normally blind. Their sensitivity to polarization enables them to deduce the position of the sun, by which they navigate, even when the sky is predominantly overcast. And their sensitivity to ultaviolet light, spectrally intermediate between violet light and X-rays, enables them to distinguish between flowers which look chromatically identical to us but which are quite different for them in terms of the edible nectars and pollens they provide.

Among birds, owls outdo us visually in their ability to perceive infrared light, spectrally intermediate between red light and microwaves. Since warm-blooded prey animals emit infrared radiation, this ability permits owls to fly low and hunt at night, when other birds must either roost or fly high. And hawks and similar raptorial birds, such as eagles, exceed us in their powers of ocular resolution, being able to see eight times as far as we. Compared to them, we are myopic.

Bioluminescence

In addition to the passive–receptive reaction to light that we call vision, there is an active–productive utilization of light known as bioluminescence. Because it differs from such light-yielding processes as incandescence and fluorescence in releasing no heat, bioluminescence is also referred to as "cold light." The fact that green plants and land vertebrates—the organisms most familiar to us—emit no such light may mislead many of us into thinking of bioluminescence as a rare and exotic form of behavior. But actually a majority of organic groups contain subgroups that luminesce. The adaptive functions served by their luminescence are many. Most firefly flashes serve as mating signals. The light-emission of deep-sea fish helps them find food. And the ventral luminescence of mid-sea squid so countershades them, in conjunction with descending sunlight, as to make them invisible to predators. In a few cases, however, such as that of the brilliantly luminescent ctenophores, or comb-jellies, the purpose of light-emission remains intriguingly mysterious.

Audio–Visual Asymmetry

Our discussion of bioluminescence leads, by its implicit contrast with our earlier discussion of vision, to a consideration of what might be called the symmetry of communication. Nearly all students of behavior agree that human communication is overwhelmingly audio–visual (rather than, for example, tactile–olfactory) in nature. But controversy persists over the relative importance of the auditory and visual components of our communicative behavior. The chief reason for this controversy is probably the fact that our auditory and visual strengths differ not only in terms of the sensory channels through which they manifest themselves but also in terms of the nature of the communication involved. For although we can produce sound at will, we cannot produce light even involuntarily, except by means of artifacts like torches and flashlights. In terms of message-transmission, our most effective visual signaling is kinesic. It employs gestures and postures to reflect light already transmitted from elsewhere—usually from the sun.

Our auditory prowess, in other words, is primarily transmissive in nature; whereas our visual prowess is primarily receptive. This behavioral asymmetry may help explain some of the physical and psychological differences between the deaf and the blind, both of whom are handicapped, but disparately so. Since our orientation to our total environment is chiefly visual, the blind are less mobile than the deaf. But, since our social relations depend chiefly on speech, the deaf are less responsive than the blind. Although both handicaps are emotionally disturbing, blindness is more likely to lead to a general restlessness, whereas deafness is more likely to induce specifically paranoid suspicions.

Nevertheless, despite the physiological passivity of our sense of sight, ocular behavior is usually responded to as though it were active. Among all the higher primates, staring is considered a form of aggression. A stare from a subordinate male monkey will precipitate assault by a dominant male. A stare from a stranger will make a female gorilla run screaming. Nor are we immune to this simian behavior pattern. Even in our own culture, which is distinctive in its derogation of the "shifty-eyed" look, a steady gaze alone, if directed at a fellow patron, will usually suffice to start a barroom brawl.

APE LANGUAGE EXPERIMENTS

An even more dramatic visual link between ourselves and our nonhuman kinsmen was forged when three different groups of American psychologists broke through what has long been regarded as "the language barrier" between apes and men. Through the 1950s experimenters interested in the linguistic capacities of chimpanzees tried only to induce them to speak. Insofar as vocalization is concerned, these attempts were almost complete failures, although the Hayeses did succeed in getting their chimp, Vicki, to produce external mouth-movements that could be deciphered by lipreading. Then, in the 1960s, the Gardners tried a wholly visual, rather than a predominantly auditory, approach to the linguistic instruction of non-human primates. They taught American Sign Language of the deaf to their chimp, Washoe, with extremely gratifying results. She mastered word order, pronominal reference, interrogation, and negation, in addition to acquiring a vocabulary of several hundred words. Furthermore, Washoe soliloquized, used synonyms, and occasionally coined comprehensible terms of her own for things that her mentors (who used manual signs only haltingly) either could not or did not name for her. Washoe is now the presiding dowager of a sign-using colony of chimpanzees at the University of Oklahoma Primate Center, where the hope is that newborn chimpanzees may soon be taught sign language by their mothers.

Two other visual systems employed in the successful linguistic instruction of chimpanzees are the plastic token method of the Premacks and the computer console method of Rumbaugh and his associates. Where Washoe gestured her words, the Premacks' Sarah "printed" hers, and Rumbaugh's Lana "typewrote" hers. The fact that manual sign-gesturing has thus far yielded the most prolific results may indicate not so much the intrinsic superiority of American Sign Language as the probability that the relatively greater personal freedom and social stimulation enjoyed by Washoe and her "co-signers" has been more conducive to creative learning.

Visual language is now being successfully taught to gorillas and is scheduled to be taught soon to orang-utans. My own hope is that, at the very least, gibbons, baboons, and macaques will also be eventually included in this fascinating plan of visual instruction.

VOCABULARY OF VISION

Let us turn now to the language of vision, beginning our discussion of it with a consideration of cross-cultural differences in visual vocabulary. The lexical area most intensively investigated in this connection is undoubtedly chromatonymics, or the study of color terms. As soon as Western traders and missionaries began learning the languages of the preliterate peoples of Africa, Oceania, and the Americas, they noticed that it was difficult to find terms in the native languages that corresponded with any precision to their European color terms. The non-Westerners seemed either to lack words for hue or to divide the chromatic spectrum quite differently from the Westerners.

By the second half of this century, three different biocultural theories had been advanced to account for these interlingual discrepancies. The first, which predominated in the nineteenth century (though it has now been abandoned by nearly all scientists), was quite simply that the tribal peoples are partially or wholly color-blind. This theory lost favor when medical tests showed, on the contrary, that preliterates actually have a lower incidence of color-blindness than do urban individuals from industrialized countries. The second theory, which predominated into the 1950s, was that color vocabularies are wholly arbitrary, reflecting the unpredictable cultural interests that different peoples exhibit in the various qualities of their sensory worlds. This theory found, and still finds, favor primarily among cultural relativists in the anthropological tradition of Franz Boas and the linguistic tradition of Edward Sapir. The third theory, recently advanced by Brent Berlin and Paul Kay of the University of California at Berkeley, is that color vocabularies evolve in roughly the same way in which cultures generally evolve, so that, other things being equal, peoples with complex cultures have large color lexicons, whereas those with simple cultures have small color lexicons. Current chromatonymic discussion, particularly in journals like *Anthropological Linguistics,* tends to oscillate between relativistic and evolutionary viewpoints, with evolutionism receiving more attention, but also serving as the target of more skeptical critiques.

Visual Metaphor

Another important aspect of the language of vision is the use of visual metaphor in intellectual discourses. To be sure, not all terms for mental activity originally had even a sensory, much less a visual, reference. The word *mind,* for example, seems to have referred solely to abstract mentation for at least 5000 years. And the verb *believe* is not only cognate with the verb *love* but was once synonymous with it. The majority of our mentalistic terminology, however, was initially concrete and sensory in reference. Of the various senses historically or prehistorically involved, the tactile sense is preeminent. The verbs *think, guess,* and *understand,* for example, once meant "take," "get," and "carry," respectively—all, presumably, in a manual sense. But, of the distal senses—those that do not require direct contact with, or even close proximity to, the object of perception—vision clearly predominates over audition in our metaphorical vocabulary. After we ask our interlocutors whether they "get" our drift, we are most likely to ask them whether they "see" what we mean. The nouns *idea, theory,* and *teaching,* moreover, originally meant "image," "spectacle," and "demonstration," respectively.

Some of our intellective terms, such as *learning, study,* and *opinion,* are of uncertain sensory reference, not so much because of the weakness of etymological scholarship as because of the widespread phenomenon of verbal synesthesia—that is, shifting or mixing of sensory references. In fact, only a minority of English words for visual activities turn out to have had a consistently visual reference throughout their lexical histories. The Latin-derived words *vision* (with its Gallicized cognates *view, survey,* and *clairvoyance*) and *inspect* (with its Gallicized cognate *espy*) may indeed be the only such words in our visual vocabulary of common use, if we exclude words like *peek* and *gaze* whose pre-Germanic history and non-Germanic connections are unknown. In any case, such visual terms as *glare* and *yellow* seem originally to have had an auditory or at least co-auditory reference and to have been semantically linked with *gleeman,* "minstrel," and *yell,* the synesthetic notion having apparently been that glaring is, so to speak, strident gazing and yellow a loud color. The verbs *see* and *stare* once had an apparently kinesthetic reference, seeing having earlier meant "following (with the eyes)" and staring "letting (one's gaze) stand." The verbs *behold* and *descry* were once tactile in reference and may have meant, respectively, "to hold fast (with one's eyes)" and "to carve (an image into one's visual memory)." And the verbs *watch* and *gawk* are of apparently nonsensory semantic origin, having meant, respectively, "to be alert" and "to pay attention."

ANOMALIES OF VISION

From the language of vision, we now turn to the anomalistics of vision, anomalistics being the systematic study of anomalies, or oddities. Whether partial or total, blindness is obviously a visual anomaly. Yet, because it is an inevitable result of crippling optical injury, such visual pathology is only minimally anomalous.

Hypereidesis

More anomalous, both because it is rarer and because there is no easy way to induce it artificially, is hypereidesis, or abnormal acuity of vision. Most people are aware of the fact that, if the formula 20/20 represents normal vision, 20/200 represents a common degree of nearsightedness. But they may not be aware that there is a parallel formula, such as 2/20, that represents an exceptional keenness of sight, equivalent to that of a healthy bird of prey. One of our astronauts turned out to have vision of this sharpness of resolution. Though government physicians did not at first believe that he could actually pick out individual houses from 100 miles above the earth's surface, they eventually conceded, after a battery of tests, that he was almost literally "hawk-eyed." (They should probably not have been so surprised. Hyperesthesia, or exceptional acuity of perception in one or another sensory channel, is well known to physiologists and psychologists. Perfumers, wine tasters, and professional fabric testers tend generally to be preselected from those who have a keener than average sense of smell, taste, and touch, respectively.)

In addition, moreover, to the "hawkeyes" among us whose vision is quantitatively superior to that of the majority of the population, there are almost certainly others—potential, if not actual, artists—whose vision is qualitatively superior. Most painters probably belong in this category, as do many photographers, sculptors, and architects. For them, the visible world is likely to have a luster which is, for others, a childhood memory at best. A conspicuous example of such enriched vision is provided by Vincent Van Gogh, for whom all objects of sight seem to have pulsated with light and color.

Synesthesia

Closely related to hyperesthesia is synthesia, which we mentioned earlier in connection with verbal crossover between terms for sight, sound, and other sensations. Although phrases like "a bright boy" or "a touching story" may seem at first to be nothing more than clever ways of playing with word contrasts for effect, the evidence is strong that they once were—and still can be—literal experiences. Our military services have had to remove some of their personnel from radar stations because these oversensitive people heard the electromagnetic radiation as an unbearably high-pitched screeching sound. Some versatile musicians report that they literally see their music dancing in the air before them. And there is every probability that this is a perennial experience. "To hear with eyes belongs to love's fine wit," wrote Shakespeare. My own study of the prehistory of European color terms indicates strongly that they were broadly audio-visual before they became specifically visual: It is no coincidence that the two English words *hue,* meaning color, and *hue,* meaning noise, are homonyms; they are so because they were once identical in signification as well as in form.

Photodermatism

An instance of synesthesia that has had little effect on our speech idioms but a great impact on physiological theory is photodermatism, or "skin-vision." Photodermatism (also called dermo-optical perception) is a perceiver's ability, when effectively blindfolded and prevented from touching anything with his upper body, nonetheless to detect accurately the color, shape, or texture of nearby objects with the skin of his fingers or face. The current leader among "eyeless viewers" is Rosa Kuleshova of Nizhny Tagil in the Soviet Urals. But, with practice, a number of experimental subjects from various countries have developed the ability not only to see but even to read materials at some distance from their skins. Although objective temperature seems not to be involved, successful color-detecters usually report subjective thermal responses to colors—red being, predictably perhaps, the warmest color and blue the coolest. And many percipients also report tactile sensations—yellow feeling slippery and green sticky. Low-voltage electricity run through objects makes them dermally detectable at greater distances but apparently serves only a facilitative rather than a primally causative function in photodermatism. Although photodermatism remains mysterious in many respects, there seems little doubt that it, like the pineal role in photoperiodism, exemplifies vestigial light-sensitivity, since it is probable that our remote aquatic ancestors had visual capacities first in their skins and later in their "third eyes," which eventually became internalized as pineal glands.

Auric Vision

Exceptional vision, found in some but absent in most of us, subsumes not only hyperesthesia and synesthesia but also the ability to see auras. The aura may be defined as a radiance of fluctuating form, color, and intensity sometimes visible around organisms. It is most often observed, as might be expected, around the heads of human beings. Most mediums and other psychics have long claimed to have auric vision. And some of them identify the aura with the "astral body" or the "etheric body" of occult tradition. It seems likely, moreover, that the saintly halos of religious art are representations of this auric radiance, although it remains uncertain whether religious artists should be assumed to have been auric percipients in their own right or merely translators into a graphic medium of what they had heard from or about such percipients.

It is also a question whether the aura is what is recorded, in a manner clearly visible even to those who lack special psychic abilities, by the technique called electrophotography. This procedure, which is still under development, was originated in Krasnodar in the Black Sea region of the Soviet Union in 1939 by Semyon and Valentina Kirlian. To take a Kirlian photograph, one places an organic object against a sheet of photographic paper in a high-frequency electrical field. No camera is needed. Yet, when the sheet is withdrawn, it yields a dramatic picture—not of the object itself, but of a brightly colored light-pattern which roughly outlines the object but goes beyond it. Two considerations which suggest a close relationship between Kirlian photographs and auras are the facts, first, that both vary with the impending mood and state of health of the organism being observed and, second, that both reveal missing anatomical segments, such as severed leaflets or "phantom limbs," as luminous extensions that dim progressively with the passage of time following transsection or amputation.

A further question concerns the relationship between electrophotography and the perennial Chinese medical technique known as acupuncture. Those who combine Kirlian diagnosis with acupunctive therapy claim that the points at which Kirlian luminosity is sharpest and brightest are precisely the same as those at which acupuncture needles should be, and in the hands of skilled practitioners are, inserted.

Ocular Radiation

The theory that even organisms that are not bioluminescent sometimes emit radiation that can be seen or at least electrically protographed is already more than most natural scientists can accept. Yet, as if this were not enough, there is a further theory that the eye is capable not only of perceiving bioradiation outside the so-called "visible band" but also of transmitting it. This theory, in fact, is so old that it might better be called a tradition. Ancient Greek and Roman authors seem generally to have believed that the eyes can be radiant in a literal as well as a metaphorical sense. And belief in "the evil eye" is found among most peoples in most parts of the world and periods of history. The essence of this belief is that some people have the power (often an involuntary one) to inflict illness or other harm on their fellows merely by casting a baleful glance at them. This power is clearly related to the destructive processes supposedly involved both in witchcraft, or harm inflicted by purely mental means, and in sorcery, or harm inflicted by ritual means. Belief in it, moreover, is probably connected with the equally immemorial popular belief that snakes and other predatory animals have the power to transfix, or, as we might say, to hypnotize, their intended victims and thereby to immobilize them before killing and eating them.

The chief reason why belief in ocular radiation is currently referred to as a theory rather than as a superstition is that it has been revived by a small but energetic group of psychotherapists known as orgonomists. Orgonomy, or orgone therapy, is a heretical offshoot of Freudian psychoanalysis and was the brainchild of the late Austro-American physician and biophysicist Wilhelm Reich. Where Freudians talked about "ideas" in or of the "mind," Reichians talk about energies in or around the body. The view taken by orgonomists about what John Donne poetically styled "eyebeams" is that their effect is likely to be beneficient or deleterious depending not so much on the moral as on the biopsychic state of the gazer: Healthy individuals will beam healing rays, and psychopathic individuals, damaging rays from their eyes. From an orgonomic standpoint, then, William Wordsworth was not being literary but intuitively scientific when, in his "Ode on Intimations of Immortality," he described an infant as flourishing "with light upon him from his father's eyes."

Clairvoyance

No less controversial than auric vision and ocular radiation is clairvoyance, or "remote viewing." Clairvoyance is the ability, held to be common among psychics, to see objects and events that are presumably out of sight, either in the sense that they are miles away or in the sense that there is an opaque obstacle between the viewer and his perceptual target. It might be described as television without any electromagnetic or other known means of transmission. Its simplest form is statistically improbable success in guessing the shapes on ESP testing cards of the type developed by John and Louisa Rhine. Its most elaborate form involves the penetration not only of spatial but also of temporal barriers: An example is a vivid and detailed precognitive vision of some future event. Even among mediums and their preliterate counterparts, called shamans, clairvoyance is a notoriously unreliable sensory or extrasensory power, occurring with dazzling clarity on one occasion but dimly, if at all, on another. An explanation sometimes offered for such fluctuations is that psychic ability is a relatively feeble talent even among the comparatively gifted and that the still unidentified channel through which it operates is often clogged by noise, possibly because messages moving through it are poorly directed.

"Photographic" Memory

Similar fluctuations occur in visual memory, for reasons which remain obscure. A minority of people, whose eidetic recollections are so detailed that they can often recite briefly glimpsed book-pages word for word, are said to have "photographic memory." Yet, although most people seem to lack this retentiveness altogether, Wilder Penfield of the McGill University Medical School has shown, through brain surgery (for epilepsy or tumors), that when appropriate areas of the cortex are stimulated, all patients experience vivid and detailed memories, both visual and multisensory, of events which were previously wholly forgotten but which can be shown, by subsequent checking, to be real and not hallucinatory. It looks, then, as though photographic memory is a latent capacity in everyone, but one that needs special triggering if it is to be made available for practical utilization. Predictably, many parapsychologists believe the same thing to be true of so-called "extrasensory" perception.

Visionary Experience

Visionary or revelatory experience is likewise difficult both to explain and to predict. Physiologically, it consists of a dazzling sensation of light just behind or in front of the eyes and, intellectually, of insight so arresting as to lead to a total reorientation of thinking on some or all subjects. Biblical books from Daniel to Revelations are full of such personal illuminations. Religious conversions usually begin with them, including the internal spiritual revolutions that seem to have occurred in Gautama and Mohammed, leading to the foundation of Buddhism and Islam. Contrary to widespread impression, however, such sudden enlightenments are not restricted to religious devotees. Scientists also experience them, though usually in a more restricted context. The German chemist August von Kekulé, for example, "discovered" the structure of the benzene ring when he saw a vivid hypnagogic image of it as a snake with its tail in its mouth. And the Danish physicist Niels Bohr first "conceived" of the atom as a miniature solar system—the model which is now standard—when he so perceived it in a vision.

Rapid Eye Movement in Dreams

The line between trancelike visions of this kind and the ordinary night-dreams all of us are now known to experience every hour or two as we sleep, is hard to draw. The distinction is doubly difficult to make in the case of artists and others who find that their best ideas come in dreams. From an eidetic standpoint, what is most striking about dreams is not only that visual impressions normally predominate in them but that the only bodily organs which commonly move when dreaming occurs are the eyes. Indeed, rapid eye movement (REM, for short) is now the preferred behavioral evidence of the dream state in mammals, even though it usually requires electrographic detection because of eyelid closure. Taxonomically, moreover, closed-eye REM is also diagnostic of homeothermic status, since only warm-blooded animals are known to dream.

Inner Vision

One way to classify visionary experiences is into endogenous and exogenous types, the former being internally generated and the latter externally generated. In these terms, mystical experiences of the kind reported by religious initiates would be endogenous, whereas similar experiences triggered by mind-altering drugs would be exogenous. Drug-triggered visions are now customarily called psychedelic. Psychedelic visions, consequent to the ingestion of such substances as cannabis or lysergic acid, typically beginning with the perception of multicolored auras, move on through rhythmic pulsations of "objectively" motionless objects and through vivid "subjective" hallucinations, and culminate in experience of a ubiquitous white light in the presence of which the observer's ego seems to merge with the cosmos. The difficulty with this bifurcatory classification of visionary experiences, of course, is that, just as the Newtonian synthesis eliminated the Aristotelian dichotomy of celestial and terrestrial mechanics, so, analogously, a synoptic psychophysiology is beginning to eliminate the equivalent split between "inner" mind and "outer" matter, finding internality and externality to be matters of role or context rather than of ultimate reality.

Fire as a Psychedelic

Such relativism seems especially warranted in considering interactions like the psychedelic response to flame on the part of many people who gaze fixedly into wood fires. They feel hypnotically drawn to its kaleidoscopic effects and soon begin to dream, hallucinate, or feel "illuminated." In considering man's prehistoric acquisition of pyrotechnology, archeologists and anthropologists might do well to consider the possibility that fire was, for early man, more than a source of heat and a means of making damp bear-caves humanly habitable. Just as hemp may have been a drug as well as a source of rope, so also may fire have been a crucial source of visionary experience.

Aerial Lights

The distinction between internal and external vision becomes even harder to maintain when we reach the subject of anomalous aerial phenomena, ranging from Old Testament angels and the New Testament "Star of Bethlehem" to the mysterious glowing airships of the nineteenth century and the "flying saucers" of our own century. Feelings about such phenomena are so highly polarized that it is now difficult to carry on dispassionate discussions of them. But it is generally agreed that percipients of these anomalies report them as luminous in appearance and aberrant in motion and, in cases of close approach, claim to have been paralyzed or transfixed while feeling a strangely ambivalent emotional reaction of fascination and fear. In those rarer cases where actual contacts with associated humanoids are reported, one of the few common factors has been a strong and often nightmarish impression that these beings had hypnotically glowing eyes of quite unhuman shape and color.

What these reports inevitably remind one of is the "eye of God" motif in the art of ancient Egypt and of modern Nepal, in which the attribute of deity most stressed is what might be called "omnividence" as against the omniscience and omnipotence more often emphasized by theologians. Those who doubt that this ocular aspect of divine power is of any material concern to sophisticated moderns need only glance at the-eye-in-the-pyramid on our dollar bills to be reminded that at least one portion of the arcane Masonic or Illuminate tradition lives on in our most public documentation.

VISUAL TECHNOLOGY

The technique of currency printing inevitably raises the question of visual technology at large. The visual education program to which this chapter is intended to contribute would probably not have been established at all had it not been for the prior development of photography, cinema, and television and the new ways of seeing that these techniques made possible. Yet we would be ill-advised to let our understandable enthusiasm for these teleidetic media deprive us of temporal perspective on them. For they grew out of older modes of visual representation and will almost certainly grow into newer modes. Paleolithic murals, Neolithic sculptures, and historic monuments not only preserved but also, in all probability, shaped the vision of their times, as mass media shape ours.

Most of those futurists known as technology assessors now predict that three-dimensional laser videophony will soon become commercially viable, as it is already electronically operative. When it does, we will be able to sit in our living rooms and seemingly "materialize" our absent associates before us as we talk with them by telephone. Such a development, clearly, will have revolutionary implications not only for communication but also for business, transportation, and travel. For, if we can be in intimate audiovisual contact with anyone anywhere at any time, much of the inter-regional visitation and metropolitan commutation in which we now engage may come to seem superfluous and may consequently be abandoned.

The "Magic Mirror" Tradition

Before seeking to trace the probable outcome of such innovations, however, let us pause to note the growing number of scientists and historians currently in the process of reassessing ancient science, with surprising results. Even the most cautious historians of science now concede that printing, plumbing, and town planning were part of the technology of pre-Hellenic Crete. More venturesome scholars claim that the ancients made use (for a restricted elite only) of electrical devices, robots, and flying machines. At this point, of course, history shades into legend, and legend, perhaps, into mythology. But, if we are willing to regard all chronicles as sources of possible fact, then we cannot automatically dismiss persistent traditions of "magic mirrors" whose owners could reputedly use them to see and hear things which were not only remote in space but also in time— the future as well as the past. When Albert Einstein and his colleagues were congratulated on having discovered the secret of atomic energy, he modestly disclaimed the plaudits and remarked, "Perhaps we have not discovered it but only rediscovered it." The videophony and electrophotography of our century may likewise turn out to be rediscoveries.

VISUAL HABIT AND VISUAL CAPACITY

If we are to visualize vision, the most powerful of our senses, in anything more than a limited way, we must learn to see through the "smoked glass" of our parochialism to catch even a glimpse of the larger world outside. In comparison with what we are capable of seeing, what we are in the habit of seeing is doubtless only fragmentary. Recognizing this disparity, we might do well to take, as our eidetic motto, Goethe's dying words: "More light!"

REFERENCES

Altmann, S. (Ed.). *Social communication among primates.* Chicago: Univ. of Chicago, 1967.

Berlin, B., & Kay, P. *Basic color terms: Their universality and evolution.* Berkeley: Univ. of California Press, 1961.

Birdwhistell, R. *Kinesics and context: Essays in human body communication.* Philadelphia: Univ. of Pennsylvania Press, 1970.

Carpenter, E., & McLuhan, M. (Eds.). *Explorations in communication.* Boston: Beacon Press, 1960.

Clarke, A. *Profiles of the future.* New York: Harper, 1962.

Frings, H. & Frings, M. *Animal communication.* New York: Blaisdell/Ginn, 1964.

Von Frisch, K. *Bees: Their vision, chemical senses, and language.* Ithaca, New York: Cornell Univ. Press, 1950.

Halacy, D. *Radiation, magnetism, and living things.* New York: Holiday House, 1966.

Harvey, E. N. *Bioluminescence.* New York: Academic Press, 1952.

James, W. *Varieties of religious experience.* New York: Longmans, 1902.

Kleitman, N. *Sleep and wakefulness.* Chicago: Univ. of Chicago Press, 1963.

Krippner, S., & Rubin, D. (Eds.). *Galaxies of Life: The human aura in acupuncture and kirlian photography.* New York: Gordon and Breach, 1973.

Lane, F. *The kingdom of the octupus: The life history of the cephalopoda.* Moonachie, New Jersey: Pyramid, 1960.

Linden, E. *Apes, men and language.* New York: Saturday Review Press, 1974.

Ostrander, S., & Schroeder, L. *Psychic research behind the Iron Curtain.* Englewood Cliffs, New Jersey: Prentice-Hall, 1971.

Tomas, A. *We are not the first: Riddles of ancient science.* New York: Putnam, 1971.

Wescott, R. (Ed.). *Language origins.* Silver Spring, Maryland: Linstok Press, 1974.

3

Visual Stimuli and
the Construction of Meaning

SAMUEL L. BECKER
University of Iowa
Iowa City, Iowa

MICROSCOPIC VERSUS MACROSCOPIC
RESEARCH STRATEGIES

David Bell (1966), in a discussion of liberal education, talks about the
relative importance of knowing questions and of knowing answers:

> What is a question? A question . . . is really an ambiguous proposition; the
> answer is its determination. . . . The talmudic parable reverses the order of
> events: a man runs down the street shouting, "I've got an answer! Who has a
> question?" In the more esoteric versions, the parable reads: If God is the
> answer, what is the question?

> Which is the most difficult to find: the right question, or the right answer? In
> this—also a question—lies the heart of the educational inquiry [p. 54].

Bell's answer, and mine, is that the question is the more difficult to find
and, hence, the more important. It is relatively easy to learn what to do
after one has a question or hypothesis; this is probably the reason that
most of us concentrate on research methods in our graduate teaching rather
than on methods of question asking. There are reasonably clear rules and
procedures for moving from question to techniques for data gathering and

39

Visual Learning, Thinking,
and Communication

techniques for data analysis. There are no clear procedures for the development of questions—questions that are both important and researchable.

I note these points because I am convinced that, for the most part, we have been asking the wrong questions about visual communication. Hence, we have been coming up with the wrong answers, answers that have not helped us to communicate or to learn more efficiently or effectively. I assume that we are most interested in the kinds or processes of visual communication that help youngsters (or adults for that matter) to develop the most useful meanings for critical concepts, such as government, the Soviet Union, the Middle East, the presidency, teacher, marriage, mother, woman, or man. As I examine the bulk of research that has been done on visual communication, it does not seem to me that it has contributed much, if anything, to our understanding of ways in which such meanings develop. We know, for example, that children have quite well-developed concepts of sex roles before they enter kindergarten, but we have only a very general notion of how they developed them, of the part played by images from picture books, television, parental actions, the actions of siblings, etc. I believe that the reason our research has not added more to our understanding of such problems is that we have concentrated too exclusively on the type of communication situations we can most tightly control and in which obtained variances in response can be attributed most reliably to particular variables. We study the responses to stimuli in isolation from anything we might call a meaningful communication situation—often even from anything we might call a meaningful message, even though there is increasing evidence that the ways in which people respond to stimuli in isolation are not generalizable to the ways in which they respond to them in various contexts. Our assumption, of course, is that what we learn from such microscopic research will ultimately add up to or be generalizable to the more complex situations encountered outside the laboratory. To date, though, nothing gives me enough confidence in the validity of that assumption to justify continued concentration on microscopic studies alone. We must give at least equal attention to more macroscopic approaches to understanding visual communication.

There are dangers in this macroscopic approach. I am urging researchers in visual communication to venture on an unknown path, a path on which we do not know how to travel, a path whose way is poorly lit. It might be relevant to recall the story of the highly inebriated gentleman who was discovered by a friend one dark night, crawling about on his hands and knees under the ring of illumination cast by a lone streetlight. The friend asked what he was doing and the drunk replied that he was looking for his car keys. So the friend got down on his hands and knees also and joined in the search. After a fruitless quarter of an hour, the friend turned to the drunk and asked, "Are you sure you dropped your keys here?" "Oh no," was the response, "I dropped them up the street." "Then why in the devil are you looking for them here? That's stupid!" "No it's not stupid," asserted the drunk, "the light's better here."

In fact, that drunken response is not completely stupid. It is not unlike the sensible behavior of most productive scholars who have learned that it does no good to search for answers in the dark where they have no means of illumination; that one ought to search for answers in places where one has sufficient light to provide a high probability of finding something. One always does this with the hope that these findings will ultimately create sufficient new light to make possible the exploration of the shadowy areas. Just so, because we do not yet see sufficient light around some of the major problems of visual communication, the problems directly related to learning and to teaching, we move down the street to the more limited problems to be found under the streetlight. To a great extent, this behavior has been deified in the academic community and we call it "doing basic research." There is a press, for those of us who wish to be accepted by the community, to do not only basic research, but more and more rigorous and precise research. The result is that we are forced further and further away from practical problems and more and more toward the study of microscopic phenomena.

Having been well-socialized into the academic community, I, too, believe in the need for rigor and precision in our research; I, too, believe that it is foolish searching in total darkness for car keys or answers to questions about visual communication. However, I also believe at least as strongly that we need to move away from the streetlight occasionally to see whether we can find new rays of illumination; we sometimes should trade off a bit of the rigor and precision that come from working on familiar and well-researched microscopic problems to open new areas of scholarship, new possibilities of knowledge, possibilities that may move us closer to providing answers to real-life problems. As statistician John Tukey (1962) put it, "Far better an approximate answer to the *right* question, which is often vague, than an *exact* answer to the wrong question, which can always be made precise [pp. 13–14]."

RECONCEPTUALIZING "MESSAGE"

Most of the decent research and theorizing about visual communication to date has been restricted to a small set of relatively simple stimuli to which subjects are exposed within a relatively brief span of time. These stimuli are either presented to the subjects in isolation or are structured into something we can call a "message"—such as a slide show, a motion picture, or a videotape program. In addition, the stimuli used in many studies are geometric shapes with which the subjects have little prior learning history. These studies tend to be well designed, rigorous in both conception and execution, and a reasonable proportion of them turn out to be replicable—so long as the replication is done in the laboratory. As soon as one moves out of the laboratory, though, and attempts to use the research and theory from these laboratory studies to predict the ways in which people perceive meanings in, or construct meanings from the stimuli they encounter, the theory and research findings become less useful. There are a number of reasons for this lack of generalizability, the major ones being some critical differences between the kinds of communication studied in the laboratory and that which goes on in the schoolroom or in our everyday life.

A clue to these differences can be found in the writings of Marshall McLuhan. In attempting to distinguish among the effects of different media, McLuhan (1964) describes television as a "cool" medium (as opposed to a "hot" medium) because, he says, the stimulus has low definition:

> The TV image offers some three million dots per second to the receiver. From these he accepts only a few dozen each instant, from which to make an image. . . . The TV image is now a mosaic mesh of light and dark spots.

> The mosaic is not uniform, continuous, or repetitive. It is discontinuous, skew, and nonlineal. . . . The mosaic form of the TV image demands participation and involvement in depth of the whole being. . . . It is total, synesthetic [p. 313].

I do not know what McLuhan means by that statement. Some readers have taken it literally and have attempted to test whether, in fact, viewers become more "involved" or retain more from an instructional program which they view on a television screen than from the same program viewed in its less grainy projection by an optical film system. Obviously, they found no differences. In pondering McLuhan's generalization, it occurred to me that the only way to make sense of it is as a metaphor for the way in which most individuals in this society use television. That is, we do not generally turn it on at the beginning of a well-constructed unified program that is complete in itself and then turn it off afterward. Instead, we watch television in fits and starts throughout the evening—and, often, throughout the day, and day after day. We get bits and pieces of all sorts of messages that we put together to create our own messages, our own pictures of reality.

Think, for example, of the message about the role of women that we get from television. We are confronted with Rhoda, Phyllis, Edith Bunker, Maude, Mary Tyler Moore, Mary Hartman, the Bionic Woman, Dinah Shore, the excitable contestants on the game shows, and all of the tragic figures in the soaps. The newscasts give us glimpses of Betty Ford and Rosalynn Carter, Indira Ghandi and Golda Meir, Chris Evert and Evonne Goolagong, and, of course, the million dollar network newscaster Barbara Walters. And amid all of those images we get the commercials—women squeezing the Charmin, washing clothes whiter than white, worrying about their coffee and about waxy yellow build-up. And these are but a few of the increments of information we get about the role of women through the tube which we use to build a coherent meaning for that important part of our world.

In this sense, McLuhan's description—of the cool, low-definition television mosaic from which each of us grasps a limited number of information increments with which to create our images—is a valid one. The major weakness of this concept is that it is not useful, as McLuhan claimed, for distinguishing among media. In fact, this concept strongly suggests that differences among media may not be important variables in the construction of our images of reality. As each of us creates and continually recreates his or her meaning for women, he or she uses not only all of those fragments seen on television, but the pictures and stories in newspapers, motion pictures, magazines, and books, bits of conversations with friends and acquaintances, and observation of the women actually encountered. *The most relevant differences among media may well be in the kinds of images presented, the frequency and rhythm with which images of a particular concept are presented, and the aspects of the concept most frequently presented and omitted.*

What I am suggesting is that there are some critical differences between the kinds of "messages" that are studied in the laboratory and the kinds of "messages" people encounter in their everyday lives.

1. In the laboratory, subjects generally have been exposed to a message that is concentrated and organized. Outside the laboratory, almost any message that people tend to expose themselves to is scattered and unorganized.
2. In the laboratory, there generally has been little repetition of the message or any of its parts. In the field one tends to be exposed to part of the message many times.
3. In the laboratory, the amount of exposure to the message for a given experimental condition generally has been relatively homogeneous

for all subjects. In the field, there is tremendous heterogeneity among almost any group of subects in amount of exposure.

4. Similarly, in the laboratory, for any given experimental condition, all subjects generally have been exposed to precisely the same or virtually the same message. In the field, for the reasons I have noted, there is great variance in the "message" to which subjects are exposed.

THE COMMUNICATION MOSAIC

I find it useful to visualize the processes of normal communication as depicted in Figure 3.1. If we take as an example the "message" of women, it is obvious that there is an infinite number of possible increments of information about women in our environment to which we might be exposed. These information increments can come from any of a very large number of sources, so large a number that, for all practical purposes, it also can be treated as infinite. However, at any given moment, only a limited number of sources, if any, are making any of the relevant increments of information available to us. (These available source-information combinations are noted by the Xs in the mosaic.) And of these increments available, we sense only a fraction.

Most parts of this communication mosaic are constantly changing; we do not have precisely the same images of women available to us all of the

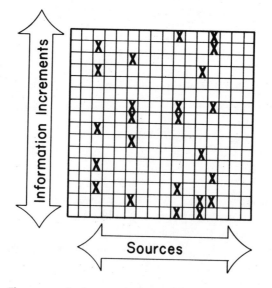

FIGURE 3.1. The communication mosaic for one "message" at one moment.

time. In some cases the images are in a *constant* state of change—as on television or the women around us. In other cases, images are less transitory, as for example a picture in a newspaper or magazine or a painting in the living room.

Some media, such as television, motion pictures, and other human beings with whom we communicate, are each multiple sources. We simultaneously get both aural and visual information from each; and these aural and visual "tracks" interact, just as the various images or increments of information that we obtain from totally different sources interact as we utilize them in the creation of our meanings. They interact not only with other information increments that we sense simultaneously, but they interact with those that have been sensed at different points in time. Thus time is an important third dimension in our communication mosaic, as Figure 3.2 suggests. With time and the accretion of information, the meaning that one has for the concept "women" shifts and develops and probably becomes increasingly complex and, yet, increasingly clear.

Another way to conceive of the time dimension is simply as an addi-

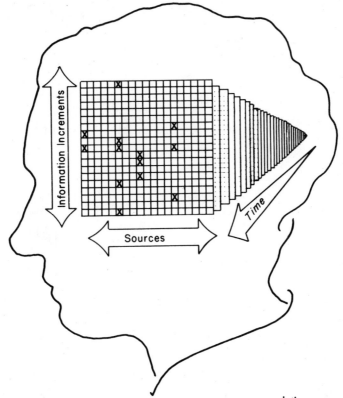

FIGURE 3.2. The interaction of message increments, sources, and time.

tional source, which is memory. For all but the most inexperienced infant, a larger set of increments of information is available from memory than from any other source. Equally important, the more information increments one has acquired, the greater the probability that further learning or the development of meanings will take the form of perceiving or creating analogies rather than being dependent on rote learning (see Lindsay & Norman, 1972).

For our model of the communication mosaic or communication environment to be more complete and useful, we need to add at least one other dimension. At any given moment, each of us has available not only many increments of information about women, but also many increments of information about an infinite number of other messages—the message of the presidential election campaign, of India and Israel, of sports, of the news media, of advertising, and many other concepts. Just as all of us are exposed to a variety of images with which we create our meanings for women, so we are exposed to a variety of images with which we build our other meanings. It is important to take cognizance of the fact that these sets of increments, which are related to different messages, are not isolated from each other, but rather are part of a single communication mosaic in which each of us exists. In terms of our model, these various messages

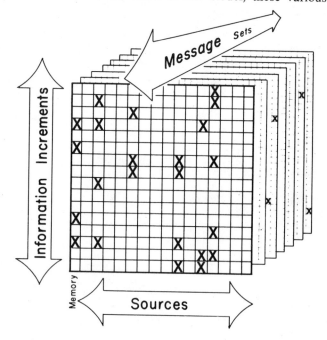

FIGURE 3.3. The total communication environment.

form a fourth dimension. (Since four dimensions are somewhat difficult to visualize, I have treated the time dimension in Figure 3.3 as a source, labeled memory.)

IMPLICATIONS OF THE COMMUNICATION MOSAIC

As this model suggests, during each waking moment we have an infinite variety of information increments about an infinite variety of concepts from which we select some fraction with which to create and alter our meanings.

One clear implication of all of this is that the structuring that the perceiver does is far more important than the structuring that the source intends. Hence, in much of our research on communication, we may be too concerned with the purposes of the source and insufficiently concerned with the sets and/or motivations of the receiver. With each set of information increments designed to communicate something about one concept come increments which, for any given receiver, communicate things about a host of other concepts.

This excess baggage—these unintended increments—may be present as part of the carrier system for the message set, or may be extra dimensions of some of the intended increments. For example, if a news medium carries a photograph showing Evonne Goolagong winning a tennis match at Wimbledon, there are innumerable elements in the photograph that are irrelevant to that intended message, but which are necessary to include. Evonne's costume has no necessary relationship to the intended message but, for most media at least, must be included and for some viewers will fit into a message set about tennis fashion.

Evonne Goolagong herself, though, might also fit into various message sets, in addition to the one intended by the transmitter of the photograph. She might fit into and affect our meaning for the role of women, for tennis, for sports, for Wimbledon, for Australia, and for the aboriginal.

One of the questions about communication that demands study concerns the conditions which affect the probability of a single stimulus of this sort becoming part of some concepts and not of others. We need to study the relationship of immediate organization in perception to recall in other contexts. We seem generally well-agreed that an individual's understanding of a concept is continually elaborated and embellished, even in the case where the concept itself is not directly encountered again (Lindsay & Norman, 1972). For example, though few if any of us probably associated Eleanor Roosevelt with the women's movement when she was alive, our memories of her may now interact with information increments about and our meanings for the women's movement, thus changing both those latter meanings and our meanings for or memories of Mrs. Roosevelt. Just so, we assume that, once stored in memory, one's image of Evonne Goolagong can affect one's meaning for concepts with which she was not immediately associated during exposure to the image. What is not clear in all of this, what demands study by some of us interested in communication and learning, are the conditions that cause these phenomena to occur or affect the ways in which they occur.

A related question concerns our more immediate associations—the factors that affect the probability of our perceiving one aspect of a stimulus or set of stimuli rather than another, or associating it with one concept rather than another. One of the favorite examples used by behavioral scientists to illustrate selective perception is the cocktail party, in which they claim that one can focus on or "tune in" to only one conversation at a time— listening to one causes the loss of the others. What these scholars fail to note is that one can also "tune in" to the total party rather than to one individual conversation in order to perceive a different sort of meaning— listening to the pitch and rhythm of the entire party, getting the "message" of whether the party is getting more or less lively, getting a notion of whether it is wild or sedate or even fluctuating between the two, getting a notion of when it is beginning to wind down or break up.

Scholars who study the acquisition of reading skills or the memorization of lists of letters or numerals are concerned with the phenomenon they term "chunking"—reading or memorizing by *groups* of letters, words, or numerals rather than by individual units. The example I cited of different ways to focus on the cocktail party can be usefully conceived of as a type of chunking. Similarly, the various ways in which we focus upon and process a visual stimulus or a set of visual stimuli probably can be usefully conceived and studied in this way. This approach may help us to understand better the reasons we associate a particular stimulus with one concept rather than another and, perhaps, even help us to understand the degree to which a single stimulus can contribute to the shaping of a large set of one's concepts.

I have been concerned here largely with the relationship of a stimulus to different concepts or messages and of the relationships among stimuli. Another type of interaction that needs study is that among messages or concepts. For example, as one is exposed to a variety of relevant stimuli and alters one's meaning for the role of women, this alteration is likely to affect the way one processes increments of information about other concepts—politics, sports, the role of men—and the meanings one creates for these concepts.

In a sense, all of what I have been discussing in the preceding pages is closely related, and all of it suggests that we must assume the existence of a system of cross-indexing of knowledge within memory, the cross-indexing of information increments or ideas that fit different cognitions. Thus, it might be fruitful to define "literacy" as the degree to which an individual perceives and stores stiimuli in a way that retains their ties to the greatest number of "messages." Thus, a photograph of a construction worker might be stored in such a way that it will be retrieved as part of the message of "construction workers," "American men," "skilled craftsmen," "the working man," "the labor movement," etc. A fruitful definition of creativity might well be the degree to which one is able to retrieve or associate a wide variety of information increments with a message—increments that a less creative person would never think of in association with the message—at least, until the relationship is pointed out. This is what underlies the ability to perceive or create analogies.

To this point I have been concerned with the mosaic concept in general. I turn now to a discussion of some of the major variables—both stimulus variables and organismic variables—that need to be considered in this context. As with other aspects of the mosaic, I have far more questions about these variables than I have answers.

STIMULUS VARIABLES

Redundancy

One of the first variables which the mosaic conception makes salient is that of redundancy. In the normal course of any individual's existence in the contemporary society, he or she is exposed to some stimuli repeatedly. The repetitive symbol may well be the most distinctive sign of our times, with the Xerox machine, high speed printers, audio and video recorders, and other devices for rapid duplication of material. We see the giant Marlboro man on billboards again and again as we drive across the country; we pass and observe numerous little "beetles" or Volkswagens on the same trip, varying slightly if at all, except for shifts in color—but even these shifts are within a limited range; we see Mrs. Olson saving a marriage with her coffee-making advice so many times that she becomes a national celebrity; and we hear "Convoy" and other such hit tunes on the radio again and again and again—and yet again. Not only do we have innumerable stimuli of these kinds that seem to recur endlessly, we get some which develop quickly, assault our senses repeatedly and intensively, and then disappear. For example, when Jack Ruby shot Lee Harvey Oswald after the John Kennedy assassination, the film of the shooting was shown repeatedly on television newscasts and specials for a 24–48-hour period, and, because interest in the event was high, many individuals attended carefully to it each time.

Not only do we have redundancy in exposure to the same stimulus and redundancy in exposure to the mass-produced carbon copies, we also have redundancy of particular elements of some stimuli, even though other elements vary. Thus, for example, we have the so-called genre film or television program—the western, the private eye, etc.—in which the conventions are so set and the inhibitions against their violation so strong that there is little of surprise value in most of them. In a sense, we have "genres" of a sort in many aspects of our environment—the ranch-style house, the leisure suit, the classroom, the usual office building, some kinds of home furnishings and furniture, and the supermarket.

In considering the role of redundancy or prior exposure in information processing, a good starting place is probably the assertion that "You can't step into the same river twice," attributed to the Greek philosopher Heraclitus in the fifth or sixth century B.C. Not only is there constant change in the river or, in our case, the communication environment, there is constant change in "you." Each prior experience, however slight, changes a person in some respect. Each increment of information we sense affects our responses to later increments, especially to later related or similar or presumably identical increments. One biologist, for example, using the model of evolution, suggests that redundancy has an effect even when one does not recall the prior exposure to an increment of information. He suggests that "the man who once knew a datum, but has forgotten it now, is different from the man who never knew it." There is support for this generalization in studies on relearning versus initial learning.

Herbert Krugman, who studied the impact of television advertising, has generalized about the effects of redundancy of material with which those who are exposed repeatedly have little involvement. He indicates that as "trivia are repeatedly learned and repeatedly forgotten and then repeatedly learned a little more. . . the *structure* of our perception [Krugman, 1971, p. 490]" of an object or idea can alter, sometimes through alteration of the relative salience of the attributes emphasized in the material to which we are exposed. Since, as the mosaic paradigm suggests, we have little involvement with most of the stimuli to which we are exposed, the processes of learning without involvement are important. In addition, though Krugman and others sometimes have used the term "trivia" to describe those information increments with which receivers have little involvement, we should not equate lack of involvement with lack of importance. As I suggested earlier, most of our major concepts probably develop from repeated exposures to stimuli with which, at the moment of exposure, we have little involvement. Even when we are involved with some aspect of a stimulus, other aspects on which we are not focusing a great deal of attention probably operate on us in the same way as other low-involvement stimuli.

The degree of involvement evoked by particular stimuli is, of course, at least partly a function of the situation and the conditions that alter their importance for particular receivers. For example, when stimuli appear on the television screen in a context that we recognize as a commercial, we generally reduce our level of attention or involvement well below that which we would devote to the stimuli if we perceived them as part of the program. In addition to these factors of situation and condition, though, there is some evidence that some classes of stimuli tend to be more important than other classes—independent of situation and conditions. Hence, they tend to evoke greater involvement. Evidence from research on person-perception suggests that people, or images of people, though like other visual stimuli in some senses, tend to evoke greater involvement (see, for example, Tagiuri, 1969). I also found evidence for this generalization in a study comparing various methods of getting continuous responses of children to instructional television programs (Becker, 1964). In this study, respondents indicated their interest or lack of interest in each portion of each program by continuously pushing or releasing a button device, by checking a chart in the appropriate place when a signal was given each 30 seconds, or through changes in the electrical resistance of their bodies measured by a galvanic skin response (GSR) recorder. The three methods of indicating interest produced reasonably consistent results, with one major exception. Almost every time the teacher appeared on the screen in one of the programs, paper and pencil and push-button responses indicated a drop in interest, whereas the GSR scores went up. That is, even though the students reported less interest in seeing the teacher on the screen, there seemed to be a higher level of tension or involvement accompanying such appearances.

I assume that children learn to attend more closely to other human beings than to most other kinds of stimuli fairly early in their lives, and the means by which this conditioning occurs are fairly obvious. The question that needs to be answered in order for us to understand the ways in which individuals process the information they absorb from their environment and build the worlds in their heads is whether there are additional categories of stimuli which tend to evoke greater or less involvement from most of us. For example, there may be systematic differences among sensory modes in the power to evoke involvement or the power to dominate, so that one mode or the other may have relatively greater impact on our creation of meanings under certain circumstances. Research on such problems can help us to determine weights for the various information increments in the communication mosaic.

Organization or Structure

Another critical concept in visual communication is structure or organization. Some scholars of visual perception have suggested that there are two major aspects of structure that are relevant to the sorts of problems we are discussing here: *message structures* and *perceptual structures*. I suggest that there is a third major type of structure, especially important in most normal, everyday communication, which we might call *exposure structures*. This is the structure that people create through the way in which they expose themselves to and are exposed to the increments of information in their environment; it is the pattern in which they sense a set of stimuli. This structure is unique for each individual.

As I indicated earlier, the organization which the *creators* of most messages impose is largely irrelevant for most individuals for whom they were intended because our exposure to them is not systematic. This seems to me to be especially true of children but, to a large extent, is also true of the rest of us. Not only do we look at the television screen in unique patterns of bits and bursts, we scan newspapers and magazines, focusing only on fragments here and there (some, like me, for example, examine the front page of the newspaper and then read the rest of it from back to front, rather than front to back as the editors intend), we hear only fragments of the conversations in which we are participants. There are, perhaps, as many ways in which the world is sensed as there are people in this world. *The wonder to me is not that we disagree as often as we do about what that world looks like, but rather than we agree as well as we do about its appearance.*

The artists, whom many label nonrealistic, may well be presenting the most realistic image of all of the way in which people sense their worlds. The Dadaists, for example, through photomontage, collage, and juxtaposition of incongruous objects, attempt to create not an "organized" work of art but a wide range of disparate images which stimulate viewers to create their own finished products (Richter, 1964). The mixed media presentations and some of the avant-garde theatre are better approximations of normal communication processes than is the usual theatrical film or the well-made play. In these contemporary art forms, the directors arrange random multiple images and whatever meaningful organization is given to them is supplied by the individual member of the audience. Russian film-maker and theorist Sergei Eisenstein used similar techniques in both his films and his theatre productions, which he labeled montage (though his images were not simply random selections, as I suspect the images of most artists whose works stand up through time are not). The montages that Eisenstein created forced his audiences to synthesize new meanings from the often simple, individual images that he juxtaposed.

There is evidence from a wide range of studies that, when a receiver is cognizant of or believes that the set of stimuli to which he or she is exposed was created or organized by someone for a purpose, the meanings that the set of stimuli evoke and, to some extent, the meanings each stimulus evokes, will be partly a function of that perceived pattern (Luchins, 1957b).

This is an especially interesting problem in visual communication involving drawings, still pictures, or motion pictures of familiar objects or scenes. In these forms of communication we have at least two potential levels of meaning. The first level derives from the fact that most objects depicted, as, for example, in the shots in a television program, are meaningful in and of themselves. The second level derives from the organization of these images, the framing and the juxtapositions that cause at least some members of the audience to perceive symbolic values. Dudley Andrew puts this point more elegantly in his discussion of the film theory of Jean Mitry when he notes that "the film image exists alongside the world it represents. . . . The filmic analogue . . . [is] forever distinct from the world it runs beside and so faithfully mirrors [Andrew, 1976, p. 190]." The framing and ordering of these images in these forms of communication are done by someone other than the viewer. Rather than the viewer directly organizing the chaos that is our world out there, he is reorganizing material that has been previously organized by someone else.

Mitry and a number of other film theorists apparently consider only these two levels of meaning in such sequences of images, that attributable to the meanings associated with the individual images and that associated with the organization imposed by the creator or compiler of the images. As Worth and Gross (1974) have pointed out, though, the meanings evoked either by the single images or by their organization will depend largely upon what the viewer infers about intent. If the viewer accepts the organization or any part of it as simply existential—a "natural order" or "natural point of view"—he or she employs a different interpretive strategy than if symbolic intent is assumed. In the latter case, we would predict that more complex meanings are likely to be evoked.

There are many examples that could be cited of this phenomenon. For one, imagine yourself walking down an alley and seeing some small pieces of torn screening piled atop each other and nailed to the wall. How do you think about those stimuli? Now imagine yourself in one of the galleries of the Guggenheim Museum in New York, seeing these same pieces of torn screening piled atop each other and nailed to the wall. Now how do you think about them? Clearly not in the same way. The situation of exposure created quite different sets of expectations and altered the probabilities of inferring symbolic intent. In the Guggenheim, we could increase the probability of your inferring symbolic intent even more by placing a frame around the set of torn pieces of screen and focusing a spotlight on the result.

In this example, there may be even a fourth level of meaning involved. The inference or assumption that some set of stimuli comprises a work of "art" seems to call forth another interpretive strategy, one that is in addition to the others, not merely a substitute for or variation of one of the others. Although research on this problem is limited, it seems to me that viewers of visual stimuli are most likely to create multiple *levels* of meaning—for example, to perceive both a simple story of the here and now and a biblical theme for which the story is a metaphor—when their strategy for interpreting artistic objects is evoked. When they infer intent, but not artistic intent, viewers are more likely to create only a single level of meaning.

Another way to conceive of some of these phenomena is in terms of convention or expectation. Consider, for example, the way in which individuals sometimes make sense out of what may appear to be random stimuli, whereas at other times they perceive no sense at all in these stimuli.

For many years, we believed that there were certain principles of film editing that could not be violated or the film would be meaningless. However, when some of the old principles of film editing were violated—principles whose violation was supposed to render a film sequence meaningless or confusing for an audience—such as a jump cut [1]—we found that most members of the audience were not confused; they had little difficulty in creating a meaning. In fact, it now appears that it may be impossible to create a meaningless film. To some degree, this is also true of theatre. It is less true of discussion, public speaking, conversation, radio, or television, probably because conventions are so much better learned for these forms—our expectations are so much more set and rigid. At one time, I thought that the difference between forms that could be perceived as

---

[1] When two pieces of film are joined with a significant piece of continuous action missing, as when an actor is shown beginning to climb a flight of stairs and then a cut is made to a shot of the actor at the top of the stairs, it is termed a "jump cut." The actor appears to "jump" up the stairs.

meaningless and those that could not be was the former's dependence on language, the argument being that linguistic structure is so well learned—perhaps even innate to some degree as Chomsky and others have postulated—that any form of communication depending strongly on language can be rendered meaningless for most people by violating grammar and syntax. However, as soon as one thinks of poetry, this generalization breaks down too. Linguistic rules can be totally ignored and, so long as the readers or listeners believe that it is poetry to which they are being exposed, one can present random words and they will tend to perceive meaning. Given the same stimuli without the expectation of poetry, but rather the expectation of rhetorical discourse, the reader or listener will perceive no meaning. *This interaction of prior learning and expectations may provide a key to many of the communication questions that are yet unanswered.*

A closely related phenomenon is the effect of contextual cues or of contiguous stimuli, especially when the two stimuli (or the stimulus and the context) are unrelated, or even contradictory. Bertolt Brecht, a dramatist and expressionist writer in the early part of this century built much of his dramatic theory around what he termed the "alienation effect" (Willett, 1964). There have been many interpretations of what he meant by that effect. The interpretation I find most useful is that it is the effect that results when members of an audience are presented with contradictory stimuli, as when an actor evokes one kind of meaning with a line of dialogue, and a contradictory kind with a gesture or facial expression. The effect is to "alienate" audience members, to shake them out of becoming lost in a play and accepting it at its simple, face value; it causes them to think and to create more complex meanings for the character they are watching and for the play. (Talented actors use this phenomenon to create the illusion of greater complexity of character. In one sense, the definition of stereotyped acting is to dress and to act in a way that is completely consistent with the lines that one is reading.)

Contextual cues can not only create alienation and force an individual to create more complex meanings to account for them, they can also serve to limit the meanings which individuals are likely to create for stimuli. As an obvious example, if we title a film "Faces" for one group of viewers and "Contemporary Fashions" for another, each group will tend to create somewhat different meanings from the film.

Some theorists have considered contextual effects in terms of two opposing processes that are part of our communication—specification and generalization. Any object or concept to which we are exposed, directly or indirectly, has the potential to be perceived as unique or as a symbol for a class. When we are exposed to a particular Iowan, for example, we may perceive her as "unique," or we may perceive her as symbol for "Iowa people in general," or "midwesterners," or "Americans," or even "mankind." [2]

Not only can a stimulus be perceived to have as a referent either a specific or general concept, it is conceivable that specification and generalization can occur simultaneously. For example, while one watches the television program *All in the Family,* one's image of Archie Bunker becomes increasingly clear so that a unique individual is perceived, at the same time that one may slowly be recognizing that Archie is a symbol for all of us in this society. Just so, as one gets an increasing number and variety of increments of information about a concept such as the city of St. Louis, one may develop a clearer and clearer perception of St. Louis as a unique city, while at the same time developing a perception of the general concept of "large city."

An important factor or set of factors in this specifying or generalizing process are the other increments of information with which we associate the stimuli that directly represent the concept. Some of these increments can be found in the context in which we encounter the stimuli. Some theorists believe that context tends to make meaning more specific for verbal signs or, in their terms, it "disambiguates" words (Rommetveit, 1971). At least one theorist, Calvin Pryluck (1973), believes that context works differently for visual or pictorial signs than it does for verbal ones, that it leads us to generalize the pictorial stimulus but to particularize the verbal one. Thus he concludes that visual communication is "structurally inductive," whereas language is "structurally deductive." Pryluck (1973) also makes the important point that sequencing and juxtaposition—contextual factors—are especially important in pictorial communication because we do not have conventional relational devices as we have for languages; "the conceptual relationship between images is indirect and inferential [p. 131]."

Though Pryluck's insights into pictorial communication processes are sensitive and useful, we need to question the inductive–deductive distinction between language and pictorial communication. Whether a word or a picture or any other stimulus tends to be perceived increasingly specifically or generally or both as context is provided depends, for both words and pictures, on the type of context, on the type of word or picture, and on the type of set of the receiver. As obvious examples, the context of the words "Calvin Jones" can lead most of us to perceive a particular and unique

---

[2] Some theorists have argued that the relative iconicity of symbols affects the degree of generalization or abstraction. I do not have time to go into this matter in this chapter. However, I should note that, to date, there has been little research designed to test or refine the claim. This could be an especially fruitful area for research by scholars interested in visual communication.

individual or to think of American men in general. Similarly, the context of a shot of a man in a film can evoke in most viewers the general image of any or all men or the very clear and specific image of the particular man they perceive as being depicted on the screen. The stimulus alone, as free as possible of context, whether visual or verbal, will probably evoke a specific image for some receivers, a general one for others. Here is another fruitful area for research. The complex interactions between sign of the concept, context, and prior set of the perceivers need a good bit of study if we are to develop useful, theoretical ideas about these phenomena.

One of these interactions, which has been studied in a limited way by two of my students, is that between order and context of information increments. The results suggest the potential richness of such study.

The studies of this interaction were stimulated by an observation about contextual effects made by two Russian film makers in the 1920s, Pudovkin and Kuleshov, when they were experimenting with film editing. This is Pudovkin's (1960) report of their results.

> Kuleshov and I made an interesting experiment. We took from some film or other several close-ups of the well-known Russian actor Mosjukhin. We chose close-ups which were static and which did not express any feeling at all—quiet close-ups. We joined these close-ups, which were all similar, with other bits of film in three different combinations. In the first combination the close-up of Mosjukhin was immediately followed by a shot of a plate of soup standing on a table. It was obvious and certain that Mosjukhin was looking at the soup. In the second combination the face of Mosjukhin was joined to shots showing a coffin in which lay a dead woman. In the third the close-up was followed by a shot of a little girl playing with a funny toy bear. When we showed the three combinations to an audience which had not been let into the secret the result was terrific. The public raved about the acting of the artist. They pointed out the heavy pensiveness of his mood over the forgotten soup, were touched and moved by the deep sorrow with which he looked on the dead woman, and admired the light, happy smile with which he surveyed the girl at play. But we knew that in all three cases the face was exactly the same [p. 168].[3]

These findings seem obvious to us today. However, some of the variations of the Pudovkin–Kuleshov study which we have carried out at Iowa in recent years suggest more complex and less obvious relationships. For example, one study demonstrated the way in which perceptions of the actor's facial expression in such films varies appreciably with the length of the closeup of his face (Tiemens, 1959). This variance may be due to a number of factors, such as facilitation of a more stable perception of that expression, or an increase in the probability that other increments of information in the closeup of the face will be processed. One might expect that the longer closeup will lead to more "accurate" perceptions of the

---

[3] Reprinted by permission of Grove Press, Inc. Copyright © 1960. All rights reserved.

facial expression. This appears not to be the case, because the differences resulting from lengthening of the closeup are not the same when the contextual cues are different; that is, as the closeup shot is lengthened, the perceptions of it evoked by the different versions of the film do not converge.

In another study at Iowa, the interaction between context and the *order* in which shots are presented was tested (Foley, 1966). Three films similar to those of Pudovkin and Kuleshov were created and then two versions of each film were made, in one of which the contextual shot came before the closeup and in one of which it came after the closeup. Results showed that the perception of facial expression is changed substantially when the order of closeup and contextual shot is reversed. The kind of change is not consistent; there is an interaction between order and context. Many variations of this study need to be made before we can describe with any precision the nature of this interaction and, hence, before we will have much predictive power. Even more important, some testable explanations of this interaction need to be developed.

Gaps

Most of the examples I have been citing of structural and contextual effects, and most of the related research that I have mentioned, are based on the traditional concept of "message" that I earlier decried as the major base on which to build useful theories of communication—the concept of message as a discrete, unified set of stimuli to which one is exposed within a limited span of space and time. An important implication of the mosaic conception of "message" is that we must strive to understand the effects of structure and context when the increments that comprise that structure and context are scattered through space, time, and mode of communication. At this point, it is not clear how much, if any, of the research on structure and context of traditional messages is generalizable to such situations; it is not clear how the magnitude of the gap in space, time, or mode of communication interacts with the other variables that have been studied.

For example, as a set of information increments about women to which one is exposed is dispersed through time, is there a qualitative as well as quantitative change in the kind of meaning that one is likely to construct? Do gaps in space and gaps in time function in the same way?

We have some potentially useful ideas about the interaction between gaps in time and gaps in sources of information from some of the general communication studies on source credibility. Though there are innumerable studies that demonstrate the greater short-range impact of messages that come from credible sources than messages that come from noncredible sources, Carl Hovland and his colleagues found that, as time elapses, the effect of source diminishes more rapidly than the effect of content (Hovland & Weiss, 1952; Kelman & Hovland, 1953; Cohen, 1957). Thus, though the source from which information comes may affect the immediate meanings that one constructs, it may have little effect on the meanings retained after some period of time. In fact, there is even some evidence that after a relatively brief gap in time, people will tend to attribute information that they got from one source to another source. In studies of information diffusion, for example, it has been found that subjects interviewed shortly after an event report getting a considerable amount of their information from interpersonal communication. Within a week or two, though, they tend to forget that they got the information from other persons and believe that they got it from television (Steinfatt, Gantz, Seibold, & Miller, 1973). To the extent that this is a general tendency for certain classes of information, it has major implications for understanding content–source interactions and, hence, for understanding the processes by which we create the worlds in our heads.

In studies of persuasion and impression formation, it has been found that information received first has greater impact than contradictory information received immediately afterward. However, again, this differential impact disappears or is reversed when there is a reasonable gap of time between the increments of information (Luchins, 1957a; Miller & Campbell, 1959). These generalizations also need to be explored in more complex situations that more nearly approximate the sorts of communication situations which most of us encounter most of the time.

There are other important variables that need to be considered in terms of the more macroscopic approach to understanding communication phenomena, organismic variables, response variables, as well as additional stimulus variables, none of which we have space to treat in detail in this chapter. However, I hope that I have suggested some fresh ways to consider them, some ways that will result in more important research questions and, ultimately, more useful theoretical ideas or understandings about human communication.

REFERENCES

Andrew, J. D. *The major film theorists.* New York: Oxford Univ. Press, 1976.
Becker, S. L. Interest, tension, and retention. *AV Communication Review,* 1964, *12,* 277–291.
Bell, D. *The reforming of general education.* New York: Columbia Univ. Press, 1966.
Cohen, A. R. Need for cognition and order of communications as determinants of

opinion change. In C. I. Hovland (Ed.), *The order of presentation in persuasion*. New Haven, Connecticut: Yale Univ. Press, 1957.

Foley, J. M. The bilateral effect of film context. Unpublished M.A. thesis, Univ. of Iowa, 1966.

Hovland, C. I., & Weiss, W. The influence of source credibility on communication effectiveness. *Public Opinion Quarterly,* 1952, *19,* 635–650.

Kelman, H. C., & Hovland, C. I. 'Reinstatement' of the communicator in delayed measurement of opinion change. *Journal of Abnormal and Social Psychology,* 1953, *48,* 327–335.

Krugman, H. E. The impact of television advertising: Learning without involvement. In W. Schramm & D. F. Roberts (Eds.), *The process and effects of mass communication.* Urbana: Univ. of Illinois Press, 1971.

Lindsay, P. H., & Norman, D. A. *Human information processing.* New York: Academic Press, 1972.

Luchins, A. S. Experimental attempts to minimize the impact of first impressions. In C. I. Hovland (Ed.), *The order of presentation in persuasion.* New Haven, Connecticut: Yale Univ. Press, 1957. (a)

Luchins, A. S. Primacy-recency in impression formation and experimental attempts to minimize the impact of first impressions. In C. I. Hovland (Ed.), *The order of presentation in persuasion.* New Haven, Connecticut: Yale Univ. Press, 1957. (b)

McLuhan, M. *Understanding media.* New York: McGraw-Hill, 1964.

Miller, N., & Campbell, D. T. Recency and primacy in persuasion as a function of the timing of speeches and measurements. *Journal of abnormal and social psychology,* 1959, *59,* 1–9.

Pryluck, C. Sources of meaning in motion pictures and television. Unpublished Ph.D. dissertation, Univ. of Iowa, 1973.

Pudovkin, V. I. *Film technique and film acting.* New York: Grove Press, 1960.

Richter, H. *Dada, art and anti-art.* New York: Harry N. Abrams, 1964.

Rommetveit, R. Words, contexts and verbal message transmission. In E. A. Carswell & R. Rommetveit (Eds.), *Social contexts of messages.* New York: Academic Press, 1971.

Steinfatt, T. M., Gantz, W., Seibold, D. R., & Miller, L. D. News diffusion of the George Wallace shooting: The apparent lack of interpersonal communication as an artifact of delayed measurement. *The Quarterly Journal of Speech,* 1973, *59,* 401–412.

Tagiuri, R. Person perception. In G. Lindzey & E. Aronson (Eds.), *Handbook of social psychology.* Reading, Massachusetts: Addison-Wesley, 1969.

Tiemens, R. K. The relationship between the length of a motion picture shot and the meaning that is communicated. Unpublished manuscript, Department of Speech and Dramatic Art, Univ. of Iowa, 1959.

Tukey, J. W. The future of data analysis. *Annals of Mathematical Statistics,* 1962, *33,* 13–14.

Willett, J. (Ed.) *Brecht on theatre.* New York: Hill & Wang, 1964.

Worth, S., & Gross, L. Symbolic strategies. *Journal of Communication,* Autumn, 1974, *24,* 27–39.

4

The Imaginarium:
An Environment and Program
for Opening the Mind's Eye

ROBERT H. McKIM

Stanford University
Stanford, California

> *You cannot teach a man anything.*
> *You can only help him discover it within himself.*
>
> GALILEO

BACKGROUND

Einstein reported that he "rarely thought in words at all" and that his thinking processes were represented to his consciousness by "more or less clear images . . . of visual and some of muscular type." Kekulé told his colleagues that he glimpsed the ringlike structure of the benzene molecule in a dream of a snake biting its own tail. Rudolph Arnheim, in a book entitled *Visual Thinking,* theorizes that visual imagery is essential to all creative thinking. Verbal and mathematical thinking, he suggests, is valuable for mental operations involving logical, linear, step-by-step reasoning, but is totally inadequate for the metaphoric, wholistic, transformational operations generally associated with the initial *"insight"* stages of creative thinking.

Recent neurological research has provided objective evidence that the

Visual Learning, Thinking,
and Communication

right hemisphere of the brain is involved in the wholistic, spatial operations of visual thinking and the left hemisphere with the more analytical, linear operations of verbal and mathematical thinking. "Hard" scientific information about thinking, however, is in short supply. What follows has not been deterred by science's inability to observe and understand mental processes that are inherently multifaceted and personal, and frequently below the threshhold of consciousness. As a designer, I have taken the unscientific liberty of declaring as self-evident the existence and creative value of visual thinking. As a design educator whose students possess imaginations that have been cramped by education's imbalance in favor of verbal and mathematical thinking, I have impatiently forged paths into territories that my more cautious colleagues in science have not yet mapped.

In 1962, I began to develop a course at Stanford University eventually called Visual Thinking. As this course evolved, three principal kinds of imagery emerged as interactive in visual thinking:

1. The kind of imagery we *see* (eyes open)
2. The kind we *imagine* (usually eyes closed)
3. The kind we *record* (graphically or photographically, for example)

Of the three, the kind of imagery that we imagine with our "inner senses" is by far the most educationally deprived. Image-thinking is virtually unknown, much less encouraged, in most classrooms. Our outer-directed society also undervalues, even actively represses, inner experience. Partly because it was an educational and social underdog, and mostly because I realized its powerful potential, I became especially interested in ways to educate, or, more correctly, liberate inner imagery for productive use in thinking and for enrichment of life generally.

The visual thinking course eventually resulted in a book (*Experiences in Visual Thinking,* Brooks/Cole, 1972) in which I devoted six chapters to directed experiences in the productive use of inner imagery. I had collected this material from diverse sources, ranging from ancient meditation practices to current psychotherapies. The sources are listed in the book, along with a gentle admonition that inner imagery exercises are best practiced in a quiet and comfortable environment safe from intrusion. A crowded classroom in a noisy school building is clearly not conducive to attending inner experience; as the book went to press, I was looking for a special environment at Stanford in which to encourage the journey inward.

In 1972, Professor Nelson Van Judah of California State University at San Jose invited me to visit a geodesic dome that he and his students had built to experiment with audiovisual materials. A similar environment seemed well suited to educate inner imagery. With Judah's assistance, and that of Stanford colleagues, William Verplank, Larry Leifer, William Potts, and several graduate students, we designed our own version of the geodesic dome environment and built it in the corner of a large, high-ceilinged classroom at Stanford. We called it the *Imaginarium*.

PHYSICAL DESCRIPTION OF THE ENVIRONMENT

A schematic cross-section of the Imaginarium is shown in Figure 4.1. Essentially, it is a 16-foot diameter geodesic dome (¾ of a sphere) made of heavy cardboard, carefully taped at the seams and painted white inside. A 14-foot diameter viewing platform is centered within the dome, as shown. The platform is made of wood and is blue-carpeted. At the center of the platform is a 10-inch spherical lens, surrounded by a large, circular pillow. As many as 15 participants may enter through a trap door entrance (not diagrammed) and place their heads on the central pillow, their bodies pointed outward like spokes of a wheel. In this position, imagery projected through the spherical lens to the dome's ceiling completely fills the viewer's central and peripheral vision. Super 8-mm and 16-mm movie projectors

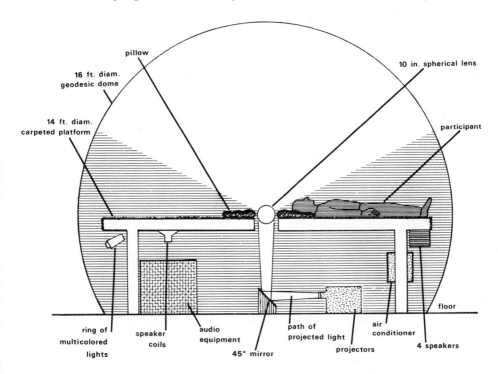

FIGURE 4.1. Schematic of Imaginarium.

and a 35-mm slide projector situated beneath the platform project imagery to a 45° mirror and thence through the spherical lens.

The Imaginarium is equipped with an excellent amplifier, tape deck, and record player connected to four high-fidelity speakers. In addition, the sound system is connected to speaker coils attached underneath the platform. Switched on, the coils vibrate the platform, allowing the participant to experience the music or sound tactually.

Multicolored, rheostat-controlled lights around the platform bathe the dome ceiling in any desired color of light, also giving the platform the appearance of "floating" in the dome. The lights can also be controlled musically, by means of a color organ.

The dome is air-conditioned. To round out the sensory input capability, we have provided means to introduce scents into the dome via the air-conditioning system.

All this equipment (except the rather occult-looking spherical lens) is hidden from the viewer and automatically controlled by an electronic programmer.

The Imaginarium is a flexible environment. It can be pitch-dark and totally quiet, or the source of polysensory stimuli at varying degrees of intensity. Via the sound system, the participant can be verbally guided, or left to imagine on his or her own. On their own, participants can evoke imagery to the accompaniment of music, sound effects, tactile sensations, olfactory stimuli, or amorphous patterns of color projected on the ceiling overhead. Visual material with specific content can both simulate and stimulate imaginative processes in a more directive way. The Imaginarium is a comfortable place to lie down, relax, and entertain imaginative experiences; it is also an excellent environment for small-group interaction and problem-solving.

OBJECTIVES AND METHODS OF
THE EDUCATIONAL PROGRAM

With a fancy environment, we needed something appropriate to do inside. The educational program of the Imaginarium has been developed, and is still developing, in fits and starts. We have reviewed and refined the educational objectives and methods of the Imaginarium, written four 1-hour programs, and had them taped in a professional sound studio.

The latest educational objectives of the Imaginarium are

1. To provide an educational environment in which outer stimuli are readily eliminated, means to enhance awareness of inner sensory

imagery are unobtrusively available, and an ambiance conducive to inner experience is provided.

2. To present an educational program that guides the participant to experience the pervasiveness of his or her own imagination. Everyone is imaginative, almost all the time. The sense of this objective is not to impart something new, but to open doors to ongoing imaginative activity.

3. To demonstrate ways to use inner imagery productively. Once awareness is enhanced, the participant realizes that abundant imagination is not necessarily *productive* imagination. Worry is an example of an abundant, round-and-round use of imagination that is rarely productive. Productive use of imagination requires the development of voluntary control of certain imaginative processes and openness to others, such as dreams and sudden insights, that are rarely voluntary. This objective is clearly the most difficult to achieve.

4. To stay as experiential as possible, keeping lectures *about* imagination to a minimum. This objective is realized when the primary educational content of an Imaginarium program is the participant's own imaginative experience.

5. To guide the participant into self-discovery of his or her own imagination, then gradually to withdraw guidance, creating self-reliance in its place.

The methods used to realize the Imaginarium's educational objectives are:

1. *Modeling*. The Imaginarium is designed as a "model" of human polysensory imagination that teaches by example. The Imaginarium models the mind's eye, for example, by projecting imagery that completely fills the participant's visual field. Auditory, tactual, and olfactory imagery are also "modeled."

2. *Evoking*. The polysensory inputs of the Imaginarium also evoke imagery. Olfactory stimuli, for example, are notoriously evocative of imagery in other sensory modes.

3. *Unblocking*. Awareness of imaginative processes is blocked by needless body tension, judgmental inner chatter, and emotional stress. Imaginarium programs always open with relaxation exercises directed to enable the participant to let go of these blocks. (There are many other blocks to imaginative experience; indeed, the "metamethod" of the Imaginarium *is unblocking*.)

4. *Guiding*. The verbal or otherwise programmed guidance in the Imaginarium contains several functions. First, as a tour guide points out landmarks and points of interest, the Imaginarium guide points

out qualities and relationships in imaginative experience that might otherwise go unnoticed. Second, the guide provides a model that does not mind-wander; the guide relaxedly and attentively moves *at will* through the incredible landscape of human imagination. Hopefully, the participant internalizes the voluntary, relaxed, and attentive attributes of the guide. Third, the guide gradually withdraws, explicitly giving more and more of the guidance function to the participant. Finally, the guide disappears, leaving the participant to explore further under his or her own guidance.

5. *Recentering.* Imaginative viewpoint is frequently, and often dramatically, changed in Imaginarium programs to give the participant insight into the value of imaginative flexibility.

6. *Enhancing.* The Imaginarium's polysensory approach to imaginative experience enhances richness and clarity of inner imagery, as does progressively deeper states of relaxed attention. Strictly speaking, these methods do not enhance as much as they unblock what is already there (with the unblocking experienced as enhancement).

7. *Sharing.* Participants are asked to share their experience at the end of each program. Sharing expands each participant's horizons about the variety of human imaginative experience, helps reinforce personal experience, reduces the "social block" against so-called irrational imaginative activity, and provides a channel for imaginative expression.

8. *Reinforcing.* Post-session exercises, intended to reinforce the Imaginarium experience, are given out after each program. Reinforcement is also given in the Visual Thinking class.

9. *Integrating.* Programs and reinforcement exercises show how inner and outer imagery are intimately interrelated and mutually reinforcing. The central role of imagination in everyday experience is stressed, and the participant is urged to make his or her use of imagination more voluntary, flexible, and productive.

EXCERPTS FROM PROGRAMS

Because the scripts for the Imaginarium's four 1-hour programs are too long to include in this chapter, I reproduce here excerpts that illustrate some of their basic ideas. As you read, you may want to imagine that the narration is in the deep, relaxed voice of a male announcer, that the music and sound effects are professionally mixed, and that the visual materials are projected overhead, filling your vision to its periphery. (The footnotes refer to visual, auditory, or olfactory images.)

Each program begins with relaxation. In "Imaginarium One," the relaxation instruction is quite directive: "Wiggle around now until you find a position that is completely comfortable / and not touching anyone else. / Close your eyes. / Clench your right fist as tightly as you can / hold it / and study the feeling of tension (*5 second pause*). Now relax your fist and feel a soothing/tingling feeling of relaxation coming to your right hand (*10 second pause*)." The instruction continues in this vein, until you have relaxed every muscle group, at which point you hear—"You are now in a positive and peaceful state of deep relaxation / in which none of your energy is diverted into needless tension / and all of your energy can be devoted to what you choose to attend. / This state of relaxed attention is like a drop of water falling into a quiet pool. The single drop [1,2] is the focused nature of your attention. The quiet pool is your peaceful and relaxed being. The single drop [1,2] creates a clear pattern in the quiet pool, a pattern of expanding, concentric ripples. This pattern is your consciousness expanding."[1,2]

After a brief description of the purposes of the Imaginarium, the participant is invited to "begin a guided tour of your inner universe. A primary power of your imagination is its ability to travel immense distances. You are about to take a voyage to the outer and inner reaches of your universe via a film entitled *Cosmic Zoom*. As you take this voyage, you may feel that the Imaginarium is actually carrying you through space. This very real sensation is, of course, imaginative. Open your eyes / to the power of your imagination / to zoom through space." [3] (*Cosmic Zoom* is an animated film that begins with the camera looking down at a boy in a boat. The camera begins to move up and away. You quickly see that the boy and boat are on a lake. As your altitude increases and your view of the geography expands, you soon see that the lake is on the American continent, then the planet Earth; you zoom past the Moon, planets, the Milky Way, way into outer space. Then the camera stops in space, reverses direction, and takes a fast-motion return trip to the boy in the boat. Continuing toward the boy, the camera zooms in on a mosquito on the boy's skin. Entering into the boy's body through the skin puncture made by the mosquito, the camera takes you on a magnifying zoom through the human microcosm—eventually to a blood cell, DNA, nucleus of the atom—then a fast-motion return trip to the boy in the boat.)

After viewing *Cosmic Zoom,* you are reminded that "In addition to

---

[1] Super 8 movie of quiet pool, single drop of water creating expanding concentric ripples.

[2] Sound effect of water splashing and rippling.

[3] 16 mm Cosmic Zoom.

traveling through infinite space, your imagination can traverse great spans of time,[4] and fantasize incredible transformations of everyday reality.[5] In your imagination, you can also discover and invent new realities." [6]

"Now close your eyes and take a *sound-guided tour* through the spatial and temporal reaches of your imagination. Remember, do not judge the clarity of your inner imagery. Even if you experience nothing, let that be perfectly okay with you. Just relax, and take whatever you get. Each of the following sounds is occurring as part of a larger event. In your imagina-ion, where are you, what are you doing, what else do you experience, as you hear:" [7]

After being briefly assisted to relax once more into a state of relaxed attention, you are told: "Now you are going to have a series of sensory and imaginative experiences involving a red apple. Overhead, you see the image of a red apple.[8] Now close your eyes, and experience that image in your mind's eye. Please do not judge the quality of your memory image. Relax and accept what you experience *totally without evaluation*. (*10 second pause*). Now open your eyes, and see the projected image of the apple once more.[8] This time examine the details of the apple / its texture and patterns of color / the way light strikes it / its particular shape. Now close your eyes and relaxedly and nonjudgmentally recall the apple to your mind's eye. / (*10 second pause*). Now, open your eyes and view a series of apple images.[9-15] Close your eyes once more and remember the apple with all your senses / the sound of the apple's juicy snap / [16] now fantasize the apple's sweet taste and fragrance / its texture in your mouth. (*10 second pause*). When you bring *all of your senses* to the act of imagi-nation, and when you become *active* in space and time / acting upon the object of your imagination / the image becomes more real.

"Now, on your own, return to a state of relaxed attention.[1,2] (*30 second pause*). With a little practice you will find that relaxation, combined with polysensory recall, will bring clarity, vitality, and immediacy to your

[4] Slide series of past and future events.
[5] Slide series of fantasy events (e.g., Dali).
[6] Slide series of inventions, famous structures, etc.
[7] Series of sound effects (e.g., surf, crickets, traffic).
[8] Slide of red apple (side view).
[9] Slide of red apple (top view).
[10] Slide of red apple (bottom view).
[11] Slide of red apple cut in half.
[12] Slide of red apple (close-up of seed section).
[13] Slide of red apple (close-up of stem area).
[14] Slide of red apple (45° angle view of complete apple).
[15] Slide of red apple (a mouth taking a bite).
[16] Sound effect of apple being bitten.

inner imagery. You will also find that the same practice will direct your attention to the quality of your everyday, sensory experience. When, for example, was the last time you gave all of your attention to the sensory experience of eating an apple? Most of us talk, read, or think when we eat—and fail to assimilate our food with all our senses.

"To make the polysensory approach to imagination truly effective, you will need to increase your awareness of the polysensory nature of your everyday experience. Sensory experience that is *consciously assimilated* is much easier to reconstruct in imagination than is sensory experience that is blocked from conscious awareness.

"You will now be given a freshly washed apple. (*10 second pause*). For the next few minutes, please do not talk. / Instead, relax / and direct all of your attention to assimilating an apple / with all of your senses."

You are then led on a fully conscious sensory experience of exploring, then eating an apple. The final experience in "Imaginarium One" follows: "Now place the remainder of your apple, its core and seeds, in the center of the dome. As you do, imagine that you are planting an apple tree. (*45 second pause*).

"Now lie down once more, this time with your head outward and your feet pointed toward the center, toward the apple seeds. (*30 second pause*). You may close your eyes, if you wish.

"In this position, your bodies are like branches on an apple tree. Close your eyes. The apple that you have just eaten is now being assimilated by your digestive system; the apple is becoming you. / Imagine that you are the apple that you have just eaten. / Join hands. / Imagine that you are one apple on an apple tree. / The group is the radiating branches of the tree. / Take a deep breath. / Let it out. / As you let it out, relax all tension. Quiet all distracting thinking. / Direct all of your attention, in a very relaxed way, to the pleasurable thought of being a real apple on a real apple tree in a beautiful apple orchard. / You are far out in the country. / You can feel the warm sun on your skin. / You can feel a soft breeze. / The sky is clear blue / the sun feels good as it radiates into your apple body. / You can hear the leaves of your tree rustling in the breeze. / You can smell the fragrance of the ripening apple orchard. / It feels good to be part of nature. /

"Now imagine that you are regressing in time. You are an apple that is going backward in time, becoming smaller, smaller / greener / tarter / smaller yet. / You are evolving-in-reverse into an apple blossom. / You are an apple blossom together with many other apple blossoms on your apple tree. You can smell the lush fragrance of apple blossoms.[17] / You can feel

---

[17] Apple blossom scent.

the warm sun on your delicate petals. / You can hear the honey bees buzzing as they go about pollinating the orchard. / In the distance, you can hear the farmer's dog barking.[18] / You can taste your own sweet nectar. / You can feel that you are an integral part of an incredible complex natural process, involving sun, earth, air, bees, the seasons—and it feels good. /

"Now you are becoming aware that you are more than a single apple blossom; you are an apple tree. Allow your imagination to move into the branch that supports the blossom. You can feel the sap that brings energy to your leaves and blossoms moving through you. / Follow this flow down into the trunk of the apple tree. / Feel the strength of the trunk in your own body. You must be strong to support branches loaded with ripe apples, and to resist the force of heavy winds. / Feel the rough texture of your bark, the hardness of your wood. /

"Now direct your attention down your trunk into your roots. Reach out into the *dark,* damp soil.[19] See the darkness / smell the fragrance of the fertile soil. / See the fat worms and the other subterranean creatures that work the earth. / Feel the cool wetness and texture of the moist dirt and rocks, as you reach out for life-giving water and nutrients. /

"Now leave the tree; become the water itself in the damp orchard field. / Feel yourself feeding the grasses and wild flowers / part of a larger context, / you are essential to life. / You are part of the much larger unity of nature. /

"As water saturated in the orchard field, experience the sun's heat drawing you upward. / Feel the sun evaporating your body / transforming your liquid nature into a vaporous one. / Feel your molecules raising upward into the blue sky.[20] Toward the sun. / You and the others are now forming into a soft cloud. Down below you can see the earth / the tiny patch of apple orchard. / You are floating in the blue sky effortlessly / white / billowy / incredibly free. / In the distance, a hawk is soaring. / You are part of the creative cycles of nature.

"The sky is darkening.[21] It is becoming cooler. / You can feel the wind swirling and moving your cloud. / You are condensing with other cloud molecules into a droplet of rain. / Falling downward in the cold gray sky. / You splash the leaves [22] of a green apple tree and fall downward to the earth / to the soil / to the roots / to the strong trunk / to the sap that

[18] Sound effect of distant dog barking.
[19] Turn off blue lights.
[20] Turn on blue lights.
[21] Turn off blue lights.
[22] Sound effect of rain storm, with voice over.

feeds the branches, the leaves / the blossoms / the apple. You are the apple on the tree, in the orchard, on a rainy day. / You can hear the rain splattering on the leaves / feel the cold, stormy wind swaying the branches / smell the rich odor of damp earth.[23]

"The apple, created by this marvelous, interwoven working of nature, is inside you, becoming you. You are a unique part of this creative unity. (*pause*) And as you return to the dome, to your aliveness here-and-now, you feel good to be part of a unity that is inherently and eternally creative.[24]

"You are fully returned to the dome now. / Open your eyes / look around you. / Reach out / touch the carpet. / You have completed your first Imaginarium venture into the inner world of your imagination. / Sit up / stretch / feel wide-awake and marvelously refreshed.[25]

"If you like, you may now share your experience of "Imaginarium One" with your group."

"Imaginarium Two" begins with relaxed attention experience, briefer and less directive than in "Imaginarium One." This time the basic theme is the active nature of imagination, its power to transcend space and time, and two basic viewpoints of imagination in space and time. In polysensory detail, you are first guided on a fantasy involving figure skating on a vast plane of ice with total freedom. You are then guided, in fantasy, to become an acrobatic seagull. In the next fantasy, you remain stationary in space, and move a guitar: Rotate it to view it from all viewpoints, move close in to view details, etc. Again, the fantasy is polysensory detail: For example, the guitar plays quietly in the distance, loudly close up. You then enter a fantasy involving cross-sectioning various fruits and vegetables (the operation first performed by the Imaginarium with slides) and end up this series of spatial fantasies by moving your imaginative viewpoint above the Imaginarium, transparentizing the dome, and looking at the people on the platform inside.

The next fantasies explore the role of positionality or viewpoint in imagination. The spatial position of *observer* is first illustrated by a slide of the planet Earth. You are in the observer position when imagining or viewing something that's "out there." A quiet drum sound begins: In the far distance, on the African continent, an African drummer is playing. You are asked to zoom in to observe the drummer close up (drum sound increases with zoom in). Participant is then asked to take second spatial position: to *merge* with the drummer, to become the drummer. The drum

[23] Fade rain storm, begin music softly, with voice over.
[24] Bring up music volume, play for 30 seconds, fade.
[25] Turn up house lights.

sound increases, this time with speaker coils under platform turned on to vibrate the platform.

These experiences are followed by the computer-generated film *Catalog,* by John Whitney, which creates unusual spatial effects in the dome, including appearing to take the roof off.

The *observer* and *merged* positions are then explored in relation to the time-transcending power of imagination. You are first asked to revisit a childhood home, in imagination, noticing the difference between *observer in time* (looking back with nostalgia) and *merged in time* (being the size of the child, having the child's feelings).

You are then asked to take the spatial and temporal position of *here and now,* and to notice how difficult it is to maintain this position. (Your mind tends to wander into *past and future.*) The value of the *observer* position to break cycles of nonproductive *merger* into *past and future* is demonstrated by having you observe your own body, thoughts and feelings at close range and nonjudgmentally. This last instruction is usually difficult ,so you are led to move, as observer, into outer space where you can view yourself, from great distance, on planet Earth (slide). From this perspective, body, thoughts and feelings are experienced as very small, and nonjudgmental self-observation is easier. Zooming back into the dome, you are led once again to experience *here and now* (an experience that is *merged* in the immediate place and moment). Ability to merge into the *here and now* is treated as the supreme test of the individual's ability to control the time-transcending power of imagination.

Your final experience in "Imaginarium Two" is rehearsing a desired skill in the *merged* position of *now and there.* (This kind of imaginative practice is now commonly used in sports, and is attributed with much current record-breaking.)

In "Imaginarium Three," relaxation introduction takes the form of a fantasy in which you are led to imagine that your body is a clear glass container filled with liquid that is gradually drained and refilled with fresh liquid. This metaphoric approach to relaxation is followed, somewhat later, by relaxation with music: "As you listen, let the music flow irresistibly into your ears / filling your body / as though your skin held the sound inside it. / (*30 seconds of music*). The music is flowing into your ears / descending through your throat / into your chest and trunk / into your arms / down through your legs. / The music is adopting the contours of your body / flowing through it. / Your fingers / hands / arms are exuding music / your feet / your legs. / Your body is relaxing into the flow of the music. /"

The metaphoric nature of imagination is then approached by returning to the spatial theme of "Imaginarium Two": "An exciting spatial power of imagination is the ability to *rearrange things*. For example, overhead you see a Stanford landmark: Hoover Tower. What if Eiffel had designed it? [26] Or what if Hoover had decided to erect a large statue instead? [27] Or he had been inspired by a visit to Pisa? [28] Or he had run out of cash during construction? [29] Or if he had created a memorial to Chiquita? [30]

"Rearranging things can take infinite form. You can make things small [31] / change their use [32] / or destination.[33] / You can also recombine: for example, put the Imaginarium on top of Hoover Tower [34] and send it into outer space.[35]

"So far we have been rearranging things from the viewpoint of *observer*. Let's change the viewpoint to *merged*. Last night we cleared out the space under the platform so we'd have a place to cage the Imaginarium's new mascot.[36] We have also converted the Imaginarium into a mobile unit: installed a new engine [37] / and wheels so that we could take you for a short ride.[38,39]

"Notice that rearranging things *feels more imaginative,* especially when the rearrangements defy the laws of conventional reality.[40]

"Now let's try some other spatial powers of imagination: *juxtaposing, then transforming things.* Start with our old friend, the apple [41] / now juxtapose the image of a fat bird.[42] Now transform the apple into a fine-feathered fruit.[43] That was an *identity transformation* in which form, or shape, stayed essentially the same. Now transform the *shape* of the apple

[26] Slide of Eiffel Tower in place of Hoover Tower.
[27] Slide of Statue of Liberty in place of Hoover Tower.
[28] Slide of Hoover Tower, leaning.
[29] Slide of top of Hoover Tower barely peeking over Stanford roofs.
[30] Slide of enormous banana in place of Hoover Tower.
[31] Slide of hand writing with small, inverted Hoover Tower.
[32] Slide of mustard-dropped Hoover Tower in hot dog bun.
[33] Slide of Hoover Tower in Kennedy Space Center launch platform.
[34] Slide of close up of above, with Imaginarium atop Hoover Tower.
[35] Sound effect of countdown and blast-off.
[36] Sound effect of lion roaring on speaker below platform; turn on speaker coils to vibrate platform.
[37] Sound effect of starter, then engine, on speaker below platform with speaker coils on.
[38] Sound of engine accelerating, going through gears.
[39] Movie taken with fish eye lens, camera pointed up, moving down a campus lane.
[40] Fade out movie, and engine sound.
[41] Slide of red apple.
[42] Slide of red apple double exposed with bird.
[43] Slide of feathered red apple with legs, beak, eyes.

by juxtaposing a torus-shaped doughnut,[44] the resultant *shape transformation* being a new variety of seedless apple.[45]

"Rearranging, juxtaposing, and transforming things moves your imagination in the direction of the metaphor. You have experienced how easily your imagination can break away from conventional reality by putting familiar things together in new ways. Now explore the power of this imaginative freedom to create metaphors."

What follows is an extensive fantasy involving metaphors: "Close your eyes / and imagine that *you* are the bud of a beautiful red rose.[46] / You are not visualizing a rose "out there," you *are* a red rose. / You can smell your delicate fragrance [47] / in the cool morning air. / Your velvety red petals are closed tightly together. / You are a rose bud ready to bloom. / A drop of morning dew is sparkling, like a diamond, at your center. / Each of your tender petals is delicately pressing outward. / You can feel the warm sun on your outer petals / the cool, fragrant moisture within / each petal growing / reaching outward. / Your rose-body is blossoming now / each petal slowly / luxuriantly / opening. Feel the marvelous sensation of relaxation pouring into your rose-body / as you open luxuriantly / to the warmth of the sun. In silence now, experience your rose-body with all your senses / you *are* a perfect red rose, basking relaxedly in the sun. Your body is open, and completely relaxed." [48] The metaphor then expands, through the colors of the rainbow, into a larger metaphor having to do with the nature of creative imagination.

An important theme of the Imaginarium is gradually internalizing the imaginative guide so that the participants become their own guides. One step in this direction is group fantasy: "You are now going to join your imagination with the imaginations of your companions in the dome to create a group fantasy. The person who is closest to the door will begin the fantasy, the person to his or her right will develop it further, and so on around the platform. To start things off, the first person will be given a sound effect by the Imaginarium's sound system. After verbally describing the image that he or she experiences in relation to that sound effect, the person to his or her right will enter into the fantasy, carry it further and pass it to the person on *their* right, and so on. While maintaining a story line, each subsequent fantasizer can feel free to rearrange and transform things so that the fantasy becomes more and more fantastic.

[44] Slide of red apple double exposed with doughnut.
[45] Slide of doughnut-shaped apple.
[46] Series of slides of red roses.
[47] Scent of roses.
[48] 60 seconds of light, poignant guitar music.

"The only rule in group fantasy is that no one should be judgmental: Cooperate fully and the fantasy will flow freely. Describe your contribution to the fantasy in full sensory detail. The group will help you by creating sound effects appropriate to the image that you are describing.

"So decide now who is closest to the entry door. / The sound that evokes the first image is . . .[49] (10 minutes of silence for group fantasy)."

"Imaginarium Four" takes the participant further toward self-reliance in a program involving problem-solving. It concludes: "Now return, one more time, to the *here and now* of the dome. This last experience, like all the previous ones, needs to be practiced regularly to obtain its full power.

"In your imagination, you can transcend all mortal limitations of space and time. You can travel into outer space, or zoom into the nucleus of an atom; you can rearrange, juxtapose, and transform things; you can create illuminating metaphors. You can also move forward or backward in time, or use your imagination to focus your awareness in the reality of *here and now*. You can observe the object of your imagination, merge with it, or, in abstraction, transcend the limitations of space and time entirely.

"The potential of your imagination to transform the quality of your life, and the lives of others is literally limitless. The Imaginarium's purpose has been to assist you to become more aware of your imagination and the importance of learning to use this powerful and pervasive human gift more productively. As announced at the start, you have been more and more charged with guiding yourself into increased awareness. Now it is time for the Imaginarium to disappear entirely, and for you to continue this lifetime task on your own.

"Please sit up / stretch / and look around. You are feeling wide awake, refreshed, and ready to share your experiences in 'Imaginarium Four' with your group."

CONCLUSION

Since we began preparing Imaginarium programs in 1972, student response has been extremely favorable. The basic flaw in the Imaginarium concept is what you might suspect: Enormous variety in individual imaginations makes it extremely difficult to develop an educational program suited to everyone. Individual imaginations have different paces. In fact, a single individual varies from day to day in speed of mental response and in rate of comfortable assimilation. Some individuals have extremely passive imaginations, and come to the Imaginarium with an "entertain me" at-

[49] Sound effect of ocean liner leaving dock.

titude. These individuals may be bored, while at the same time individuals with more active imaginations are not finding adequate time to explore their fantasies. For this reason, we often find that the part of an Imaginarium that pleases one participant, bores another, and displeases a third.

There are other problems: Relaxation puts some participants to sleep. If they snore, this distraction can diminish the quality of the experience—as can other unprogrammed sounds: giggling and coughing, for example. Somewhat surprisingly, we have not experienced one participant entering into imaginative areas that they could not handle. The programs are carefully written to avoid this potential problem, and students seem to have an in-built ability to respect their own psychological limits.

Overall, the Imaginarium, with its flaws and limitations, seems to perform its basic educational objectives to direct attention inward to imaginative activities that already exist, and to suggest ways to use this inner resource more productively. Education, with its imbalance toward verbal and mathematical thinking, could undoubtedly profit from additional experimentation toward this objective.

5

A Program for the EEG Study of Attention in Visual Communication[1]

THOMAS MULHOLLAND
Veterans Administration Hospital
Bedford, Massachusetts

In this chapter I propose a method and a rationale for an experimental study of visual attention, which is part of the process of visual communication. Though speculative, this rationale grows out of a solid base of research; it is necessarily incomplete because visual attention is only one aspect of the processes involved in visual communication; it can provide answers to some of the questions about visual attention and visual communication that have not yet been answered.

The old-fashioned concepts of "attention," "paying attention," and "getting attention" are basic to the language of visual media. Debes (1974), speaking for the visual literacy movement, recognizes the importance of attention in a visual communication. In an analysis of Eisenstein's theory of film editing, Andrew (1976) stated that the film maker must concentrate on all that is needed to lead the spectator to a confrontation with the theme of the film:

And the film maker must lead him there with his eyes open, exposing to the spectator his means, his mechanism . . . the film derives its energy from the

[1] Research reported here was supported by Veterans Administration Central Office, Washington, D.C. Research Program.

77

conscious mental leaps of the spectator. The audience literally brings to life the dead stimuli, forcing lightning to leap from pole to pole until a whole story is aglow and until the theme is illuminated beyond doubt and ignorance. Without the audience's *active participation* there would be no artwork, for the human mind is the means by which the film exists and the destination of its message [p. 63].

Some of that "active participation" of the audience involves a transaction between the film which is the "attention-getter" and the person viewing the film who is the "attention-giver."

Mulholland (1970, 1974) has pointed out that visual attention has a function in visual communications similar to that of a *question* in verbal communication.

Attention is to the visual what a question is to the verbal. It is a process for getting information. When there is something new to learn, we may ask a question and decide if the answer is relevant to our needs or, we may know that the answer will be relevant no matter what it is. In both cases we ask a question. . . . Similarly, we pay attention to novel visual messages to see if they are relevant to our needs or, we may recognize that they are relevant, even though they are familiar to us. In either case of novelty or relevance, we pay attention. The reverse is also true—if the verbal material is familiar or not relevant, we do not ask questions. If the visual message is familiar and not relevant, we do not pay attention to it. Thus, the amount of information (novelty or uncertainty) and the degree of relevance to one's needs, plans, and feelings, are important determinants of the success of a visual communication. The most creative and potentially effective communication is wasted if the viewer does not pay attention [1974, p. 8].

Despite the obvious importance of visual attention in the process of visual communication, research is lacking. In particular, there is practically no research that has investigated the moment-to-moment shifts of attention as we "read" a visual message.

MEASUREMENT OF VISUAL ATTENTION

Quantitative measurement of visual attention is not easy. There are formidable methodological problems. For instance, if subjective reports of attention are given by the person who is viewing a visual message, they disrupt the continuity of the processes involved in the perceiving of and the meaning of the visual message. Measurements of behavior or of eye movements, which would be an index of attention, are often unsatisfactory. For these kinds of reasons there is no scientifically valid answer to questions like, "Does a shift from a long shot to a zoom-in increase visual attention?" Or, "Is a *talking head* (a close-up of a human head which is talking) effective in holding the viewer's visual attention?"

Visual attention is a covert process. We can perceive almost anything in our environment with finely graded emphasis, or view it with selective scrutiny without giving any external, behavioral clue of internal, attentional processes. There *are* some external, behavioral signs of attention such as the direction and fixation of gaze, eye movements that acquire and track a visual stimulus, and positioning of the head and trunk, but these are small effects and are difficult to measure accurately. Because of these problems, attempts have been made to use electrophysiological measures of attention.

The electroencephalogram (EEG) can reveal large-scale gradations of cortical processes related to attention. In particular, the process of attention to visual stimuli is usually associated with a reduction of alpha rhythms recorded in the posterior EEG. Unfortunately, because the EEG is recorded from the scalp, only large-scale processes in the cortex of the brain can be appraised. Thus, the EEG sign of visual attention does not reflect fine gradations in the amount or time span of attention.

To provide a framework I will briefly review how we study "visual attention" with the EEG and the rationale for our methods.

Alpha and Attention

Alpha rhythms are prominent in EEGs recorded from the posterior scalp, over the occipital and parietal lobes of the brain. They are measured in terms of voltage, which fluctuates rhythmically from 8–13-Hz frequency. Amplitudes are minute, ranging from about 5 to 150 μv. Alpha rhythms are recordable from at least 85% of the population.

Berger, who discovered the human alpha rhythms (1929), observed that the alpha rhythms were suppressed or disrupted by a visual stimulus, an observation confirmed by many others. If stimulation continued, alpha returned; if there were no further change in the stimulus, alpha gradually increased. Actually a visual stimulus is not necessary to disrupt or suppress the alpha rhythm. Simply opening one's eyes in the dark can momentarily suppress the alpha rhythm. If one tries to see in the dark by looking into the darkness, alpha is suppressed even more. These observations, made in the early days of EEG science, meant that the presence of a stimulus was not necessary to cause suppression of alpha; nor did the absence of a stimulus necessarily prevent suppression. Rather it was something that was triggered by the stimulus, which declined as the stimulus continued, and which could be present even without visual stimulation. An early concept of "visual attention" focused on that momentary suppression of alpha. In fact, scientists began to use the suppression while seeing–sensing and looking as an index of visual attention. It is important to emphasize *visual* attention (as early researchers did), because auditory stimuli produce a much smaller change in alpha.

Repetitive Stimulation

The suppression of posterior alpha rhythms declines with repeated stimulation. This is consistent with attention–alpha theory because active attention usually declines with repetition. Alpha rhythms are very reliably reduced by visual attentional processes at the beginning of a series of visual stimulations, no matter what the visual stimulus is. If the stimulus is repeated, however, alpha will gradually recover. This decline of the suppression of alpha with repetition of the stimulus is so suggestive of a decline in attention that my students have termed it the "boredom function." In the language of electroencephalography it is called the habituation of the alpha-blocking response.

Habituation is not a general effect. It applies only to the particular stimulus or ones very similar to it. For example, if a red light is repeatedly presented until practically no alpha suppression occurs, and then a blue light is presented, the alpha suppression reaction will recur. This suggests that we became accustomed to the red light, and paid attention to the blue light because it was different. In EEG jargon, *dishabituation* occurred.

The amount of alpha rhythms can reflect general states of emotional arousal, which involve visual processes in general, but a discussion of these would take us too far afield. The effects described so far are valid for a person whose eyes are open, looking at visual stimuli.

Alpha and Visual Control

Visual control of pupillary diameter, lens accommodation, convergence of the eyes, fixating a stationary target or tracking a moving one with smooth pursuit movements all involve a visual input and a visual output— a seeing–sensing and looking. The best way to predict the probability and amplitude of alpha increase or decrease is to evaluate the degree of visual control, that is, the number of reflex systems involved in maintaining the best vision. In general, the more visual control systems are involved, the less alpha there is. Since all systems involve input and output, the amount of alpha must be related to both visual stimulus input and eye response output (Mulholland & Peper, 1971).

We assume that "looking" is an operational definition of visual attention, and we use alpha and alpha suppression to define "not looking" and "looking," which defines "low visual attention" and "high visual attention" for the subject whose eyes are open.

Notice in these assumptions that we talk about "looking," not "seeing." This is because we are convinced that alpha is linked not only to seeing (or sensing) stimuli, but to looking at stimuli. Both seeing and looking are part of vision and visual attention, but our research shows that the oculo-motor process and those adjustments of the eye which include positioning movements of the head and eyelids are the major determinants of alpha suppression on the occipital EEG (Mulholland & Peper, 1971; Mulholland, 1972). Auditory stimuli also evoke a looking response as part of the orienting response, but this response declines if no visual stimuli to be seen or looked at. Sounds will, at first, be followed by a suppression of alpha, but the response is not robust and rapidly habituates.

Why not measure what the eye is doing, rather than the EEG if the EEG is an index of looking? The reasons for *not* directly measuring eye behavior are (*a*) the technical difficulty involved; (*b*) the confounding interaction between looking at the stimuli and looking at the apparatus used to measure the eye's position and movement; (*c*) the fact that looking is not identical with eye position and movement—a "loose" fixation and a "tight" fixation may be associated with the same direction of gaze, but have different variability and be associated with different amounts of lens accommodation.

FEEDBACK METHODS

The EEG is a rather imperfect index of attention for additional reasons than those just described. It is too variable, and it is difficult to decide if the EEG alpha changes because of or in spite of visual attention. For these reasons, it is not feasible to measure attention on-line by monitoring EEG changes on-line.

Our solution to this problem was to use feedback to increase the control of the EEG by the visual stimulus. We reasoned that *increased control,* analogous to that observed with feedback control of complex machines, would also be seen with an EEG biofeedback system. That is, there would be a reduction of random variation of the EEG response relative to the mean value of the response.

Feedback is created when the occipital alpha rhythms are connected to a device that controls a visual stimulus or display, so that the occurrence of alpha controls the display. Technical features of this biofeedback method are reported elsewhere (Mulholland, 1968, 1973, 1977). We have found that this feedback method reduces unwanted, unpredictable variation in the brain rhythm relative to the main trend or average magnitude of response, and permits rapid, controlled accumulation of data.

Figure 5.1 is a block diagram of the feedback system (Boudrot, 1972). It includes an EEG machine, brain wave detectors, a display, and a person. Notice the word *person.* It would be incorrect to say that there are only EEG waves in the loop. Actually the *whole person,* not just the "brain," receives and interprets the display cognitively and emotionally, and decides whether or not to play the feedback game. The "person-in-the-loop" makes this method psychophysiological rather than just physiological or electroencephalographic.

Figure 5.2 shows how the alpha rhythm responds when feedback stimulation is used. Note how repetitive and predictable the EEG response is. The variability in the duration of alpha and intervals of little or no alpha are reduced relative to their average. Imagine yourself in the experiment. When your alpha rhythms occurred, the slide would flash on the screen. Look at the slide and your alpha disappears, which makes the slide go off. Now you are in the dark, with nothing to look at or see, and alpha returns. The slide flashes on and the whole cycle repeats. The visual display controls the period of alternation between alpha brain rhythms and rhythms that are not alpha; these EEG waves, in turn, control the display. This regular alternation between alpha and little or no alpha is observed without feedback.

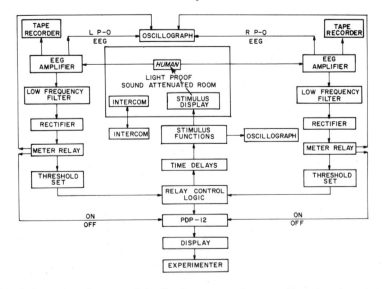

FIGURE 5.1. Flow diagram of feedback apparatus for controlling the presentation of visual stimuli by feedback from the EEG response to the visual stimuli.

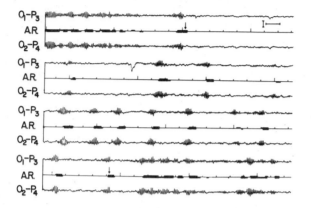

FIGURE 5.2. Electroencephalograph tracing just before, during, and just after feedback stimulation. Feedback starts at top arrow and ends at bottom arrow. Calibration is 50 μv and 1 second. (From Mulholland & Benson, 1976.)

In terms of attention theory we could say that attention is low during alpha. Then the visual stimulus is automatically presented. Attention to the stimulus increases and alpha is suppressed causing the stimulus to be removed. With the slide off, the subject stays at a higher level of attention for a brief interval, then attention begins to wane. Gradually alpha recurs, signaling that a low level of attention has been reached again. Thus, during feedback, attention is varying between lower and upper limits; negative feedback is forcing an oscillation of attention.

In terms of looking behavior, when looking is reduced, alpha occurs, and the visual stimulus automatically goes on. Looking is then increased, alpha is suppressed, and the visual stimulus is automatically removed. Looking continues in the dark and alpha remain suppressed. Then, looking decreases until it is reduced enough for alpha to occur. Thus, feedback has forced a controlled oscillation of looking behavior.

QUANTITATIVE INDEX OF VISUAL ATTENTION

From our studies of static "visuals," which are complex visual stimuli, we have developed a computerized graphic display that shows the reaction of the EEG to the visual. The graph can be interpreted as showing the amount of looking at the visual stimulus. When the value on the vertical axis is high, the durations of alpha suppression are long; looking is occurring and, we infer, attention increases. When the durations of alpha suppression are brief, looking is reduced, as is attention. The graphs are

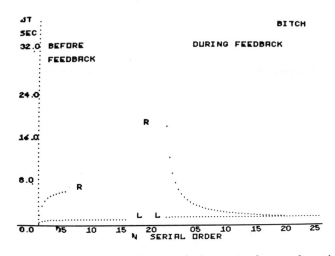

FIGURE 5.3. Computerized graph of a smoothed attentional curve from data in a single trial of 30 presentations of the stimulus word "bitch." Patient has a focal lesion in the left cortex. (From Mulholland & Benson, 1976.)

best-fit functions fitted to the series of alpha durations. The *x* axis gives the serial number of each successive stimulation.

The procedure involves first measuring the durations of alphas and no-alphas on-line during a baseline darkness condition. The durations of alphas and no-alphas are then measured after presentation of a visual. Figure 5.3 is the graph of a patient's reaction to a visual that was repeated 30 times. This patient had a localized brain lesion on the left side. His attentional response in the EEG recorded from the right side is normal: Alpha suppression durations are longer than the baseline, that is, at the onset of stimulation, he is more visually attentive (more looking behavior) compared with baseline. With repetition of the stimulus, the alpha suppression response declines. There is no evidence for response on the left side because of the brain damage on that side.

These studies and others have shown that the feedback EEG attention index is greater for emotional than for neutral words; it is larger when the subject reports paying attention; it increases with novel stimuli and decreases with repetition; it is greater for sexual stimuli compared to pictures of flowers or pastoral scenes; it increases when the subject is instructed to pay attention. A review of these studies is given elsewhere (Mulholland, 1973). Several other facts can be noted: (*a*) the attention index is less for brain-lesioned patients than for normal subjects (Mulholland, McLaughlin, & Benson, 1976); (*b*) it increases when the person counts the stimuli; (*c*) older children (9–12 years) show a greater alpha suppression response than younger children (6–7 years) (Mulholland & Gascon, 1972).

SOME APPLICATIONS

Feedback EEG methods can be used to study visual messages in terms of attentional responses. Cinematographic and videographic techniques are used in television to engage and hold the subject's visual attention. For instance, a documentary may show a long shot of ducks paddling on a pond. Not much is happening and, the scene might become boring. Then the scene changes to a close-up of a duck preening or diving. One reason for such a change is to hold the viewer's attention.

One way to study the effectiveness of such techniques would be to make a special film that included repetitive footage of a long shot; it would have to be repetitive enough that most people would not look at the picture in an attentive way, and alpha rhythms would occur. When the close-up occurred, alpha would be measured to find out if it decreased. In this rather straightforward way, different kinds of cinematographic and videographic techniques that are alleged to increase visual attention could be evaluated. We have done some pilot studies, but more research is required.

Another method we have used could be applied to the study of a "picture-story" (made of a series of static visuals), in terms of attentional responses. As described previously, a slide can be presented each time alpha occurs and removed when alpha is blocked or suppressed. We already know that alpha suppression remains after removal of a visual stimulus when looking behavior has been increased. The viewer sees each slide in sequence, pacing the transition from one slide to the next by the alpha blocking reaction. By progressing through the visual slides in this way, a person could reveal changes of visual attention. As attention increases or decreases (as a function of developing and confirming *expectancies*), no-alpha durations between stimuli would increase or decrease. Although this particular experiment has not been tried, the method is very similar to the experiments described earlier.

Applying the same method to moving pictures is more complicated. The major problem is that moving pictures maximally suppress alpha, so that alpha occurs only in short bursts. This causes the film to be shown in brief and erratic fragments, and continuity of presentation and continuity of meaning is lost. There is, however, a method that might work. The film is *on* when no-alpha occurs until either (*a*) alpha occurs or (*b*) 60 seconds have elapsed. It is then shut off. When alpha occurs again, the film is turned on. The relevant measure would be the duration of no-alpha. As attention increased, the duration of no-alpha would come closer to the maximum 60 seconds allowed. This experiment has not been tried yet but it is technically feasible.

Another method for identifying "attention-getting" visuals is to train the viewer to maintain attention by showing a rewarding visual sequence. For instance, connect a television to the EEG so that when alpha (not looking) is present, there is no picture. When alpha is suppressed (looking), the picture appears. If the viewer is interested in the television and wants to see it looking behavior with its consequent suppression of alpha will be maintained, keeping the television on. If the viewer is bored, that is, if the television "message" is not sufficiently rewarding, the viewer will not look at it attentively, causing alpha to appear and the television to be turned off.

Many studies show that persons receiving feedback can learn to control the occurrence and suppression of alpha rhythms and other brain rhythms. A review of the literature has been presented by Johnson (1977). Studies show that it is easier to learn to suppress alpha below baseline than it is to increase it above baseline. Thus it appears that it is easier to learn to become and remain visually attentive than it is to become inattentive and remain inattentive, in a low arousal state, *without going to sleep*. It is clear, however, that alpha can be increased with feedback when compared to no-feedback conditions. Brain reactions associated with increased arousal and visual attention can be trained; a person can learn to increase or decrease voluntarily some of the brain rhythms recorded in EEGs. Scientists disagree as to how a person self-regulates the EEG and as to what that regulation implies about brain processes and mental states (Plotkin, 1976).

We hypothesize first that attention is trained when the suppression of EEG occipital alpha is trained. Second, even if visual attention could be improved by EEG biofeedback training, we do not know if learning or performance in school would be improved, although it is reasonable to assume that it would.

In a pilot study, four children were told to try to keep a musical tone on. The tone would go on only when alpha occurred. To perform this task, the child had to inhibit responses to the visual stimulus, that is, reduce looking at the visual stimulus. Another task required the child to try to keep a television on by maintaining suppression of alpha. The television remained on so long as the child did not produce alpha. The two tasks were done 2 minutes each in alternation about five or six times each. It is important to note that these training tasks did not require that the child know about attention. We did tell the child to pay attention. Rather, we asked the child to keep the television on. After several weeks of training the children between 1 and 2 hours per week we found that their performance improved with practice. Their control was better with feedback than without.

We do not consider this pilot study on a small sample to be definitive; much more research needs to be done. With the feedback method, we found that the children liked to participate, especially when they became aware that something *they* did controlled the television.

Viewing television is not necessarily associated with a high level of visual attention. We noticed that while watching television, children often have low levels of EEG activity associated with prominent alpha, and their facial muscles are often relaxed. The high level of alpha (with the television programs we used) led us to hypothesize that preschool children may be spending huge amounts of time learning how to be inattentive (or operate at a low level of visual attention) while watching television. Thus, extremely complex and dynamic television displays may become conditioned stimuli for decreased EEG activity and low levels of visual attention. This may adversely affect normal development of attention and the reaction to such visual material as educational television and films. A market researcher has reported that more alpha was recorded from subjects while they were watching television than while they were reading (Krugman, 1971). More research in this area is indicated.

VISUALS AND BRAIN PROCESSES
ASSOCIATED WITH LANGUAGE

One of the issues in the visual literary movement concerns the existence of a visual language, which differs from verbal language. From the point of view of cortical neurophysiology, one way to examine this issue is to determine if the same brain regions are involved in processing verbal messages compared to visual messages.

Brain Lateralization and Visual Language

Laboratory research, especially in the last decade, has confirmed clinical evidence that for most humans, verbal language processes occur predominantly in the left hemisphere; that is, there is a *relative dominance* of the left cortex for verbal language. Research also shows "superiority" of the right cortex for spatial and musical (i.e., nonverbal) cognitions (Witelson, 1976). Electroencephalographic investigations have figured prominently in those researches. Generally speaking, there is slightly less synchronous alpha in the left EEG compared with the right EEG when cognitive activity includes a large verbal language or numerical component. Using bilateral EEG responses as a dependent variable, Galin and Ornstein (1972) and others (e.g., Davidson, Schwartz, Pugash, & Bromfield, 1976; Doyle, Ornstein, & Galin, 1974; McKee, Humphrey, & McAdam, 1973; Robbins & McAdam, 1974; Callaway & Harris, 1974; Morgan, McDonald, & Mac-Donald, 1971; Morgan, MacDonald, & Hilgard, 1974; Butler & Glass, 1974; Duman & Morgan, 1975) have demonstrated that subjects show relative left EEG activation during verbal and numerical tasks and relative right EEG activation during spatial and musical tasks. These findings have been obtained with both overt and covert response requirements.

Schwartz, Davidson, and Pugash (1976) trained subjects to produce more alpha in the EEG of one side compared to that of the other. When subjects produced more alpha in the right EEG than in the left, they reported significantly more verbal cognitions. When they produced more alpha on the left than on the right, they reported more visual, nonverbal cognitions.

In a study of Hopi Indian children, Rogers, Ten-Houten, Kaplan, and Gardiner (1976) found that alpha was lower on the right compared to left when the children listened to stories told in Hopi language. More alpha occurred in the right EEG compared to the left when they listened to stories in English. The authors conclude that processing of Hopi speech involves greater right hemispheric participation than does processing of English.

Electroencephalographic and other studies have shown sex differences in the lateralization of verbal and nonverbal functions. In general, men show greater lateralization of nonverbal processes than do women, and men show lateralization at an earlier age than women (Witelson, 1976). These studies suggest the hypothesis that women may process *visual* language differently from men, analogous to sex differences in lateralization of haptic, visual–spatial processes.

A review of studies of the lateralization of brain function in relation to verbal, numerical, spatial, and musical cognitions is given in Walter, Rogers, and Finzi-Fried (1976), which also lists references to EEG studies relevant to the lateralization of brain functions.

Preference for Visual Imagery

A recurring theme in the EEG literature is the comparison of "visual-izers" and those who do not use visual images in their thinking, or who use verbal processes (Walter, 1968). Some researchers have concluded that persons who use abundant visual images have less alpha while thinking than persons who use little or no visual imagery in their thinking. This preponderance of alpha in nonvisual thinking is not found in all studies, an ambiguity which probably results from the exclusion of some important relevant variables.

Individual differences in imagery may be paralleled by individual differences in the use of or preference for visual as opposed to verbal language (Walter, 1968). For instance, the effect television watching has on children may reflect differences between verbalizers and visualizers as well as sex differences. This is an area of research which is not developed yet.

SUMMARY

There are EEG methods and research results available now that can be applied to the study of visual language in the areas of (*a*) visual attention in relation to sequences of visuals; (*b*) biofeedback training of visual attention; (*c*) relative lateralization of brain functions in relation to visual compared to verbal cognitions; (*d*) individual differences in the relative dominance of visual versus verbal, nonvisual processes in thinking, and the relation of those differences to (*e*) the preference for visual over verbal language. Clearly, there is a role for psychophysiology and electroencephalography in the scientific study of visual communication.

REFERENCES

Andrew, J. *The major film theorists.* London: Oxford Univ. Press, 1976.

Berger, H. Uber das Elektrenkephalogramm des Menschen. *Archiv für Psychiatrie und Nervenkranken,* 1929, *87,* 527–570. [*Translation:* Gloor, P. In: Hans Berger on the electroencephalogram of man. *Electroencephalography and Clinical Neurophysiology,* 1969, Suppl. 28, 37–73.]

Boudrot, R. An alpha detection and feedback control system. *Psychophysiology,* 1972, *9,* 461–466.

Butler, S. R., & Glass, A. Asymmetries in the electroencephalogram associated with cerebral dominance. *Electroencephalography and Clinical Neurophysiology,* 1974, *36,* 481–491.

Callaway, E., & Harris, P. R. Coupling between cortical potentials from different areas. *Science,* 1974, *183,* 873–875.

Davidson, R. J., Schwartz, G. E., Pugash, E., & Bromfield, E. Sex Differences in patterns of EEG asymmetry. *Biological Psychology,* 1976, *4,* 119–138.

Debes, J. L. Superminds: New potentials for educating children through visual literary. Paper presented at the Oklahoma State Visual Literacy Conference, Stillwater, Oklahoma, Jan. 9, 1974.

Dimond, S. J., & Beaumont, J. G. (Eds.) *Hemisphere function in the human brain.* New York: Halsted Press, 1974.

Doyle, J. C., Ornstein R., & Galin, D. Lateral specialization of cognitive mode: II. EEG frequency analysis. *Psychophysiology*, 1974, *11*, 567–578.

Duman, R., & Morgan, S. EEG asymmetry as a function of occupation, task and task difficulty. *Neuropsychologia*, 1975, *13*, 219–228.

Galin, D., & Ornstein, R. Lateral specialization of cognitive mode: An EEG study. *Psychophysiology*, 1972, *9*, 412–418.

Johnson, L. C. Learned control of brain wave activity. In J. Beatty & H. Legewie (Eds.), *Biofeedback and behavior*. New York: Plenum, 1977.

Krugman, H. Brain wave measures of media involvement. *Journal of Advertising Research*, 1971, *2*, 11.

McKee, G., Humphrey, B., & McAdam, D. W. Scaled lateralization of alpha activity during linguistic and musical tasks. *Psychophysiology*, 1973, *10*, 441–443.

Morgan, A. H., McDonald, P. J., & MacDonald, H. Differences in bilateral alpha activity as a function of experimental task, with a note on lateral eye movements and hypnotizability. *Neuropsychologia*, 1971, *9*, 459–469.

Morgan, A. H., MacDonald, H., & Hilgard, E. R. EEG alpha Lateral asymmetry related to task and hypnotizability. *Psychophysiology*, 1974, *11*, 275–282.

Mulholland, T. Feedback electroencephalography. *Activitas Nervosa Superior, Prague*, 1968, *10*, 410–438. [Reprinted in Barber, T., DiCara, L., Kamiya, J., Miller, N., Shapiro, D., & Stoyva, J. (Eds.), *Biofeedback and self-control*. Chicago: Aldine-Atherton, 1971. Pp. 305–333.]

Mulholland, T. The concept of attention and the electroencephalographic alpha rhythm. In C. R. Evans & R. B. Mulholland (Eds.), *Attention in neurophysiology*. London: Butterworth, 1969. Pp. 100–127.

Mulholland, T. Automatic control of visual displays by the attention of the human viewer. In C. M. Williams & J. L. Debes (Eds.), *First National Conference on Visual Literacy*. New York: Pitman, 1970. Pp. 70–80.

Mulholland, T. Occipital alpha revisited. *Psychological Bulletin*, 1972, *28*, 176–182.

Mulholland, T. Objective EEG methods for studying covert shifts of visual attention. In J. McGuigan & R. A. Schoonover (Eds.), *The psychophysiology of thinking*. New York: Academic Press, 1973. Pp. 109–151.

Mulholland, T. Training visual attention. *Academic Therapy*, 1974, *10*, 5–17.

Mulholland, T. Biofeedback as scientific method. In G. Schwartz & J. Beatty (Eds.), *Biofeedback: Theory and research*. New York: Academic Press, 1977.

Mulholland, T., & Benson, F., Detection of EEG Abnormalities with feedback stimulation. *Biofeedback and Self-Regulation*, 1976, *1*, 47–61.

Mulholland, T., & Gascon, G. A quantitative index of the orienting response in children. *Electroencephalography and Clinical Neurophysiology*, 1972, *33*, 295–301.

Mulholland, T., McLaughlin, T., & Benson, F. Feedback control and quantification of the response of EEG alpha to visual stimulation. *Biofeedback and Self-Regulation*, 1976, *1*, 411–422.

Mulholland, T., & Peper, E. Occipital alpha and accommodative vergence, pursuit tracking and fast eye movements. *Psychophysiology*, 1971, *8*, 566–575.

Plotkin, W. On the self-regulation of the occipital alpha rhythm: Control strategies, states of consciousness, and the role of physiological feedback. *Journal of Experimental Psychology: General*, 1976, *105*, 66–99.

Robbins, K. I., & McAdam, D. W. Interhemispheric alpha asymmetry and imagery mode. *Brain and Language*, 1974, *1*, 189–193.

Rogers, L., Ten-Houten, W., Kaplan, C., & Gardiner, M. Hemispheric specilization and language; An EEG study of Hopi Indian children. In D. O. Walter & L. Rogers (Eds.), *Function*. Brain Information Service Conference Report No. 2. BRI Publications, University of California, Los Angeles, 1976. Pp. 33–40.

Schwartz, G., Davidson, R., & Pugash, E. Voluntary control of patterns of EEG asymmetry: Cognitive components. *Psychophysiology*, 1976, *13*, 498–504.

Walter, D. O., Rogers, L., & Finzi-Fried, J. *Conference on human brain function*. Brain Information Service Conference Report No. 4. BRI Publications Office, University of California, Los Angeles, 1976.

Walter, W. G. The social organ. *Impact of Science on Society*, 1968, *18*, 179–186.

Witelson, S. Sex and the single hemisphere: Specialization of the right hemisphere for spatial processing. *Science*, 1976, *191*, 425–427.

6

The Development of
Pictorial Comprehension[1]

IRVING E. SIGEL
Educational Testing Service
Princeton, New Jersey

Two themes govern the material to be presented in this chapter. First, comprehension of the external world evolves through an *active* engagement and subsequent "construction" of the external into "mental" representations. Second, the cognitive system functions as both a filter and a moderator for behavior. Although this chapter emphasizes the individual, it should be presumed that phylogenetic and cultural considerations are embedded in the more general conceptual system which will be presented in this chapter. However, the problem addressed here is, I believe, best highlighted in a cognitive developmental framework. It is a deceptively

---

[1] The vast body of research on picture perception has deliberately been omitted. Much research focuses on the structure of the picture as Hagen (1974) writes in regard to developing a theory of picture perception, ". . . a more fruitful pathway for research is the systematic investigation of pictorial information in the Gibsonian terms of ecological optics [p. 495]." While there is no doubt that physical features of the pictures are relevant, as is the position of the viewer, I believe the development of comprehension of pictures fundamentally resides in the interpreter of that "ecological" stimulus. It is the hypothetical mental structures that will provide the key to understanding of how the viewer comes to interpret the pictures—which are interpretations of others (Goodman, 1968; Gombrich, 1969; Gregory, 1970).

*Visual Learning, Thinking,
and Communication*

simple problem: How does an individual come to understand that a picture is a representation of an object, an event, or an idea?

The question of comprehension of pictorial representations is addressed here as a cognitive developmental question, suggesting that there is a developmental process involved in what I call *picture comprehension* (i.e., coming to know pictures). Picture comprehension is analogous to reading the printed word, where, in each case, the "reader" must transform a set of symbols or signs from one system to another. It is only through a process of transformation that comprehension can begin. Before proceeding to elaborate on this argument, a number of terms must be clarified.

DEFINITION OF PICTURE

First, the term *picture* refers to any two-dimensional representation. Pictures can vary in at least three ways: (*a*) in the *detail* presented, e.g., the usual detailed portrait as opposed to a sketch or outline; (*b*) in the *representational level,* i.e., the degree of approximation to the object or event depicted; and (*c*) in *spatial perspective,* i.e., is the representation flat or does it provide illusions of a third dimension. Of course pictures can also vary in themes depicted, in organization of elements, and in complexity. This last set of features must be distinguished from the forms, where the forms define classes of pictures *qua* representations; it focuses on inherent structural or thematic material that may, in fact, be found among any set of pictures. Thus for heuristic purposes, we can summarize our definition of pictures as shown in Figure 6.1.

Picture types

	Detail		Representational		Perspective	
	Full	Schematic	Realistic	Nonrealistic	Flat	Depth
Organization/ structure (high–low)						
Themes (any)						
Complexity						

FIGURE 6.1. Definition of pictures.

Pictures can be used to exemplify each of the categories, but for this discussion, the focus will be on the structural–functional characteristics, using verbal definitions to differentiate the types.

It should be made clear at this point that these definitions exclude the aesthetic aspects. Our interest here is not in engaging in a discussion of how aesthetic tastes and values develop.

The term *comprehension* must be clarified at the outset. To comprehend is to understand. To comprehend a picture is to *extract meaning* from the picture, to relate to it as a *representation* of a referential object or event either in the knowledgeable past or as projected in the future. *Comprehension* is used here as in reading: *To comprehend is to understand.* Comprehension must be distinguished from recognition, where recognition refers to the *identification* or labeling of a picture and does not imply or require understanding. When a child labels a cat or a dog or its mother in a picture, the child recognizes. Such recognition cannot be presumed to be *comprehension.* The reading analogue is, for example, when a child articulates a word phonically but does not know its meaning. As the pronunciation does not necessarily mean the child comprehends the meaning of the word, so too the labeling of a picture does not necessarily indicate the child comprehends the picture. Frequently, research employing pictures fails to make this distinction, which results, as we shall see, in false positives relative to children's comprehension of pictures.

PICTURES AS REPRESENTATIONS

If a picture literacy is analogous to reading comprehension (literacy), then it seems reasonable to ask whether the same processes are involved. The proposition to be asserted in this chapter is that at the core level, comprehension of written language and of pictures involves comparable cognitive processes, but each of these classes of representational material has a different rule system. Figure 6.2 illustrates the issue.

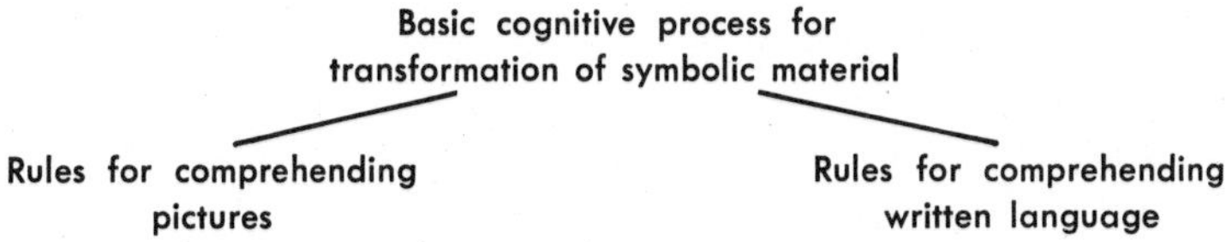

Basic cognitive process for
transformation of symbolic material

Rules for comprehending
pictures

Rules for comprehending
written language

FIGURE 6.2. Rule systems for comprehension of written language pictures.

Although a different set of rules governs picture literacy than word literacy, the rule common to each is the knowledge that objects and/or events can be represented in some alternative media or mode. For example, *horse* can be represented by the picture or by a word (Paris & Mahoney, 1974). Not only does the child have to learn that a picture represents some referent, but most important, the child must learn *how* a given picture represents an object in such a way that he can tell specifically which referent (or type) is referred to by the particular picture.

To develop the argument further, let us return to our characterization of pictures. As indicated before, pictures are two-dimensional characterizations. Pictures do represent something. To that extent, a picture is an external representation (to be distinguished from internal representations, e.g., images). As an external representation, a picture contains only some features of its referent. No one is exactly a replica of its referent. In fact, "any two-dimensional image [picture in this case] *could represent an infinity* of three-dimensional shapes [Gregory, 1970, p. 25]."

In addition, *pictures* have a "double reality."

Drawings, paintings, and potographs are objects in their own right—patterns on a flat sheet—and at the same time entirely different objects to the eye. We see both a pattern of marks on paper, with shading, brushstrokes or photographic "grain," and at the same time we see that these compose a face, a house or a ship on a stormy sea. Pictures are unique among objects; for they are seen both as themselves and as some other thing, entirely different from the paper or canvas of the picture. Pictures are paradoxes [Gregory, 1970, p. 32].

Thus, pictures, as complex stimuli, demand a set of cognitive processes that enable the viewer to comprehend the paradox and respond appropriately.

PICTURES AS MINIATURIZATIONS

Pictures are not only flat, but generally tend to be miniatures of the referent. The residual of the miniaturization process is distinctive morphological characteristics of the referent. Thus, for example, a picture of a horse retains the defining horse characteristics that enable the viewer to label the picture as *horse*.

Some pictorial forms, especially art forms, not only miniaturize, but also represent the pictorial representation as a transformation in which the morphological similarity is transformed symbolically (for example, a cubist rendition of a known solid object). This type of pictorial representation, while characteristic of painting (art), still requires the individual to know *how* a given picture represents the object.

The process of comprehending miniaturization is another point of contact between pictorial comprehension and language comprehension. Linguistic concepts are used to represent complex ideas succinctly and efficiently.

The terms *road* or *urban* subsume a number of descriptions, and language statements of concepts can be conceptualized as a particular subset of miniaturizations.

Although pictorial representations are within the broader miniaturization system, a different set of rules is still necessary for comprehension of pictorial stimuli than other miniaturization systems, especially linguistic systems. Rule systems have been offered for development of linguistic comprehension (Bloom, 1970; Brown, 1973; Chomsky, 1968; Cocking & Potts, 1976). Unfortunately, the same is not true for pictorial comprehension (Deregowski, 1971; Serpell, 1976).

RESEARCH WITH PICTURES

Relatively little research has been done to determine *how* children come to comprehend pictures. It is as if picture comprehension is so fundamental and primitive that comprehension can be explained on the basis of simple association. Hochberg and Brooks (1962) report that a child kept away from pictures until age 2 had no difficulty identifying pictures when shown them for the first time. Bower (1971) has shown that infants recognize pictures of their mothers at very early ages. Numerous other studies have demonstrated accurate recognition of pictorial material on the part of children.

Not only have these studies demonstrated the capability of young children to recall and recognize pictorial material, but they have also demonstrated advantages of pictures as learning aids (Reese, 1970). When asked to learn sentences or lists of words, children do better when integrated pictures are used as learning aids (integrated pictures are those in which components of a sentence interact with the picture) (Rohwer, 1970).

Since pictures seem so easily recognizable, since there seems to be no explicit instruction in learning how to comprehend pictures, and since they seem to be effective learning aids, how can pictorial comprehension be considered a particular developmental phenomena? Is it not, one might ask, like talking? Most healthy humans begin talking at about the same age. No one teaches the child how to talk. It just happens in the course of growing up. Or does it?

In the course of investigating the achievement of verbal labeling, Ninio and Bruner (1976) studied a mother–infant dyad by analyzing a joint picture-book reading. Although the purpose of this study was to explore the development of lexical labels, the authors report other behaviors of the child over a 10-month period (ages 8 to 18 months).

Ninio and Bruner describe the child's reaction to pictorial representation very vividly in the following passage:

> Pictures, being two-dimensional representations of three-dimensional objects, have special visual properties: they can be perceived both as a two-dimensional object *and* as representing a three-dimensional visual scene. This poses a conflict for a child, one which he solves increasingly by assigning a privileged, autonomous status to pictures as visual objects. There is steadily less evidence of the child trying to manipulate, grasp, or "scratch" pictured objects on a page. This process might be one of the stepping stones to grasping arbitrary symbolic representation in language, since visual representations are themselves arbitrary in the sense that a crucial object property, i.e., graspability, is missing.
>
> In preverbal book-reading the child is taught three different skills:
>
> a. The manipulatory skills involved in holding the book, turning the pages, indicating items, etc.
> b. Language skills, i.e., the names of objects and dialogue skills
> c. Perceptual–cognitive skills involved in decoding pictorial representations
>
> Whilst the mother is usually aware of the first two of these processes and is contributing to their development in an active way, the third learning process is going on without the mother's active awareness. She seems to take it for granted that the child is capable of interpreting pictorial information in an adult manner. That pictorial decoding is not as obvious an accomplishment as the mother believes, is well known from studies plotting the development of pictorial interpretation in children. Such studies reveal the gradual and slow development of this skill into adolescence. Richard, the child in our study, often sought information by scratching, fingering, touching the pages, by moving his hand lightly over the picture surface, or by looking underneath the page, probably to check on the picture's dual nature.[2]

It will be noted that the mother assumes that the child is able to interpret the picture. Yet the child's behavior is to the contrary—he is acting on the picture as though it were an object. Although the mother does not direct her attention to the quality of the representation, her inquiries demand an "as-if" attitude on the part of the child. Ninio and Bruner recorded maternal speech. While direct labeling is the most prevalent type of maternal speech (approximately 48%), 19% of the maternal utterances are "what" questions. Within this category about 60% are requests to label (e.g., "What's that?"). The remaining questions are action-based—that is, asking the child to attend to "as-if" actions of the static picture.

This study reveals three important aspects of picture comprehension behavior: (*a*) the mother, as do so many adults, assumes the picture is readily understood; (*b*) the child learns through physical motor activity that the picture *is* an object; and (*c*) the child is learning, aided by the maternal inquiry, that the picture is also a representation. By making these

[2] Reprinted by permission of the Institute for Research in Human Development from A. Ninio and J. Bruner, The achievements and antecedents of labelling. *Journal of Child Language,* in press.

query–demands, the child is being asked to take an "as-if" attitude. Armed with these maternal stimulations and his own motoric explorations, the child begins to learn that the picture is not just a thing in itself. He is resolving the paradox described by Gregory.

Thus Ninio and Bruner demonstrate that decoding of pictorial representations may well be facilitated by the nature of adult–child interacts. At any rate, the Ninio and Bruner description supports the notion that pictorial decoding is a learned phenomenon—a different perspective than implied by the Hochberg and Brooks' (1962) report that the young child deprived of pictures is able to recognize them upon first presentation.

Is the notion that picture comprehension is a learned phenomena correct? What additional evidence exists that supports the notion?

In studies using integrated pictures, there is no explanation of why integrated pictures facilitate sentence learning (Rohwer, 1970). Pictures are said to provide bases for imagery—but imagery is also possible for non-integrated pictures. Does Rohwer imply that the integrated picture produces an image the child reads as though scanning? If so, then, association theory can explain the facilitative effect: After all, the child is not comprehending the sentence or the pictures, but is merely recognizing and recalling the items. These thoughts do not address the issue of picture comprehension, but rather deal with picture recognition. The studies by Rohwer and his colleagues are typical—pictures are used for their capacity to evoke imagery, without consideration of what it is about pictures that evokes imagery. I maintain that a picture evokes an image that shares characteristics with the picture but that is not necessarily a true copy. The internal image is an interpretation of the picture, with a resemblance and a shared meaning.

Another body of research, more suggestive that picture comprehension is learned, stems from cross-cultural research. It is argued that pictorial comprehension is a cultural convention. Some cultures do not have pictures, nor do they comprehend the idea that an object or a person can be represented, or even reflected, in a pictorial modality (Miller, 1973; Serpell, 1976). It is also argued that these cultural studies reveal that picture comprehension, being a result of cultural convention, is easily corrected by pointing out the general principle that the picture is a representation. The respondent will grasp the principle in a single trial. The evidence is not all clear and there is some question regarding the degree to which non-Western societies have difficulty comprehending pictures, but the bulk of the data supports the notion that instant recognition is not present, and that some learning must occur (Arnheim, 1969; Deregowsky, 1971; Gregory, 1970; Hudson, 1967; Segall, Campbell & Herskovits, 1966). To argue that picture comprehension is a cultural convention actually supports the learning conception, for if it is an innate process of recognizing and/or comprehending the observable, then there should be instant recognition; not even one-trial learning should have been necessary.

Cross-cultural research, while providing a rich data base, has tended to focus primarily on the problem of *depth perception* (Serpell, 1976). Using pictures that presumed three-dimensionality, it was found that African natives, unschooled in Western ways, had more trouble perceiving depth than European children (Miller, 1973). That perception of depth must be learned is the argument that Jahoda and Deregowski, separately and collectively, have presented (Jahoda, 1966; Deregowski, 1968, 1976). Deregowski, Muldrow, and Muldrow (1972) worked with a group of Me'en, a remote Ethiopian tribe, most of whom may never have seen a picture. When pictures of familiar animals were printed on a familiar material to obviate the influence of a novel material, most of the individuals could recognize the picture. Interestingly, however, when the pictures were on paper, the paper provoked considerable exploratory behavior and the pictures were ignored. The recognition of these pictures was not instantaneous. The individuals, in this case adults, went through a process of identifying fragments of the picture and linking them into a comprehensive whole. The individuals had to *accumulate* information, and link the elements *before* they comprehended the whole. They did not have an instantaneous recognition or comprehension of the picture, nor could they identify it as a whole. These results suggest that picture recognition and comprehension is not instantaneous but comes through a process of discovery. This point will be discussed further.

The explanation offered for assorted cross-cultural findings tends to focus on difficulties with interpretation of depth cues, but little is offered as to why this is the case (Deregowski, 1971). For my purposes, these data have one major significance; namely, they demonstrate that responses to pictures are neither automatic nor instantaneous. Rather, they are products of learning. The results of the cross-cultural work, then, provide one link in the argument *that pictorial comprehension is learned*. Thus, Arnheim's (1969) contention that picture comprehension is learned finds further support.

Another relevant body of research that indicated that pictorial literacy is more than recognition and/or labeling of instances comes from work in my own laboratory (Sigel, Anderson & Shapiro, 1966; Sigel & McBane, 1967; Sigel & Olmsted, 1970). These studies were originally intended to investigate the degree to which level of symbolization of stimuli influence criteria for classification. This idea has its roots in the work of Goldstein and Scheerer (1941), who suggested that in sorting three-dimensional stimuli (the Goldstein–Gelg Object-Sorting Test), neurologically intact individuals would organize the array of objects on the basis of logical abstract categories and take an "abstract" attitude. On the other hand, neurologically impaired respondents would tend to be concrete, and would arrange things on the basis of familiar functions, having difficulty in creating logical classes.

In reviewing these studies I asked two questions: (*a*) To what degree does the degree of symbolization influence categorization behavior? (*b*) What developmental trends exist among neurologically intact children in their attempt to categorize materials that vary in degree of symbolization? These questions arose because the performance of brain-injured individuals was often described as childish or childlike—the assumption being that the concrete attitude was less mature than the abstract. Thus began what was a series of studies to investigate, initially, the degree to which level of symbolization influenced classification behavior. The significance of this issue resides in the question of whether similar or different practices are involved in extracting meaning from linguistic and pictorial stimuli.

The first study involved sorting tasks administered to boys 7, 9, and 11 years of age, from middle-income families, with an average range of mental ability scores. Five sorting tasks were administered, each of which varied in level of symbolization and/or mode of interacting with the items (Sigel, 1953). Twenty-four items in the classes human, vehicle, furniture, and animal were used. Three-dimensional miniature replicas, black-and-white photographs, and words were used as media of symbolization. The children were asked to sort the 24 items any way they wished into as many groups as they wished. After each trial, each child was asked to explain the basis used for grouping. Age trends were consistent, irrespective of media. The results were that, in effect, from age 7 to 11, the level of symbolization of material is irrelevant. Comparable meanings were extracted from the picture, the word, or the three-dimensional replica. Cue properties such as texture, color, and material were irrelevant. Even when items were identical only in color or texture and the children were asked if they could be grouped together, they had difficulty providing classification responses. For example, when a red ladder, a red miniature horse, and a red truck were presented, even the oldest children did not produce "red" as a common attribute (Sigel, 1953). This difficulty was probably due to the fact that the items represented different classes. Since class differences were more salient than the similarity in color, color was not seen as relevant. The diverse class membership of the items precluded the children from focusing on the color commonality.

In a subsequent study that examined the issue of salience of physical attributes (in this case color and form) as opposed to meaning (representation), children aged 6 to 11 invariably chose meaning as a criterion for matching (Bearison & Sigel, 1968). Combining the results of these two experiments led to the conclusion that the meaning of familiar objects is the salient characteristic in grouping (Sigel, 1954). The rich cue-properties of the three-dimensional objects, in fact, apparently have little salience in classification tasks presented to children aged 7–11. Meaning seemed to transcend the mode of presentation as well as discrepancies between the item as presented and its realistic referent (the miniature horse was red, yet always treated as a horse).

The dominance of meaning seemed obvious; it depended simply on manifest morphological properties between pictures and their three-dimensional counterparts. However, I discovered that younger children and low SES children do differentially classify objects and pictures. This finding has been replicated (Sigel *et al.,* 1966). Specifically, when children from economically disadvantaged environments were asked to classify familiar objects and photographs of those objects, significantly fewer classifications were made with the photographs than with their three-dimensional counterparts (Sigel & McBane, 1967; Sigel & Olmsted, 1970).

Such results might be explained as a function of unfamiliarity with pictures or of difficulty in class grouping behaviors. But each of these arguments can be rejected since (*a*) all objects and pictures were identified at the appropriate level and (*b*) groupings of three-dimensional objects were constructed, but not of pictures. Pictures seemed to represent a different class of instances, despite sharing common labels and physical attributes.

These results opened up a new line of investigation and conceptualization, especially with younger children (Sigel *et al.,* 1966; Sigel & Cocking, 1977; Sigel & Olmsted, 1970). The results have been consistent. Training studies were done to determine if, by focusing on the morphological similarities of the picture and its three-dimensional referent, the discrepancy in grouping behavior could be reduced. Some efforts were undertaken with low SES preschool black children. They were given three-dimensional objects and pictures of those objects. The training was to "demonstrate" the identifiable common feature between the picture and the object. The children had no difficulty in labeling the picture and the object. At this level, no differences were observed. It was only when the tasks shifted to classification that pictures still posed more difficulty. The issue seems not to be resolvable through focusing on manifest cues. On the other hand, training studies that did emphasize "meaning" properties of objects and pictures indicated tendencies toward reduction of object–picture grouping discrepancy (Sigel & Olmsted, 1970).

These results suggest that the comprehension of pictures involves more than an awareness of morphological congruence between the two sets of stimuli. The inference here is that categorizing pictorial stimuli, in addition to recognizing them, involves cognitive processing. The suggestion is that the comprehension of the equivalence of the picture and the object involves two sets of judgments: (*a*) recognizing similarity and/or identity of elements to allow for appropriate labeling and (*b*) realizing that although pictures and objects can be labeled with the same labels, each instance is in fact different while being similar. For example, the picture of the apple and the three-dimensional apple are correctly labeled as "apples." In this sense they *share meanings,* but the picture does not allow for behaviors that the object does. Although this is obvious to adults, there is no reason to assume that it is obvious to young or inexperienced children. The understanding that instances similar in meaning can at the same time appear different demands the comprehension of the principle that instances, while conceptually equivalent, are not necessarily identical in appearance. The principle that is a prerequisite for picture comprehension is the *concept of equivalence,* which holds that instances, while partially sharing characteristics and while appearing differently, can be judged as members of the same class. Items classified in a common class need share only the defining attributes of that class, and can simultaneously possess characteristics that set them apart. An apple (round, red) does not share either redness or roundness with a banana, yet, both can be classed as fruits. The shared meanings that allow for such equivalent classification indicate that the defining attributes are neither color or shape. But the fact that other meanings are shared, in this case the relationship of apples and bananas to their origins, makes them classifiable as *fruit.* This example is homologous to the process involved in judging the relationships between a three-dimensional object and its pictorial referent.

The awareness that items can be similar and different at the same time is a cognitive achievement that evolves gradually. This achievement necessitates mental coordination on the part of a child of two apparently unrelated events. A child who takes a literal approach sees that the *object* is *not* the picture. Equivalence resides in the head of the respondent, not in the ostensive reality, because the respondent extracts the meaning from the stimuli. As the three-dimensional object is a representative of a class, so the picture represents the same class, since class membership is defined by meaning. This is the essence of the problem, and once this awareness is grasped, the individual is functioning in accord with the equivalence principle.

From the perspective of Piagetian theory, mental coordination of diverse elements is achieved during the latter stage of preoperational thought (ages 5–7). If, as I contend, the awareness of pictures and objects as equivalent and yet different is learned, then it seems reasonable to expect differential performance in tasks using pictures and/or objects as a function of developmental level.

As indicated previously, the evidence from cross-cultural research, as well as our studies with low SES children, demonstrates the difference. These data tend to suggest a cultural or "deprivation" hypothesis. In effect, individuals who come from cultures where pictures are not indigenous, and also individuals who come from low SES groups manifest the difference. These results demonstrate that recognition of pictures is neither universal nor instant. Rather it is in some way related to experience. For example, use of pictures and/or objects as stimuli in language-knowledge assessment produce different results. A study by Cocking and McHale (1977) dealt with (*a*) two aspects of children's language knowledge and (*b*) children's uses of pictures and objects when demonstrating their language skills. Previous research has indicated a developmental difference in the two aspects of language reception and language production, with reception antedating production for most syntactic categories. Similarly, research suggests that children find working with toys much easier than working with pictures and picture stories. Cocking and McHale wished to determine whether stimulus medium (pictures or objects) interacted with response mode (language reception or language production). The implication of such an interaction would be that the assessment of children's linguistic competencies is confounded by the materials used to make the determinations, as well as by the task demands.

Subjects were 48 white, 4–5-year-old middle-class children from suburban communities. The tasks varied across two dimensions, medium of the stimulus and mode of response. They measured language comprehension using object stimuli, language production using object stimuli, comprehension with picture stimuli, and production with picture stimuli. The stimuli were designed to assess the children's knowledge of 44 syntactic categories. Each child was tested individually on one of the four tasks.

Children did significantly better on the comprehension task involving pictures than on the picture-production task, and better on the production task using objects than on the picture-production task; they performed better on the comprehension task involving pictures than on the object-production task; and finally, they performed better on the comprehension task involving objects than on the picture-production task. These results demonstrate clearly that objects and pictures do engage the child differentially. Now the question is which is the valid method for determining children's language knowledge?

Of particular significance is that in studies on classification of pictures and objects where there were discrepancies in performance, with objects being more readily classified than pictures, the populations involved were young children. On the other hand, the cross-cultural research, while involving children, also involved adults. Thus, while a similar performance phenomena was found with two diverse populations, it should not be concluded that the reasons for the outcomes are the same. The only conclusion we can come to at this time is that *picture comprehension is a learned phenomenon*—not a natural automatic understanding, as is comprehension of the object.

These findings raisc thc possibility that the findings regarding picture comprehension can be explained as a function of experience. Children have limited experience with pictures as well as with learning tasks involving pictures. Individuals in nonliterate or nonpictorial societies also have virtually no experience with pictures, which are in effect meaningless stimuli. It is therefore not surprising that they have difficulty in comprehending them. These results can reduce the explanation to an experiential one; namely, the lack of utilization of pictorial medium as a meaningful or frequent means of communication, accounts for the findings. This might be a most parsimonious explanation, but insufficient.

THEORY OF PICTURE COMPREHENSION

The basic argument is that comprehension of pictures is a cognitive function—an awareness of the *rule* that items can be represented in various media. The alterations of the media will create a different form, but it does not alter the basic meaning. I propose the term *conservation of meaning*. The principle is similar to Piaget's notion of conservation of quantity, number, or other physical properties. Conservation of meaning refers to the phenomena that the meaning of an object remains despite the transformation of the media in which it is presented. Thus, the apple retains its identity as an apple whether the picture, a wax model, or the word is used. The medium alters *only* the form, it does not alter the *meaning*.

Variations in media, of course, provide variations in identifiable attributes—in some cases a reduction. A picture provides fewer cues than an object, and a word, fewer than a picture. This reduction of cues, although reducing morphological similarities, does not reduce the central meaning.

The question, then, is what the developmental features of this acquisition are. Are the developmental requirements the same as those involved in the acquisitions of other types of conservation (e.g., mass and/or weight)? Is it just familiarity? My contention is that the ability to comprehend pictorial stimuli emerges as the child acquires the principle of conservation of any quality.

The Development of Conservation of Meaning

In this context, *meaning* refers to the definition of a case whereby an instance is identified, labeled, and/or in some other way differentiated from other particulars. How an individual comes to "know," in a sense to extract and use meaning of the array of instances in the environment, is the fundamental question. The answers, and they are many, vary with the conceptual framework of the proponent. For me, the works of Piaget (1951), Werner and Kaplan (1963), Polanyi (1958), and Kelly (1955), disparate as they may be, can be (with qualification) brought to bear on this issue. Simply put, knowledge is constructed through experience with proximal and distal instances. Knowledge is acquired differentially at various developmental epochs through actions on objects. Actions may be motor, haptic, or visual. Whatever the modality employed in such engagement, information is constructed, yielding definitional constructs that guide the subsequent relations with objects (or their representations). The hypothesis here is that it is during the course of such engagements that the child comes to learn *rules* by which to cope with diversity.

Detailing this developmental process is beyond the scope of this chapter. The relevant issues, however, can be schematized as follows: Interactions with objects are in cultural contexts where cultural agents, including the physical environment, provide the definition of objects, their use, and their significance—in effect, their meaning. The nature of the formal, informal, and idiosyncratic interaction is multidetermined. In short, experiences are defined in an interactional context. With varying competences again defined by developmental level, the child is constantly engaged in the crucial transformation of sensory (irrespective of modality) input into meaningful wholes. The meanings so constructed are not isomorphic to the input. For example, the child at the preoperational level will attribute a different set of meanings to a dog than an adult will. To be sure, there may be some overlap, but what is significant is the discrepancy. If the child's meaning diverges from the adult's meaning, then communication problems can arise. A child's generalization of a fear response as in the classic case reported by Watson (1919), where Albert was afraid of the rabbit and generalized his fear to furry things, is a case in point. These "fears" or phobias are also found among adults. In these cases, not only is the cognitive element present (attribution of meaning), but also the affective (the fear response). The evaluation of meaning, then, extends beyond the sheer labeling or identification of the object as "out there." By the very nature of human interaction with objects and/or events, affective involvements are inevitably present. Thus, the object is constructed. The *conservation of meaning* is an outcome of the child's interaction with the object world.

It may seem that I am raising an epistemological argument—the issue is how knowledge of a "real" world is transformed. I have not touched on the issues of *constancy* as a critical factor in enabling the transformation of "real" world stimuli to mental representations. Just to complete the argument, the acquisition of constancy is inherently tied to meaning. If one conserves the meaning of an object, by definition one is aware of *object constancy*. Conservation of meaning is a more appropriate construct because it is: (*a*) epistemological in character, (*b*) more comprehensive, and (*c*) consistent with a constructivist argument.

PICTORIAL COMPREHENSION AND ART

Gombrich (1969) contends that comprehension of pictorial representations is a function of experiences. He argues that pictures, be they photographs or paintings, are not mere copies of the reality they depict since the photographer is limited by his camera, the light available at the time of taking the pictures, and the chemical composition of the film used in transforming the scene into a two-dimensional representation. The artist, too, no more or less than the photographer, is constrained by medium. "For the artist too cannot transcribe what he sees; he can only translate it into the terms of his medium. He, too, is strictly tied to the range of tones which his medium will yield [Gombrich, 1969, p. 36]."

In view of the fact that "reality" cannot be depicted in a true copy, all pictures are approximations of that reality, depicting aspects defined by the constructor of the picture. These aspects interact with the medium employed to create that depiction. Gombrich then poses the problem, "how far must we learn to read such images as line drawings on black and white photographs and how far this capacity is inborn [Gombrich, 1969, p. 53]." He contends that it is necessary to learn to read pictorial images, but that the learning is rapid.

The learning discussed to this point deals with the comprehension of pictorial productions that are efforts at creating "copies" of reality (copies in the minds of the creator, perhaps, but really only approximations of *that* reality). Creators of most pictorial representations use their own signs to depict that reality. When viewing an impressionistic painting close up it is difficult to identify a particular flower or tree; they are usually mere daubs of colored paint. But at a distance an impression of a "tree" is created. This is the sign employed by this type of painter.

Thus, Gombrich concludes that, "All art originates in the human mind in our reactions to the world rather than in the visible world itself, and it is precisely because all art is 'conceptual' that all representations are recognizable by their style [Gombrich, 1969, p. 87]."

The starting point for recognition is the development of categories by which the percept (the picture) can be comprehended. As Gombrich (1969) says:

> Without some initial system, without a first guess to which we can stick unless it is disproved, we could indeed make no "sense" of the milliards of ambiguous stimuli that reach us from the environment. In order to learn, we must make mistakes, and the most fruitful mistakes which nature could have implanted in us would be the assumption of even greater simplicities than we are likely to meet with in this bewildering world of ours . . . it may still prove logically right to [insist] that the simplicity hypothesis cannot be learned. It is indeed the only condition under which we could learn at all. To probe a hole we first use a straight stick to see how far it takes us. To probe the visible world we use the assumption that things are simple until they prove to be otherwise [p. 272].

Thus, the initial argument, even for sophisticated adults, is that a picture is a simple item, readily identified and labeled. Since it is so readily labeled, it appears that the perceiver understands the picture; often, all labeling is an index of knowing. My argument, however, is that the simplicity of recognition should not be mistaken for the ease of comprehension.

Let us return to the basic argument that "the world never presents a neutral picture to us; to become aware of it means to become aware of possible situations that we can try out and test for their validity [Gombrich, 1969, p. 275]." The visual field is influenced by light, shadows, colors, and perspective. It is a familiar experience to be fully aware that the tiny retinal image of a friend emerging from a distance is not a midget rapidly growing in size but rather a person approaching. The red flowers are red despite the fact that the light in the room "makes" them look black. Psychologists refer to this phenomenon as "object" constancy, but such a label offers little help in explaining the phenomena. What establishes the "constancy" phenomena is knowing or awareness, essentially the possession of a schema of *that* particular object or class of objects. We *know* an individual does not grow from 2 feet to 6 feet in 5 minutes; we *know* that roses are characteristically red and do not shift from red to black. We know an even more fundamental principle, that object characteristics do possess a degree of stability, of permanence, the principle of inertia is operative. *But* the outside force that alters the observed instance is an attack directly on the object. Thus, as Gombrich argues, the percept is not neutral; rather it is based on concepts—concepts that have evolved during the course of the individual's development.

The process of seeing has been discussed by Arnheim (1974) in terms of an active process, not a response to the impression of the millions of retinal stimulations.

> the world of images does not simply imprint itself upon a faithfully sensitive organ. Rather, in looking at an object, we reach out for it. With an invisible finger we move through the space around us, go out to the distant places where things are found, touch them, catch them, scan their surfaces, trace their borders, explore their texture. Perceiving shapes is an eminently active occupation [Arnheim, 1974, p. 43]."

In essence, vision (perception) is "a creative activity of the human mind. Perceiving accomplishes at the sensory level what in the realm of reasoning is known as understanding [Arnheim, 1974, p. 46]."

SOME RESEARCH DIRECTIONS

There is a dearth of experimental and/or other types of empirical data on the development of pictorial comprehension, which, to me is a researchable question that should be couched in developmental terms (Gibson, 1966; Hagen, 1974; Randhawa, 1972). Specifically questions such as these should be raised:

1. Can the rule constraints be defined?
2. Is there a generalized competence in dealing with representations?
3. Is comprehension of art related to the more generic problem of comprehension of pictures?
4. What is the developmental course of picture comprehension and is it related to other cognitive competencies?

In sum, the assertion that the process of development of pictorial comprehension is embedded in a broader context of development of *representational competence* must be put to the empirical test.

ACKNOWLEDGMENTS

I wish to thank Marianne Amarel, Rodney Cocking, Bikkar Randhawa, Ruth Saunders, and William Ward for their willingness to critique my ideas. The final product is, of course, my responsibility.

REFERENCES

Arnheim, R. *Visual thinking.* London: Faber & Faber, 1969.

Arnheim, R. *Art and visual perception: A psychology of the creative eye . . . The new version.* Berkeley: Univ. of California Press, 1974.

Bearison, D. J., & Sigel, I. E. Hierarchical attributes for categorization. *Perceptual and Motor Skills,* 1968, *27,* 147–153.

Bloom, L. *Language development: Form and function in emerging grammars.* Cambridge, Massachusetts: MIT Press, 1970.

Bower, T. G. R. The object in the world of the infant. *Scientific American,* 1971, *225,* 30–38.

Brown, R. *A first language: The early stages.* Cambridge, Massachusetts: Harvard Univ. Press, 1973.

Chomsky, N. A. *Language and mind.* New York: Harcourt, 1968.

Cocking, R. R., & McHale, S. *A comparative study of the use of pictures and objects in assessing children's receptive and productive language.* (RB 77–10) Princeton, New Jersey: Educational Testing Service. June 1977.

Cocking, R., & Potts, M. Social facilitation of language acquisition. *Journal of Genetic Psychology Monographs,* 1976, *94,* 249–340.

Deregowski, J. B. Difficulties in pictorial depth perception in Africa. *British Journal of Psychology,* 1968, *59,* 195–204.

Deregowski, J. B. Illusion and culture. In R. L. Gregory & E. H. Gombrich (Eds.), *Illusion: In nature and art.* London: Duckworth, 1971.

Deregowski, J. B. Coding and drawing of simple geometric stimuli by Bukusu schoolchildren in Kenya. *Journal of Cross-Cultural Psychology,* 1976, *7,* 195–208.

Deregowski, J. B., Muldrow, E. S., & Muldrow, W. F. Pictorial recognition in a remote Ethiopian population. *Perception,* 1972, *1,* 417–425.

Gibson, J. J. *The senses considered as perceptual systems.* Boston: Houghton Mifflin, 1966.

Goldstein, K., & Scheerer, M. Abstract and concrete behavior: An experimental study with special tests. *Psychological Monographs,* 1941, *53,* (2, Whole No. 239).

Gombrich, E. H. *Art and illusion: A study in the psychology of pictorial representation.* Bollingen Series XXXV. 5. Princeton, New Jersey: Princeton Univ. Press, 1969.

Goodman, N. *Language of art: An approach to a theory of symbols.* Indianapolis: Bobbs-Merrill, 1968.

Gregory, R. L. *The intelligent eye.* New York: McGraw-Hill, 1970.

Hagen, M. A. Picture perception: Toward a theoretical model. *Psychological Bulletin,* 1974, *81,* 471–497.

Hochberg, J., & Brooks, V. Pictorial recognition as an unlearned ability: A study of one child's performance. *American Journal of Psychology,* 1962, *75,* 624–628.

Hudson, W. The study of the problem of pictorial perception among unacculturated groups. *International Journal of Psychology,* 1967, *2,* 89–107.

Jahoda, G. Geometric illusions and environment: A study in Ghana. *British Journal of Psychology,* 1966, *57,* 193–199.

Kelly, G. A. *The psychology of personal constructs* (2 vols.). New York: W. W. Norton, 1955.

Miller, R. J. Cross-cultural research in the perception of pictorial materials. *Psychological Bulletin,* 1973, *80,* 135–150.

Ninio, A., & Bruner, J. The achievement and antecedents of labelling. *Journal of Child Language* (in press).

Paris, S. G., & Mahoney, G. J. Integration in children's memory for sentences and pictures. *Child Development,* 1974, *45,* 633–642.

Piaget, J. *Play, dreams and imitation in childhood.* New York: W. W. Norton, 1951.

Polanyi, M. *Personal knowledge.* Chicago: Univ. of Chicago Press, 1958.

Randhawa, B. S. Nonverbal information storage in children and developmental information processing channel capacity. *Journal of Experimental Child Psychology,* 1972, *13,* 58–70.

Reese, H. W. Imagery and contextual meaning. *Psychological Bulletin,* 1970, *73,* 404–414.

Rohwer, W. D., Jr. Images and pictures in children's learning: Research results and educational implications. *Psychological Bulletin,* 1970, *73,* 393–403.

Segall, M. H., Campbell, D. T., & Herskovits, M. J. *Influence of culture on visual perception.* Indianapolis: Bobbs-Merrill, 1966.

Serpell, R. *Culture's influence on behavior.* London: Methuen, 1976.

Sigel, I. E. Developmental trends in the abstraction ability of children. *Child Development,* 1953, *24,* 131–144.

Sigel, I. E. The dominance of meaning. *Journal of Genetic Psychology,* 1954, *85,* 201–207.

Sigel, I. E., Anderson, L. M., & Shapiro, H. Categorization behavior of lower and middle class Negro preschool children: Differences in dealing with representation of familiar objects. *Journal of Negro Education,* 1966, *35,* 218–229.

Sigel, I. E., & Cocking, R. R. Cognition and communication: A dialectic paradigm for development. In M. Lewis & L. Rosenblum (Eds.), *Communication and language: The origins of behavior.* Vol. V. New York: Wiley, 1977.

Sigel, I. E., & McBane, B. Cognitive competence and level of symbolization among five-year-old children. In J. Hellmuth (Ed.), *The disadvantaged child.* Vol. 1. Seattle: Special Child Publications of the Seattle Sequin School, Inc., 1967.

Sigel, I. E., & Olmsted, P. Modification of classificatory competence and level of representation among lower-class Negro kindergarten children. In A. H. Passow (Ed.), *Reaching the disadvantaged learner.* New York: Teachers College Press, 1970.

Watson, J. B. *Psychology from the standpoint of a behaviorist.* Philadelphia: Lippincott, 1919.

Werner, H., & Kaplan, B. *Symbol formation: An organismic developmental approach to language and the expression of thought.* New York: Wiley, 1963.

7

On Exploring Visual Knowledge[1]

ALLAN PAIVIO
University of Western Ontario
London, Ontario, Canada

The psychological study of visual knowledge as a theoretical and applied problem is dealt with in this chapter. Visual knowledge refers to long-term memory information concerning the appearance and functions of things. We know something about the sizes, shapes, and colors of animate and inanimate objects in all their infinite variety. Subjectively at least, such knowledge seems to be visual and nonverbal in form. We also know how things behave and how they can be manipulated and shaped by our own actions. That knowledge, too, appears to be partly visual: We "see" ourselves or some other agent reshaping or shifting things about in our mind's eye. The memory for appearances and the capacity for transforming those appearances in the interests of a particular task together constitute the dynamic visual knowledge that permits us to adjust in a flexible way to an ever-changing visual world. It also provides the basis for creative modifications of our visual environment with a speed and control that would be impossible if all such changes required direct trial-and-error manipulations of objects in the real world.

[1] The author's research reported herein was supported by Grant A0087 from the National Research Council of Canada.

113

This informal description of the nature and functions of visual knowledge is familiar enough and probably acceptable to most of us on the basis of everyday experience, but we are far from having a precise theoretical or factual understanding of the basic phenomena. On the theoretical side, we are not sure how visual knowledge should be conceptualized psychologically. On the factual side, we are only beginning to get detailed information on the dimensions and scope of what people actually do know about the perceptual world, and the precision and flexibility with which they can use it. Solutions to such applied problems as visual literacy, which implicate visual knowledge, obviously depend heavily on advances in theoretical and factual information through systematic research.

The balance of this chapter reviews some recent research approaches to the theoretical and applied problems, with particular emphasis on our own studies. The first section provides a theoretical and methodological orientation, which stresses the relevance of verbal processes in research on visual knowledge. The second deals with research designed to explore the characteristics of visual knowledge. The third is concerned with research on the exploitation or use of visual knowledge.

SOME OBSERVATIONS ABOUT
THEORY AND METHOD

Until recently, it was theoretically fashionable to assume that language was the major if not the only form in which conceptual knowledge is represented. Verbal mediational theories of memory and perception, and the Whorfian hypothesis of linguistic determinism are familiar examples. The pervasive influence of the verbal approach has been felt in areas that are directly relevant to the present conference and the Visual Scholars Program in general. For example, in a book entitled *Man's Information System,* intended as a supplementary text for audiovisual instruction courses, Travers (1970) asserts that evidence "suggests that the human permanent memory system is mainly a verbal memory system. Incoming information, if it is to be effectively stored, is recoded as verbal information before it is placed in the storage system [p. 148]." Taken literally, this implies that visual knowledge, too, must be verbal, since it involves permanent memory. Memory for appearances simply becomes a descriptive memory.

Recently there have been strong reactions against such extreme forms of linguistic determinism, and they are no longer popular. It would be tempting, therefore, to compensate for the historical imbalance by going overboard in the other direction, emphasizing nonverbal visual processes to the neglect of language. This would be a grave mistake because the higher-order visual processes implied by such terms as visual literacy, visual scholarship, or visual knowledge cannot be understood or even studied in isolation. This restriction stems from the fact that language constantly imposes itself on the activity of nonverbal information-processing systems, both developmentally and in specific situations. Developmentally, much of our knowledge about objects and events is acquired in a linguistic context of descriptions and comments by parents and other members of the linguistic community. The result is an association between words and things that gives language a compelling and pervasive psychological prominence. We have all observed this association in action among young children as they eagerly leaf through a catalogue or picture book naming familiar objects and demanding the names of unfamiliar ones. This tendency to name, comment, or question modifies the psychological effect of the non-verbal objects and events themselves in varying degree and in different ways, depending on task demands and the situational context generally. Conversely, visual information processing in the form of visual imagery is often aroused and guided by linguistic cues. Thus the functional contribution of visual knowledge per se is usually embedded in a linguistic context, and it can be studied and understood only by taking language explicitly into account by either controlling it or varying it systematically in order to determine its influence on visual processing.

The problem has both theoretical and empirical implications. On the theoretical side, we need a conceptual model that takes account of the structural and functional properties of verbal and nonverbal systems. Some investigators, myself included (Paivio, 1971; see also Randhawa, 1971), have adopted a dual coding approach, which assumes that the two systems are functionally independent but interconnected. Each system presumably is specialized for different functions and either can initiate activity in the other, given appropriate contextual stimuli, so that cooperative action is possible. Others assume that nonlinguistic and linguistic information become transformed into an abstract, amodal form that can be characterized as a network of semantic entities and descriptive propositions. The abstract level functions as a kind of interlingua that connects language and non-linguistic perceptual events. I do not wish to argue here in favor of my own theoretical bias, but I am insisting that there is a theoretical problem and that eventually it must be solved in one way or another if we are to make any progress in the understanding of what constitutes visual literacy and how it can be nurtured and developed toward practical ends. The visual scholar presumably will want to emphasize the nonverbal visual side of the theoretical issue, but in so doing, the linguistic side cannot be simply ignored in the hope that it will go away.

The empirical implications can be illustrated with concrete examples. It is a well-established fact that pictures are generally easier to remember than words. Because of the nonverbal character of pictures, one might conclude that nonverbal (visual) memory processes have some intrinsic mnemonic advantage over verbal ones. This possibility remains likely, but numerous studies have also shown that the memorability of pictures is at least partly due to the supplementary involvement of verbal processes. Because pictures of familiar objects readily elicit naming responses, they presumably can be stored in two ways (as memory pictures and as memory words), thereby increasing the probability that the target item can be retrieved at the time of the memory test. Simply stated, two memory traces are better than one. This interpretation has been supported specifically by the finding that naming enhances memory for pictorial items and image coding increases memory for words (e.g., Paivio, 1975a).

We observed more complex dual coding effects in an experiment on the role of verbal processes in sequential memory for pictures and words (Paivio & Csapo, 1969). Typically, memory for serial order is at least as good when the items are pictures as when they are words. This suggests that visual and verbal processes are equivalent in regard to memory for the temporal order of discrete events. Csapo and I reasoned, however, that visual memory may not be specialized for sequential information processing and that sequential memory for pictures may be due instead to implicit naming responses. To test this idea we presented sequences of pictures or words to subjects at very fast or somewhat slower rates. The fast rate of 5.3 items per second was designed to prevent subjects from naming the pictures to themselves during presentation without hindering recognition of the pictures. Printed words could also be easily read at that rate. The slower rate of 2 items per second permitted implicit naming responses to occur. If our theoretical reasoning was correct, the fast rate should selectively interfere with memory for the sequential order of pictures without affecting memory for the items independent of their order. This is what the results showed. At the fast rate, pictures were inferior to words in sequential memory tasks (immediate memory span and serial reconstruction) but not in tasks involving memory for items but not their order (free recall and recognition memory). At the slow rate, where naming responses were possible, pictures and words were comparable in the sequential tasks, and pictures tended to exceed words in the nonsequential tasks. Thus the results indicate specifically that verbal and nonverbal systems differ in their capacity to store information concerning temporal order.

The findings just outlined are of theoretical interest in their own right, but my main point here is that predictions concerning the mnemonic function of nonverbal visual processes in such studies would have been inaccurate without at the same time taking into account the contribution of verbal processes.

The argument is even more pertinent when one is concerned with the role of visual imagery in memory for words, since the visual knowledge on which imagery is based must be reached in this instance through the verbal system. Without taking the latter into account, one could not reasonably infer that visual processes are involved at all. This was particularly true at the time we began our research on the problem in the early 1960s, when verbal learning and memory research was dominated by verbal associative theories and the concept of imagery was only beginning to recover from the beating it received from the early behaviorists. We studied the effects of the concreteness and image-evoking value of words on their memorability in various situations. To do so, we had subjects rate a large number of words on their imagery value and their concreteness–abstractness. We then varied these attributes in memory tasks. It turned out that word imagery has a powerful effect on memory: High-imagery, concrete words are typically much easier to learn and remember than low-imagery, abstract words.

However, concrete and abstract words differ on many attributes besides imagery. For example, word associations occur more readily to concrete than to abstract words, and it could be argued that this variable rather than imagery is the effective one in memory tasks. We tested this possibility by comparing the effects of verbal associative value (i.e., the number of associations that a given word evokes in a given period of time) and imagery value on memory. The result was that the number of associations had little or no effect when the imagery value of words was held constant, whereas high-imagery words were easier to remember than low-imagery words even when verbal associations were controlled. The generalization extends to a large number of other attributes. To date, more than 20 word attributes, such as familiarity, pleasantness, pronunceability, complexity, emotionality, age of acquisition, and so on, have been compared with imagery value in a variety of memory tasks. None of these alternatives accounts for the effects of imagery, although some are effective in their own right. Thus, whereas it always remains possible that some other variable will be found which will explain away the word imagery effect, at the moment we can have considerable confidence that visual imagery is really involved and that it may well be the most effective attribute of all. But we could not be so confident without the evidence from many studies in which verbal and other confounding variables were controlled or their effects partialled out.

Many other examples could be cited, but these should suffice to illustrate why a comparative approach should be an essential part of the research strategy in studies of visual knowledge as it is in other areas of scientific inquiry. I shall take the strategy for granted in the following selections.

EXPLORING VISUAL KNOWLEDGE

This section deals with research designed to explore the content or structure of visual knowledge. The problem has been studied in various ways by geographers as well as psychologists, particularly in relation to the structure of mental maps (see, e.g., Downs & Stea, 1973). Inferences have been based on verbal descriptions and sketch maps of geographic areas as well as more indirect and analytically powerful methods involving analyses of similarity judgments using multidimensional scaling methods. Shepard and Chipman (1970), for example, demonstrated that judgments of shape similarity made in response to the names of pairs of states of the United States were highly comparable to similarity judgments in response to cut-out maps of the states. Thus they established what they called a second-order isomorphism between the structure of internal representations activated by words and the perceptual structures activated more directly by physical maps. A comparable isomorphism has been similarly demonstrated between the memory structures underlying color names and the perceptual structure of the colors themselves (Fillenbaum & Rapoport, 1971). The information gained by such methods constitutes a kind of psychophysics of visual knowledge.

We have begun to investigate the nature of visual knowledge systematically using a reaction-time procedure introduced by Robert Moyer (1973). Moyer presented his subjects with pairs of animal names, which differed more or less according to their real-life size. Thus *bear* and *mouse* differ greatly whereas *bear* and *wolf* differ less in size. The subjects were required to press a key under the larger of the two animals. It turned out that the reaction time for the decision was related systematically to the magnitude of the difference: The larger the size difference, the faster the reaction time. The function was similar to that obtained with perceptual stimuli differing in size, such as lines that differ in length. Moyer accordingly reasoned that the task involves a kind of mental psychophysics, where subjects compare animal names by first translating the names into analogue representations which preserve relative size, and then comparing the perceptual analogues. The result is a *symbolic distance effect* similar to the psychophysical function obtained with perceptual size differences.

The study is particularly interesting in the present context because the comparisons involved apparently depend on rather precise visual knowledge. At least two important questions arise, however. First, how is the visual knowledge represented? Is it truly visual in nature, as though one were comparing things perceived through "the mind's eye," or is it in a more abstract form, such as networks of semantic information where size differences are preserved as relational propositions of the kind A larger than B, B larger than C, and so on? Second, how generalizable is the psychophysical function to other dimensions of perceptual and nonperceptual knowledge? The following experiments were designed to provide answers to such questions.

An initial series of experiments on the first question strongly supported the visual metaphor. Since the details are available elsewhere (Paivio, 1975b), I shall simply summarize the more pertinent findings and their implications. One experiment showed that the memory size comparisons are faster with pictures than with printed words as items, even when the pictures show the two objects as equal in physical size. This effect is consistent with the idea that pictures have more direct access to the internal representations containing the size information than do words, or that the representations are in some sense more visual and picture-like than they are word-like or abstract. Another experiment revealed a modality-specific conflict effect when memory size and picture size information are incongruent. For example, as shown in Figure 7.1, when a donkey was depicted as smaller than a toaster (an incongruent size relation), the time to decide which object is larger in real life was slower than

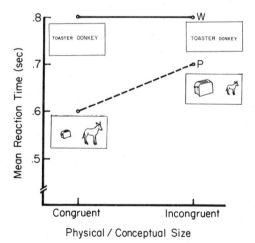

FIGURE 7.1. Reaction time for choosing the conceptually larger of two objects presented as pictures or as words when depicted size and conceptual (memory) size differences are congruent and when they are incongruent. The inset examples illustrate the experimental conditions. (Based on Paivio, 1975b.)

when the picture showed the donkey as larger than the toaster. The conflict did not occur when the printed sizes of words were similarly varied. These findings provide strong evidence for the idea that the representations of size information in memory are modality specific in the double sense that they are both visual and nonverbal in nature.

A further observation indicated that the visual knowledge can be used in a flexible way for different purposes, depending on task demands. Rather than judging relative size, subjects indicated which of two pictured objects looked farther away. The expectation was that the conflict observed in the size comparison experiments would be reversed, so that decisions would be faster in the size-incongruent than in the size-congruent condition because large objects obviously appear to be relatively farther when they appear smaller, but not when they appear larger than their partners. As shown in Figure 7.2, the results were clearly as predicted. This finding is especially important because the distance judgments must have been based partly on memory size, since the pictures lacked perspective and other cues to distance. Thus the same visual knowledge system mediated contrasting reaction time patterns in different tasks, one of which primarily involved a perceptual memory judgment (which object is larger in real life?) and the other, a more direct perceptual judgment (which object *looks* farther away?) which nonetheless depended equally on visual knowledge concerning real life size.

These and other results from this series of experiments generally support a theory of cognition that assumes, among other things, that knowledge of the visual world is represented in a system which is distinct from, though interconnected with, linguistic knowledge. Moreover, the visual memory knowledge seems to be truly analogous to the information derived directly from visual perception, at least in regard to object size.

We have used the same basic method to explore other dimensions of visual knowledge and the role played in such tasks by individual differences in relevant perceptual memory abilities. The new dimensions included concrete visual ones like shape and color as well as more abstract properties such as pleasantness and value. Each dimension was varied in terms of ratings obtained from groups of subjects with respect to the real-life characteristics of a named object or concept. The ratings were made on 9-point scales. Thus, one group rated such words as *toaster, lamp, zebra, table,* etc., on the degree to which the referent objects are angular or round in shape. Others rated items for their brightness, or pleasantness, etc. The averages of these ratings were used to construct pairs that differed to a greater or lesser degee on each dimension. The pairs were presented to experimental subjects as words and, in some experiments, as pictures, and

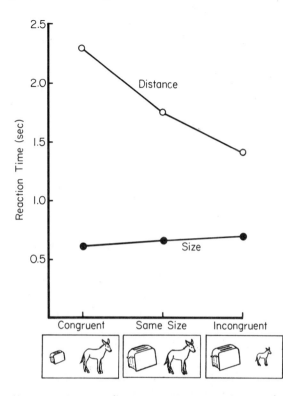

FIGURE 7.2. Mean reaction time for memory size comparisons and relative distance judgments of pictured pairs in which the items are equal in size or differing so that the pictured size difference is congruent or incongruent with the real-life differences. (Adapted from Paivio, 1975b.)

the subjects were asked to choose the member of each pair that was rounder, or more pleasant, etc., in real life.

The main results of interest were as follows. Not surprisingly, each dimension yielded the typical symbolic distance effect, so that comparison reaction times were faster with larger than with smaller differences on a given attribute. This suggests that continuous analogue representations underlie relatively abstract properties, such as pleasantness, as well as concrete ones, such as shape. Other results were less predictable. Pleasantness, for example, could be alternatively regarded as a characteristic of the referent object rather than its name, or as a verbal attribute, or as an abstract semantic attribute that words and things share in common. If the first interpretation is true, pleasantness comparisons should be faster with pictures than with words, and faster with concrete object names than with more abstract concepts such as *truth* and *vice*. This follows from the dual coding idea that the availability of imaginal representations for the conceptual referents increases from abstract words, to concrete words, to pictures. Conversely, if pleasantness is primarily a verbal attribute, comparisons should be slower with pictures than words. Finally, if it is a common abstract property, there should be no effect of stimulus concreteness.

The results were consistent with the referential hypothesis: Pleasantness comparisons were fastest with pictures and slowest with abstract words, as though affective value is a property of concrete referents rather than of words per se.

An unexpected result occurred with brightness comparisons. This dimension refers to a property of the visual objects. Accordingly, following the logic applied to size comparisons, it might be expected that brightness comparisons would be faster with pictures than with words. Not so. Stimulus type interacted with symbolic distance so that relative brightness judgments were faster with words than with pictures when the differences were very small, and comparison time for the two classes of stimuli did not differ when the differences were large. Thus the results were inconsistent with the idea that visual brightness is stored along with visual shape. Instead, brightness appears to be a conceptual property that is at least as accessible through the verbal as the image system. This conclusion is very tentative, but at the very least it is consistent with the neuro-psychological finding that aphasics, whose color perception is not disturbed, showed disturbance in memory for object color even when the color memory task does not require color naming (De Renzie & Spinnler, 1967). These findings imply that there may be dissociation among the components of our visual memory knowledge and that some components are somehow more dependent on verbal processes than are others. The problem obviously cries out for further research.

Interesting results also emerged from the study of individual differences. Participants in the experiments completed several spatial manipulation tests which can be regarded as measures of visual imagery ability. These included the Minnesota Paper Form Board (Bennett, Seashore, & Wesman, 1947), Thurstone's Space Relations (Likert & Quasha, 1941), and a cube visualization task developed by Guilford (1967). Subjects were divided into high- and low-imagery groups at the median of the total standardized scores on the three tests. They were also given a verbal association test (see Paivio, 1971, p. 459) as a measure of verbal ability. The results showed that the subjects with high imagery ability were generally faster than low imagers in comparison tasks involving concrete visual attributes (size, shape), whereas verbal associative fluency was unrelated to performance in these tasks. The high imagers were also relatively faster in the pleasantness comparison task, but in this case the relation was qualified by verbal associative fluency; the fastest reaction times occurred among subjects who scored high on both imagery and verbal ability, particularly when the comparison task involved words as stimuli. This suggests that pleasantness judgments depend on verbal associative structures as well as on imaginal processes. Finally, imagery ability was unrelated to comparison time in a task that presumably involves the verbal but not the imagery system, namely, judgments of which of two words or picture names was more familiar. Thus imagery ability was generally predictive of reaction time in experiments involving visual knowledge, but not in a task based on verbal knowledge. Conversely, verbal ability was generally not predictive of performance although it played a role in one task. The individual difference research needs to be extended particularly so as to include more tests of verbal ability but to date the results are quite consistent with the view that visual knowledge is indeed linked to modality-specific perceptual memory processes.

EXPLOITING VISUAL KNOWLEDGE

Whereas the preceding section emphasized the content and structure of visual knowledge, this section is concerned with research on the functions of visual knowledge in such applied endeavors as learning, problem solving, and creativity. In other words, interest centers here on the exploitation of visual knowledge for practical ends. The applications primarily take advantage of the memory functions of visual imagery. Accordingly, I will first describe some of the pertinent findings in that area. Then I will illustrate their relevance for conceptual thinking tasks, such as concept learning and creativity. Finally, I will show how visual knowledge can be systematically applied to educational problems by describing some recent work on the use of imagery mnemonics in second language learning.

Imagery and Memory

Earlier I referred to the well-established finding that pictureable material is generally easier to learn and remember than less pictureable material. Specifically, pictures are generally more memorable than words and concrete, high-imagery words are more memorable than abstract, low-imagery words. The generalization for linguistic material extends to phrases, sentences, and paragraphs. At all levels, memorability is directly related to the pictureability or image-arousing value of the materials (for a review, see Paivio, 1971).

The memory value of imagery has also been dramatically revealed by research on mnemonic techniques, in which subjects are instructed to use imagery in order to remember items. Such techniques are based on an ancient system known as the method of loci, or of places and things, in which one tries to remember items by imagining that they are placed in distinct and familiar locations. The locations might be houses and other objects that one encounters on a walk through one's neighborhood, or the rooms and walls of a building, or a numbered series of high-imagery words, the referents of which are imagined in association with the to-be-remembered items. The one–bun, two–shoe, three–tree rhyming mnemonic technique is a familiar example of the last of these. The items are retrieved by retracing the memory locations in systematic order, so that the locations can remind one of the objects that have been placed there. Experimental studies have established that such techniques are highly effective (see Paivio, 1971), and many experiments have provided information on the precise role of visual memory processes in the effects. Some studies have demonstrated, for example, that subjects who have been taught such a technique actually use a "read-out" of spatial locations to remember items, rather than verbal memory (e.g., Lea, 1975; Peterson, Holsten, & Spevak, 1975; Peterson, 1975).

Many of the variables that affect the efficiency of the mnemonic system are also known. One of the most important of these, from a theoretical as well as a practical viewpoint, is that the effectiveness of associative images depends on the degree to which the mnemonic peg and the to-be-remembered items are relationally organized or integrated in the compound image. Thus the word *house* is a better recall cue for the associated word *giraffe* if, for example, the giraffe is imagined inside the house with its head sticking out of a second-story window than if the two are pictured side-by-side as separate entities.

These mnemonic techniques and the processes involved in them are particularly relevant here because they draw on the individual's long-term visual memory of the appearance of the named objects and on his or her ability to generate novel imaginal structures from which the verbal information can be retrieved. The sequence of events is complex, involving the encoding of words into visual images, organization of the elements of the image into a relationship according to instructional cues, retrieval of the image during recall, and finally decoding or translating the image into the required verbal form. All this involves visual knowledge to the extent that the words have visual referents and the degree to which the context actually induces the subject to engage in visual work during the task. It remains a fruitful and fascinating research problem for those interested in visual processes in memory and thinking because our understanding in the area is still quite primitive, at least in the theoretical sense. Nonetheless, enough is already known that the theoretical concepts and methods can be extended beyond the confines of the laboratory memory task.

Conceptual Thinking

A number of writers have discussed the role of visual knowledge in areas involving the highest forms of conceptual thinking such as creativity and problem-solving (e.g., Arnheim, 1969; Paivio, 1971). I will confine my comments to two specific research examples that provide specific support for such ideas. One involves concept learning and the other creativity.

Katz and Paivio (1975) found that the imagery value of conceptual categories as well as instructions to use visual imagery during learning facilitated the acquisition of concepts. The task involved the learning of pairs in which nonsense items were associated with instances of several concepts. The subject's task was to learn the concepts that were represented by the nonsense words. What is particularly interesting is that the instances that corresponded to high- and low-imagery concepts did not themselves differ in imagery value. Only the to-be-learned concept labels differed in imagery. Thus performance of the subjects must have been influenced by the pictureability of the concepts that they sought to discover. That such a process was somehow involved was further supported by the fact that instructions to use imagery facilitated the concept learning and did so more in the case of the high-imagery than the low-imagery concepts.

It is not clear precisely how imagery operates in this case, although one possibility is suggested by work by Eleanor Rosch (1975). She has shown that perceptual processes are dominant in tasks in which subjects are required to respond to category labels. Specifically, her findings suggest that general categories are represented cognitively by the most prototypical instances, or best examples, of the categories. Thus subjects are likely to think of birds in terms of perceptual representations that look more like robins or sparrows than like turkeys or hens. As applied to our experiment, Rosch's results might mean that the exemplars of high-imagery concepts were somehow more prototypical of the categories they represent than are the examples of low-imagery concepts, despite the fact that the exemplars for the two kinds of concepts did not differ in imagery value. Whatever the ultimate theoretical resolution, the results implicate visual memory processes in conceptual thinking.

The highest forms of conceptual thinking presumably occur in creative works in the arts and sciences. Many creative workers and students of the creative process have emphasized the role of imagery and visual thinking generally in the creative process. The following example establishes a bridge between a specific laboratory task involving imagery and the concept of creativity. Hargreaves and Bolton (1972) administered a battery of widely used tests of creativity to a sample of 10–11-year-old school children. They also added four new tests, including one they called Images. The Images test consisted of a paired-associate learning trial in which the children were presented pairs of concrete nouns that they were asked to link together by forming images of each pair. The first word of each pair was then read out and the children attempted to recall the second word by remembering the image. An individual's score was the total number of words recalled. The results showed that these scores correlated highly with 11 standard tests of divergent thinking, the median correlation being .49, with a range of .27–.58. The important point is that the paired-associate task is one in which imagery has been shown to be effective under the conditions given (concrete words, imagery instructions). Thus the results provide very specific operational evidence of a relation between imagery and creativity as measured by a wide variety of tasks. Clearly, the results encourage further reseach to determine more precisely the manner in which imagery is involved, and how its potential might be more fully exploited for creative purposes by artists, scientists, and inventors.

Foreign Language Acquisition

My final example deals with the application of visual imagery to the learning of foreign languages. Imagery mnemonics were commonly advocated for this purpose by earlier mnemonists (e.g., Feinaigle, 1813) as they are by contemporary memory experts (e.g., Lorayne, 1974). However, their potential in this regard is only beginning to be explored by rigorous experimental methods. Atkinson and his co-workers (see Atkinson, 1975) developed an effective procedure for aiding the learning of foreign language vocabularies using a variant of the imagery mnemonics described earlier. It works by using a key word to establish an acoustic and an imaginal link between the foreign word and its translation equivalent in the native language. Consider the French word *couteau* and its English translation "knife." To learn *couteau,* one selects an English key word that sounds like some part of the French word and is also easily pictureable. In this case, "toe" would be an appropriate choice since it sounds like the last syllable in *couteau.* Then one establishes an imagery link, perhaps by imagining a knife cutting someone's toe. Subsequently, given the English word *knife,* one is likely to remember the imagined scene, which in turn can be decoded to yield "toe," which prompts recall of *couteau.* Experimental studies have demonstrated that it significantly speeds up learning of foreign language vocabularies among university students.

We have begun to explore further applications of imagery mnemonics in foreign language acquisition. The key-word technique serves admirably in the initial stages of learning but procedural modifications are necessary if imagery mnemonics are to be effective for extended purposes. For example, the usefulness of the foreign vocabulary depends on its psychological availability in appropriate contexts. Such contextual availability is most effectively developed in the foreign language milieu itself, but most of the time this is not possible and the learner must resort to extensive rehearsal using self-study materials or language laboratory programs. Imagery mnemonics can be used as a substitute or supplement to such study methods. I will describe one specific approach and indicate what potential advantages it has for language learners who already have some familiarity with the vocabulary and grammar of a foreign language, and who wish to extend their useful vocabulary and expressive skill. The approach is particularly relevant here because it involves the use of one's visual knowledge to construct a private referential context for the new language.

The basic method involves associative imagery in which new vocabulary items are associated with an ordered series of mnemonic peg words and related images, so that the pegs and images can remind one of the vocabulary items they represent. A complete foreign language context is established by using a mnemonic system in which the peg words themselves are chosen from that language.

A letter–number–word–image system that has long been advocated by memory experts is convenient because it permits construction of a long serially-ordered list of memory pegs (for a summary, see Paivio, 1971, Chapter 6; its contemporary use is described by Lorayne, 1974). The key items are pictureable words that can be directly translated into numbers by means of the consonant–number code based on visual or acoustic similarity. The following is a version of the system:

1	2	3	4	5	6	7	8	9	0
t, d	n	m	r	l	j, sh	$k,$ hard c	f	p, b	z, s

In this particular system, t stands for the numeral 1 because it has one down stroke; n stands for 2 because it has two "legs"; m has 3 legs; r occurs in the name for the numeral 4 in many languages; L is the Roman numeral for 50; j somewhat resembles the numeral 6; k resembles 7; a script f ($\int$) resembles 8; p resembles 9, and z is the first sound in "zero." The letters d, sh[$\int$], hard c, v, b, and s are acoustically related alternatives for the basic consonants.

Table 7.1

Examples of Memory Pegs in a Number–Letter–Word–Image Mnemonic System

Number	Letters	Peg word	Number	Letters	Peg word
1	t, d	tea	11	t–t	tot
2	n	Noah	20	n–s	nose
3	m	emu	32	m–n	moon
4	r	oar	43	r–m	ram
5	l	law	54	l–r	lyre
6	j, sh, ch	shoe	65	j–l	jail
7	k, hard c	cow	76	k–j	cage
8	f, v	ivy	87	f–k	folk
9	p, b	ape	99	p–p	pipe
10	t-s, z	toes	100	d–s–s	disease

Next, one chooses peg words containing only the relevant consonant sounds (vowels are discounted). Thus 1 might be represented by tea, 2 by Noah, 3 by emu, 4 by oar, 10 by toes, 20 by nose, and so on, as shown in Table 7.1. Finally, appropriate referent images are learned for each: a large toe, Noah with a beard, etc. The system must be rehearsed until the associations are overlearned, and it is easy to retrieve any mnemonic image given the number, or vice versa. The pegs can then be used to remember a new list of items by constructing images linking the to-be-remembered words to the mnemonic pegs. Like the other imagery–mnemonic techniques described earlier, this one may seem rather elaborate, but once learned, it is simple to use and highly effective in promoting item recall.

I have applied the technique to the study of French vocabulary items and phrases in such a way that the study items and the verbal and imaginal pegs to which they are hooked provide a meaningful verbal and imaginal context for systematic rehearsal of the language. Table 7.2 shows examples of the French peg words together with their English translations. Consider how these pegs might be used with a vocabulary list beginning with the following six items: armoire ("wardrobe"), caoutchouc ("rubber"), cheval ("horse"), poignet ("wrist"), scie ("saw"), and vignoble ("vineyard"). The first might be imagined as a wardrobe or cupboard onto which thé ("tea") is being poured from a teapot; the second as a rubber ball with a knotted rope (noeud) around it; the third as a horse trying to climb a mast (mât), the fourth, as a king's crown (roi) around someone's wrist; the fifth as a policeman ("lawman" for loi) sawing his night stick in two; and the sixth, as cabbages (chou) hanging from grapevines. On the recall test, thé (number 1) will remind one of the "scene" with

Table 7.2
Examples of French Peg-Words and Their English Translations

Number	Peg word	Number	Peg word
1	*thé* ("tea")	11	*tête* ("head")
2	*noeud* ("knot")	20	*noce* ("wedding")
3	*mât* ("mast")	30	*mousse* ("moss," "foam")
4	*roi* ("king")	41	*râteau* ("rake")
5	*loi* ("law")	52	*laine* ("wool")
6	*chou* ("cabbage")	63	*chameau* ("camel")
7	*camp* ("camp")	74	*carré* "square")
8	*feu* ("fire")	85	*fil* ("thread")
9	*pain* ("bread")	96	*poche* ("pocket")
10	*tasse* ("cup")	100	*diseuse* ("fortune teller")

the teapot and the armoire, *noeud* will redintegrate the knotted rope around the rubber ball, leading to *caoutchouc,* etc.

What are the advantages of this procedure? First, it is mnemonically effective. I have used it repeatedly to study different 100-item vocabulary lists and have been able to recall at least 90 of these correctly in sequence, or backward starting with the last item, or in any order when someone else provides the numbers as randomly ordered cues. Second, it is a highly convenient rehearsal method because it requires no apparatus and does not even require a written vocabulary list once the items have been pegged in memory. I have rehearsed lists while shaving, while walking to work, while jogging, and so on, thereby taking advantage of moments that otherwise might have been spent in idle daydreaming. Third, it can provide a naturalistic context for language use in the sense that one generates a referent situation mentally in response to the word list during the study trial, and then retrieves the words from their imaginal contexts during recall. This process can be elaborated to any degree. For example, I typically construct sentences that incorporate the peg words and associated vocabulary items, so that each sentence is essentially a description of my image. The technique in effect provides a means of generating pictorial aids for language learning entirely within one's own head, a kind of private *voix et image* program, which simply takes advantage of one's own knowledge of the world as the basis for constructing the visual referents.

Finally, the technique has high motivational value. We all know that rote study of any subject matter can be deadly dull. The imagery mnemonics can make language learning interesting because it makes the language meaningful and because its effectiveness makes every study trial highly rewarding.

I have described the technique as I have used it for my own practical purposes and as a kind of informal experiment in which I have served as my own subject. However, the real potential of the technique will only be revealed by formal experimental study. One of the important issues is to determine the degree to which the technique actually increases the avail-ability of vocabulary items in appropriate contexts, relative to the transfer effects of rote rehearsal and other control conditions. Another problem would be to extend the technique to standard phrases and sentences in order to determine its usefulness in the learning of larger chunks that occur frequently in the language. A related purpose would be to explore its value in the learning of syntactic information. For example, would it be effective in the learning of noun gender, adjective–noun order, and adjective–noun gender agreement in French? I have found that I can easily recall the gender of nouns in a study list simply by including a gender "tag" in the image. Thus, in the example of the policeman and the saw, one might imagine a policewoman rather than a policeman, to remind one that the French word *scie* is feminine.

I cannot be sure, however, that such a procedure is any more effective in the long run than rote rehearsal of noun gender. These and many other questions remain to be explored and we have begun to do so. I present these examples simply to illustrate the way in which one's knowledge of the world can be used in a mnemonic technique for the purpose of language learning. I believe this kind of approach offers rich practical possibilities in any number of educational areas, but only further research explorations will tell us precisely where the exploitation of visual knowl-edge will be most profitable.

REFERENCES

Arnheim, R. *Visual thinking.* Los Angeles: Univ. of California Press, 1969.
Atkinson, R. C. Mnemotechnics in second-language learning. *American Psychologist,* 1975, *30,* 821–838.
Bennett, G. K., Seashore, M. G., & Wesman, A. G. *Differential aptitude tests.* New York: Psychological Corporation, 1947.
De Renzi, E., & Spinnler, H. Impaired performance on color tasks in patients with hemispheric damage. *Cortex,* 1967, *3,* 194–217.
Downs, R. M., & Stea, D. (Eds.) *Image and environment: Cognitive mapping and spatial behavior.* Chicago: Aldine, 1973.
Feinaigle, V. von *The new art of memory.* (3rd ed.) London: Sherwood, Neely & Jones, 1813.
Fillenbaum, S., & Rapoport, A. *Structures in the subjective lexicon.* New York: Academic Press, 1971.
Guilford, J. P. *The nature of human intelligence.* New York: McGraw-Hill, 1967.

Hargreaves, D. J., & Bolton, N. Selecting creativity tests for use in research. *British Journal of Psychology,* 1972, *63,* 451–462.

Katz, A. N., & Paivio, A. Imagery variables in concept identification. *Journal of Verbal Learning and Verbal Behavior,* 1975, *14,* 284–293.

Lea, G. Chronometric analysis of the method of loci. *Journal of Experimental Psychology,* 1975, *104,* 95–104.

Likert, R., & Quasha, W. H. *Revised Minnesota paper form board test, series AA.* New York: The Psychological Corporation, 1941.

Lorayne, H. *How to develop a super-power memory.* New York: Signet, 1974.

Moyer, R. S. Comparing objects in memory: Evidence suggesting an internal psychophysics. *Perception & Psychophysics,* 1973, *13,* 180–184.

Paivio, A. *Imagery and verbal processes.* New York: Holt, 1971.

Paivio, A. Coding distinctions and repetition effects in memory. In G. H. Bower (Ed.), The psychology of learning and motivation. Vol. 9. New York: Academic Press, 1975. (a)

Paivio, A. Perceptual comparisons through the mind's eye. *Memory & Cognition,* 1975, *3,* 635–647. (b)

Paivio, A., & Csapo, K. Concrete-image and verbal memory codes. *Journal of Experimental Psychology,* 1969, *80,* 279–285.

Peterson, L. R., Holsten, J., & Spevak, P. Spatial coding of auditory signals. *Memory & Cognition,* 1975, *3,* 243–246.

Peterson, M. J. The retention of imagined and seen spatial matrices. *Cognitive Psychology,* 1975, *7,* 181–193.

Randhawa, B. S. Intellectual development and the ability to process visual and verbal information. *AV Communication Review,* 1971, *19,* 298–312.

Rosch, E. Cognitive representations of semantic categories. *Journal of Experimental Psychology: General,* 1975, *104,* 192–233.

Shepard, R. N., & Chipman, S. Second-order isomorphism of internal representations: Shapes of states. *Cognitive Psychology,* 1970, *1,* 1–17.

Travers, R. M. W. *Man's information system.* Scranton, Pennsylvania: Chandler, 1970.

8

Externalization of Mental Images and the Act of Creation[1]

ROGER N. SHEPARD
Stanford University
Stanford, California

In the two major sections of this chapter I consider successively the externalization of mental images in two different senses. In the first section, I review the cases of a number of highly original and significant creations of the human mind, ranging from such concrete inventions as the condensing steam engine and the alternating current motor to such abstract theories as those of electromagnetic fields and special relativity. I argue that these creations derived rather directly from nonverbal internal representations or images of a largely spatial and often visual character and that, at least in a metaphorical sense, these creations constitute a very objective and tangible "externalization" of the corresponding subjective and private images from which they arose. In the second section, I consider attempts that some artists, scientists, and others have made to externalize their own mental images, in a more faithful, concrete, and less metaphorical way, by means of drawing, painting, or related techniques. Here the focus is no longer on the role that a particular image may have played in some real-world project with scientific, technological, or artistic goals. Rather, the focus is on the detailed nature of the image itself, just as it

[1] I am indebted to the National Science Foundation for its support during the preparation of this paper, principally through NSF Grant No. BNS–75–02806.

spontaneously occurred, whether during wakeful problem solving, idle reverie, or in a dream or hypnagogic state. My hope is that, through efforts of this kind, we may begin to discern some ways in which we may yet be able to undertake a closer and more systematic look at these various sorts of mental images; images that, although they have often appeared to play a crucial role in processes of scientific discovery, have themselves seemed to remain largely inaccessible to those very processes.

SCIENTIFIC THEORIES AND INVENTIONS
AS EXTERNALIZED MENTAL IMAGES

Suppose that we do not start by asking what kinds of thought processes are most accessible to empirical study, are most conveniently externalized in the form of discrete symbols, words, or sentences, or are most readily described by existing models imported into cognitive psychology from linguistics or computer science. Suppose, instead, that we first ask what sorts of thought processes underlie human creative acts of the highest and most original order. Perhaps we shall come to be less than fully satisfied with research that is exclusively motivated by current theories of linear sequential processing of discrete symbolic or propositional structures. At the same time, an examination of specific cases may help to suggest another approach to the study of creative thinking. For, if the tangible products of human invention are in any sense external embodiments of what originally were purely internal images, then the degree of externalization necessary to support a scientific investigation may, at least in principle, be possible.

The Role of Imagery and Related Nonverbal Processes in Some Creative Thinkers

Albert Einstein. We can hardly do better than start at the top.[2] On several different occasions Einstein reported that verbal processes did "not seem to play any role" in his processes of creative thought. Rather he claimed to achieve his insights into the fundamental nature of space and time by means of Gedanken experiments on mentally visualized systems of light waves and idealized physical bodies (including clocks and measuring rods) in states of relative motion (Hadamard, 1945, Appendix II; Holton, 1972; Wertheimer, 1945, p. 184). Indeed, the paradox that eventually led him to the development of the special theory of relativity first came to him

---

[2] And Einstein's is a case that fascinated me long before the organic chemist (and discoverer of biochemical mechanisms related to multiple sclerosis—see Maugh, 1977), who once employed me as her laboratory assistant at the Stanford Research Institute, became Einstein's daughter-in-law, Dr. Elizabeth Roboz Einstein.

when, at age 16, he imagined himself traveling along beside a beam of light (at the velocity of some 186,000 miles per second). It then struck him that the stationary spatial oscillation that he mentally "saw" corresponded neither to anything that could be perceptually experienced as light nor to anything described by Maxwell's equations for the propagation of electromagnetic waves (Holton, 1972, p. 98). The elimination of the paradox required a revolutionary restructuring of the spatiotemporal configuration visualized in this thought experiment. However the translation of this restructuring into the verbal and mathematical symbols necessary for communication to others was, for Einstein, a very uncongenial and difficult business that he could undertake only when he had worked out his conceptualization of the physical situation by means of "more or less clear images which can be 'voluntarily' reproduced and combined [Einstein, in Hadamard, 1945, p. 142]."

As a child, Einstein, like a number of other eminent persons—including, among many others, Thomas Edison, Harvey Cushing, Charles Darwin, Auguste Rodin, and Woodrow Wilson (see Lombroso, 1901, pp. 13, 357; Thompson, 1971)—manifested language disabilities suggestive of dyslexia (Patten, 1973). Einstein did not speak until age 3 and only with difficulty for some years thereafter (Holton, 1972). He was so unsuccessful at the verbal and even the arithmetic tasks emphasized in his early schooling that his teacher predicted that "nothing good" would come of the boy (Sullivan, 1972). By contrast, Einstein demonstrated an early fascination with the behavior of physical devices (such as, particularly, a magnetic compass and a model steam engine), and an unusual skill in dealing with spatial structures—having erected houses of cards as many as 14 stories high and having devised an original, purely geometrical proof of the Pythagorean theorem before the age of 10 (Holton, 1972; Patten, 1973; Sullivan, 1972). It is tempting to conjecture that Einstein's early and often solitary preoccupation within a relatively private visual–spatial domain, in preference to the socially and institutionally controlled verbal domain, set the stage for his latter roles in the developments that have transformed twentieth-century physics; namely, those of quantum theory and the special and general theories of relativity.

Throughout, Einstein's work in theoretical physics was marked by an interplay between concrete perceptual visualization, on the one hand, and a relentless drive toward abstract, aesthetic principles of symmetry or invariance, on the other. This interplay seems to have been mediated, not by verbal deductions, "logical bridges," or mathematical formalisms, but by soaring leaps of spatial and physical intuition. "There is no logical way to the discovery of these elemental laws. There is only the way of intuition, which is helped by a feeling for the order lying behind the appearance [Einstein's prologue in Planck, 1933, p. 10]." *Max Planck,* incidentally, who was shortly followed by Einstein in taking the first steps toward the development of quantum theory, expressed what appears to be a consonant view: "Again and again the imaginary plan on which one attempts to build up that order breaks down and then we must try another. This imaginative vision and faith in the ultimate success are indispensable. The pure rationalist has no place here [Planck, 1933, p. 215]." I am inclined to agree with Holton that, in Einstein's case, the abstract principle of symmetry which emerged time and again—in his insistence on a symmetrical relation between rest and motion, charge and current, electric field and magnetic field, space and time, matter and energy, and gravitation and inertia—was itself rooted in an aesthetic appreciation of a more concretely visual kind of symmetry.

James Clerk Maxwell. There are some suggestive parallels between Einstein and the theoretical physicist James Clerk Maxwell, who was perhaps Einstein's greatest immediate predecessor. In his crowning achievement, Maxwell was able to crystalize, in a symmetrical set of four simple equations, the fundamental relationships governing electric fields, magnetic fields, and the propagation of electromagnetic waves—namely, light. These are precisely the "Maxwell's equations" that Einstein had in mind when he later performed his epochal thought experiment on pursuing a light wave through space.

In an instructive discussion of Maxwell's development, James R. Newman (1955) points out that the usual view of Maxwell as an abstract theoretician overlooks the route, rich with concrete geometrical and mechanical imagery, by which he reached the final pinnacle of abstract formalism. As a child, Maxwell was fascinated with mechanical devices and, in this, he resembled not only Einstein but two other great physicists, *Ernst Mach* and *Isaac Newton* (Holton, 1972, p. 109). Just as Newton in his early youth made drawings, mechanical toys, clocks, and sundials (though by no means a prodigy in his school subjects), Maxwell devised a scientific toy in which a set of figures on a turning wheel produced the illusion of continuous movement; constructed (as he wrote his father) a "tetra hedron, a dodeca hedron, and two more hedrons that I don't know the wright [sic] names for;" and discovered (as had the young Descartes before him) a method for generating a perfect ellipse using two pins and a loop of thread. Later in life Maxwell devised elaborate mechanical models to demonstrate, for example, that the stability of Saturn's rings implied that they must be neither liquid nor rigidly solid but composed of separate particles (see Newman, 1955, p. 61). And Maxwell is said to have "developed the habit of making a mental picture of every problem [Beveridge, 1957, p. 76]."

Indeed, Maxwell arrived at his celebrated electromagnetic equations, not by a chain of logical steps, but by a series of increasingly abstract hydrodynamic and mechanical models of the medium or "ether" presumed to underlie electromagnetic fields and waves. At first, Maxwell visualized Faraday's lines of electrostatic force as tubes in which electric flow was represented by the flow of an incompressible fluid such as water. Later he devised a more elaborate mechanical model to account for magnetic attraction and electromagnetic induction as well as the electrostatic effects explained by the earlier hydrodynamic model. He now envisioned the lines of magnetic force as parallel rotating cylinders separated by ball bearings rotating in the opposite direction. Changes in the rotation of a local set of cylinders, corresponding to changes in the magnetic field, induced a movement at right angles in the bounding layer of ball bearings, corresponding to changes in the electric flow; and vice versa. Then, in a particularly brilliant stroke, he went on to show that the rate of propagation of what would be interpreted as an electromagnetic disturbance in such a system corresponded to the velocity of light. Finally, when the abstract structure of this system was sufficiently formalized, Maxwell was able to dispense with the concrete mechanical model and, with it, the last vestiges of asymmetry between the electric and magnetic fields. As remarked by Sir Edmund Whittaker, he now displayed the underlying elegantly symmetrical structure of electromagnetism "stripped of the scaffolding by aid of which it had first been erected [Newman, 1955, p. 67]."

Michael Faraday. Having traced electromagnetic theory backward from Einstein through Maxwell, I will pursue it back one step further to where the modern conception of magnetic and electric fields might be said to have originated—in the mind of another of Einstein's towering predecessors, Michael Faraday. Interestingly, as Koestler has noted, Faraday was a visionary in a quite literal sense. He not only had an aversion to writing and later, seemingly, to "language itself," he also "lacked any mathematical education or gift [beyond] the merest elements of arithmetic." Yet the invisible "lines of force," which he visualized as narrow tubes curving in the space around magnets and electric currents and, indeed, pervading the universe, "rose up before him like things" (see Koestler, 1964, p. 170; Tyndall, 1868).

The great nineteenth-century mathematical physicist Helmholtz later remarked in his Faraday memorial lecture: "It is in the highest degree astonishing to see what a large number of general theorems, the methodological deduction of which requires the highest powers of mathematical analysis, he found by a kind of intuition, with the security of instinct, without the help of a single mathematical formula [Kendall, 1955]."

Hermann von Helmholtz. In addition to his role in guiding his student, Heinrich Hertz, toward the conclusive experimental proof of Maxwell's theoretically derived equivalence between light and electromagnetic oscillation, Helmholtz himself made contributions to physics of the most fundamental sort. He is, in fact, regarded as a prime architect of one of the most basic pre-Einsteinian invariance principles, namely, the principle of conservation of energy. A scientist of extraordinary breadth as well as depth, Helmholtz also made the first measurements of the speed of neural conduction, invented the ophthalmoscope, and forged unprecedented advances in the understanding of visual and auditory perception. It is of some interest, therefore, that Helmholtz, while kept at home during the earliest school years by poor health, reportedly took a particular interest in playing with a set of wooden blocks, with the result that when he finally began school at age 8, he "astonished" his teachers with the knowledge of geometry that he had already acquired on his own (Koenigsberger, 1965, p. 6).

Also of interest is the similarity between a passage that Helmholtz wrote later in life and Einstein's statements concerning the role of sensory experience and of reproducible mental operations on objects in space. According to Helmholtz, "memory images of purely sensory impressions may . . . be used as elements of thought combinations without it being necessary, or even possible, to describe these in words, [and] equipped with an awareness of the physical form of an object, we can clearly imagine all of the perspective images which we may expect upon viewing from this or that side [Warren & Warren, 1968, pp. 252–254]."

Helmholtz reported another aspect of many of his own "happiest" scientific ideas; namely, their tendency to come to him, sometimes virtually full-blown, immediately upon awakening or while hiking in the green hills near Heidelberg, no longer actively thinking about the problem to which they represented the solution (e.g., Warren & Warren, 1968, p. 11). This phenomenon of sudden "illumination" has, of course, been described by many of the most creative thinkers—including two of the greatest mathematicians of all time, Gauss and Poincaré (Hadamard, 1945, pp. 12–15); the prolific philosopher and logician, Bertrand Russell (Hutchinson, 1949, p. 112); the two originators of the theory of evolution, Darwin and Wallace (Beveridge, 1957, p. 93); the neurophysiologists, Loewi and Cannon (Cannon, 1945); the physicist, Ampère (Koestler, 1964, p. 117); and the inventors, Watt and Tesla (considered on pages 141–142). Some interesting descriptions of this phenomenon are also quoted in an early survey of chemists by Platt and Baker (1931). And a contemporary physicist has gone so far as to assert that "every new discovery originates in such a sudden nonverbal flash [Capra, 1975, p. 39]."

The unexpected eruption into consciousness of a creative solution to a previously intractable problem seems to imply the preceding occurrence of unconscious and, presumably, unverbalized thinking on a very high order—as when *Henri Poincaré,* in the very act of stepping on a bus leaving for a geological excursion and in the middle of an unrelated conversation, was suddenly struck with the startling and profound realization that his "fuchsian functions" were in fact "identical to those of non-Euclidean geometry [Poincaré, in Ghiselin, 1952, p. 37]." Moreover, the striking consistency with which the various scientists just mentioned have used the phrase "flashed before my mind" in describing these sudden insights (as well as the seeming appropriateness of the word "illumination") points to a strong visual component.

One might suppose that the inadequacy of conventional language for creative thinking in theoretical physics, suggested by the remarks of Einstein and other physicists, might be peculiar to that field—struggling, as it now is, with phenomena that are so small, so large, so rapid, so energetic, or so dense as to fall entirely outside the range of direct human experience. *Werner Heisenberg,* who set the cornerstone of quantum mechanics with his principle of uncertainty, called attention, particularly, to the inadequacy of language for dealing with the very small: ". . . the problems of language here are really serious. We wish to speak in some way about the structure of the atoms and not only about 'facts'—the latter being, for instance, the black spots on a photographic plate or the water droplets in a cloud chamber. But we cannot speak about the atom in ordinary language [Heisenberg, 1958, p. 179]." However, as we shall see, the limitations of language, though especially severe in physics perhaps, are felt quite generally.

Sir Francis Galton.   Certainly many thinkers in fields other than physics (and in times antedating the advents of relativity and quantum mechanics) would agree with the Eastern philosophers who assert that "The instant you speak about a thing you miss the mark [Capra, 1975, p. 34]" or that "All things in their fundamental nature . . . cannot be adequately expressed in any form of language [Ashvaghosha, 1900, p. 56]" or with the Western philosopher, Schopenhauer, who wrote that "Thoughts die the moment they are embodied by words [Hadamard, 1945, p. 75]." Shifting, for example, to the quite different fields of anthropology and genetics, we encounter Charles Darwin's renowned cousin, Francis Galton, who asserted that, when he was working on a scientific problem, as much as when he was planning a shot in billiards, his thought was never conducted by means of words. Very much as Einstein, Galton complained that "It often happens that after being hard at work, and having arrived at results that are perfectly clear and satisfactory to myself, when I try to express them in language I . . . waste a vast deal of time in seeking for appropriate words and phrases [Hadamard, 1945, p. 69]."

Galton, incidentally, was apparently the first to undertake a large-scale empirical investigation of the many forms and degrees in which mental imagery and related phenomena occur in children and in adults—including writers, artists, and scientists (Galton, 1883, pp. 83–114; 155–177). In the same work, moreover, Galton described a metaphorical "antechamber of consciousness" (pp. 203–207) that, along with Poincaré's mechanical analogy of thoughts as "hooked atoms" moving about in space (Poincaré, in Ghiselin, 1952, p. 41), provided a promising, if sketchy, early indication of a possible mechanism for the phenomenon of illumination.

Jacques Hadamard. A noted mathematician, who like Galton was moved to undertake his own study of the processes of creative thought, Hadamard (1945) aligned himself explicitly with Galton: "I insist that words are totally absent from my mind when I really think [p. 75]," and "they remain absolutely absent from my mind until I come to the moment of communicating the results in written or oral form [p. 82]." With difficult mathematical problems, Hadamard claimed, even algebraic signs became "too heavy a baggage" for him, and he had to rely on "concrete representations, but of a quite different nature—cloudy imagery" that indicated relations of inclusion, exclusion, or order, or that held the structure of the whole problem together in such a way as to preserve its "physiognomy."

I suspect that those who have written computer programs of any complexity know exactly the difficulty to which Hadamard alluded when, after stating that "every mathematical research compels me to build such a schema," he added that, if he was interrupted in the course of his calculations, the concrete symbols that he had written on paper became "dead" for him so that he often could "do nothing else than throw the sheet away and begin everything anew [p. 82]." (One is reminded, here, of the famous dictum by Gauss to the effect that notation is nothing, conception everything.)

Fortunately, Hadamard's labors were not always this trying. Much as in the case of Helmholtz, Hadamard reported, with "absolute certainty," the following event:

> On being very abruptly awakened by an external noise, a solution long searched for [involving the valuation of a determinant] appeared to me at once without the slightest instant of reflection on my part—the fact was remarkable enough to have struck me unforgettably—and in a quite different direction from any of those which I had previously tried to follow [p. 8].

I turn now to the cases of some inventors in whom such sudden illuminations, perhaps because they provided solutions to less abstract problems, were more explicitly of a concrete visual or spatial character.

James Watt. The revolutionary effects of the steam engine, on industry, transportation, and society, came about as a direct consequence of Watt's inventions—including the centrifugal or "fly-ball" governor (often presented as the purest early example of a negative-feedback servomechanism), the pressure-volume "indicator diagram" (which played a central role in the later development of theremodynamic theory) and, most particularly, the steam condenser. Watt's own account of the origin of this last invention is most interesting. After finding, by calculation, that the primitive Newcomen engine wasted three-fourths of the heat supplied to it, Watt worked for 2 years trying to overcome this debilitating inefficiency, but without success. Then, during the enforced idleness of "a fine Sabbath afternoon," the solution suddenly presented itself.

As Watt himself described the incident,

> I had entered the green and . . . had gone as far as the herd's house when the idea came into my mind that as steam was an elastic body, . . . if a connection were made between the cylinder and an exhausting vessel it would rush into it and might then be condensed without cooling the cylinder. . . . I had not walked further than the Golf house when the whole thing was arranged in my mind [Thurston, 1878, pp. 87–88].

I do not doubt that this mental "arranging" as well as the preconscious processes preceding the moment of illumination were not so much logical as "analogical" (cf., Myers, 1903, p. 226; Sloman, 1971). The incident is not unlike that in which *Oliver Evans* invented the automatic flour mill by putting the whole system, including bucket elevators and screw conveyors, together in his mind while lying in bed (Ferguson, 1977, p. 834).[3]

It is perhaps worth noting that Watt's childhood was parallel in some suggestive respects to the childhoods of Newton, Maxwell, Helmholtz, and Einstein. Owing to poor health, Watt received little formal schooling as a child, and was relatively isolated from his peers. At the same time, he was said, by the age of 6, to have occupied himself with the solution of geometrical problems and, later, to have done much drawing and carving, and to have constructed many beautiful models and ingenious mechanisms, including "a very fine barrel-organ [Thurston, 1878, p. 81]."

Nikola Tesla. Some of the most striking illustrations of concrete visual imagery in problem solving are to be found in accounts of the eccentric and reclusive inventor, Tesla, to whom we are indebted for such ubiquitous

---

[3] Just reported is a recent case, like those mentioned on pages 141, 145, 154, in which a novel, highly complex machine took form as a visual image. Seymour Cray, the "genius at compaction" who designed the world's fastest supercomputer, the cylindrical $8 million Cray–1, is said to proceed by building a "visual concept" of the whole machine in his head. "There are no intermediate steps. He simply conceives it and then draws it [Metz, 1978, p. 406]."

supports to our modern way of life as flourescent lighting, the three-phase electrical distribution system, and the self-starting induction motor. One should perhaps be cautious about accepting literally some of the more enthusiastic reports—such as, that Tesla, before actually constructing a physical machine, would first determine what parts were most subject to wear by "inspecting" an imaginary model that he had "run for weeks" purely mentally (O'Neill, 1944, p. 51). But there is little doubt that Tesla's creativity owed much to mental imagery of an extraordinarily concrete, three-dimensional, and vivid character, and may have been in some way connected with his susceptibility to spontaneous visual sensations and phantasms from childhood onward (Hunt & Draper, 1964, p. 184).

The conception of the self-starting, reversible induction motor reportedly came to Tesla, with dramatic suddenness, in the form of a kinetic visual image of hallucinatory intensity. While walking toward the sunset with a former classmate, Szigety, Tesla's recitation of a poem by Goethe was suddenly interrupted by a vision of a magnetic field, such as Faraday and Maxwell had so beautifully depicted as a family of curving lines (see Maxwell, 1873), brought into rapid vortical rotation within a circle of electromagnets energized by sinusoidally alternating currents of the same frequency but relatively shifted in phase. He saw, further, that a simple iron armature placed within this field was dragged around by the field and, in fact, could be caused to start, to stop, or to reverse rotation merely by switching connections to the coils of the magnets (Tesla, 1956, p. A–198; see Hunt & Draper, 1964, p. 34). In short, this one vision led him simultaneously to the invention of the self-starting alternating current motor and to the inspiration for constructing the polyphase system of electrical generation and distribution now used throughout most of the world.

Creative thinkers in whom visions or hallucinations have figured are, in fact, both numerous and illustrious (see Lombroso, 1901, pp. 56–57; 73–77; 96). Among those already mentioned, they include Descartes, Goethe, and Schopenhauer. Two further cases are relevant here. First, there is the notorious *Girolamo Cardan* whose multifarious medical, mechanical, and mathematical contributions may well be connected with his proclivity to exceptionally intense imagery. Certainly it is suggestive that, for the highly theoretical invention of imaginary numbers which "has illuminated the whole mathematical science [Hadamard, 1945, p. 135]" and hence, incidentally, the theories of electromagnetism, quantum mechanics, and (via Minkowski's geometrization) relativity, and also for the very practical inventions of a Braille-like system for teaching the deaf to read and write and a mechanical linkage (the Cardan joint) that is an essential part of every automobile, we are indebted to an individual who, by his own account, was from childhood subject to "hypno-fantastic hallucinations" and for whom "whatever he imagined, he could see before him as a real object [Lombroso, 1901, p. 74]." And second, there is the precocious genius *Blaise Pascal* who, inspired at age 10 by the noise made by a plate struck by a knife, partially anticipated Helmholtz's development of the modern theory of sound by working out a theory of his own and, at 15, completed his celebrated geometrical treatise on the conic sections; but who was also subject to fits, deliriums, and hallucinations, and who (like Descartes) was profoundly influenced by his dreams. Intriguingly, in view of the several reported cases of persons who began writing poetry only after lesions had formed in the left (or linguistic) hemisphere (Sagan, 1977, p. 167), the suppurated lesions found in Pascal's brain following his early death were also localized in his left hemisphere (Lombroso, 1901, pp. 11; 327).

Sir John Herschel. Not all creative thinkers whose visual imagery sometimes verged into hallucinatory vividness exhibited other signs of neurologic disease or madness. In a published lecture "On Sensorial Vision," the nineteenth-century British astronomer, chemist, and philosopher John Herschel, who was both notably productive in diverse fields and, as far as I am aware, eminently sane, provides us with an illuminating report of several distinct types of highly structured, subjective visual phenomena that he had spontaneously experienced at various times. The son of Sir William Herschel, who was the discoverer of Uranus, Sir John had his own most significant influences as the compiler of the enormously important *General Catalogue of Nebulae* and as one of the independent inventors of photography. In this last connection, Herschel was in fact the first to speak of "positive" and "negative" photographic images; and he made some of the earliest explicit comparisons between the photochemical processes on the photographic plate and in the retina—including those giving rise to afterimages, which persist following the removal of the external stimulus (see, e.g., Herschel, 1867, p. 402). The high esteem in which Herschel was held by his countrymen is indicated by his interment in Westminster Abbey next to Isaac Newton.

One of the phenomena that Herschel reported provides a remarkable illustration of a virtually hallucinatory and involuntary counterpart of the voluntary ability of the mind, noted by Helmholtz, to "imagine all of the perspective images" of an object. It also appears related to the more recent claim that, following a brief flash of illumination in a totally dark room, the residual image of the room may appear to undergo appropriate perspective changes as the observer then moves through the darkness with fixed regard (Gregory, Wallace, & Campbell, 1959; Richardson, 1969, p. 25). According to Herschel, while passing by the place where he had recently witnessed the demolition of a structure that had been familiar to him since childhood, he was astonished "to see it as if still standing—projected against the dull sky." "Being perfectly aware that it was a mere nervous impression," he says, "I walked on, keeping my eyes directed to it, and the perspective of the form and disposition of the parts appeared to change with the change in the point of view as they would have done if real [Herschel, 1867, p. 405]." Although I have not myself experienced so perceptually compelling an example of internally generated perspective transformation while fully awake, I have many times been struck by awesome involuntary transformations of this type in my dreams and hypnagogic imagery.

Herschel also provides us with detailed descriptions of spontaneous visual phenomena that he had repeatedly experienced of a quite different nature. These, he says, consisted in "the involuntary production of visual impressions, into which geometrical regularity of form enters as the leading character . . . under circumstances which altogether preclude any explanation drawn from a possible regularity of structure in the retina or the optic nerve [Herschel, 1867, p. 406]." These geometrical visions, which typically appeared in darkness while Herschel was still awake but which also arose with particular vividness on two occasions when he had been given chloroform as a general anesthetic, tended to be of rhombic or rectagular lattice works, sometimes containing repeating complex or even colored "close patterns" or "fillagree work" or else they were of a "very beautiful and perfectly regular and symmetrical 'Turkscap' pattern, formed by the mutual intersection of a great number of circles outside of, and tangent to, a central one" consisting of "exceedingly delicate . . . assemblages of coloured lines [and sometimes containing lozenge-shaped forms] in the intersections of the circles with each other [pp. 409–410]." I shall return later to a consideration of the possible significance of images possessing such "perfect symmetry, and geometrical regularity." From Herschel's descriptions, they appear to bear a striking resemblance to drawings (reproduced toward the end of this chapter) that I made of some of my own hypnagogic images well before I had known of the existence of Herschel's lecture on the subject.

Omar Snyder. A previously unpublished case, though of a more recent and less widely-known scientist, is also of particular interest to me both because the solution to a difficult problem suddenly appeared in a visual–spatial form seemingly resembling that indicated by Watt and Tesla and because in this case I myself was able to interview the scientist, Omar Snyder, to whom the solution occurred. This incident took place in 1943 while Snyder was working on the "Manhattan Project" for the development of the atomic bomb (a device whose possibility was prefigured, of course,

in Einstein's fundamental equation relating matter and energy, $E = mc^2$).
Before describing the particular incident, however, I should mention that
according to Snyder his experience was not unlike others that occurred to
the great twentieth-century physicists with whom he had contact on the
project—notably Fermi, von Neumann, and Wheeler. All three, he said,
reported that the answer to a difficult problem would sometimes "just
come."

Snyder's own answer came after he had been struggling for some time
with what, in the words of the official report on the Manhattan Project
(Smyth, 1945), "turned out to be one of the most difficult problems encountered [p. 117]" in the design and construction of the atomic reactor;
namely, the "canning problem" of sealing the uranium slugs in metallic
sheaths or jackets that "would protect uranium from water corrosion,
would keep fission products out of the water, would transmit heat from
the uranium to the water, and would not absorb too many neutrons [p.
117]." The problem of achieving both a uniform, heat-conducting bond
between the uranium and the enclosing can while ensuring a gas-tight seal
proved so troublesome that "even up to a few weeks before it was time to
load the uranium slugs into the pile there was no certainty that any of the
processes under development would be satisfactory [Smyth, 1945, p. 147]."
Then, one day, during lunch hour, Snyder achieved the solution in a
manner that was sudden, unexpected, and remains vividly in his memory.
He was walking down the hall of one of the laboratories and, in his words,
"I had gone one pace past the water cooler when suddenly the entire
process for the manufacture of the three-metal composite for the fuel
elements flashed in my mind instantaneously." Much as in Watt's invention
of the steam condenser, Snyder immediately set to work constructing a
physical realization of his idea. ("I didn't need any drawings; the whole
plan was perfectly clear in my head.") By the end of the next day he had
verified that the entire process did indeed work—just as it had been revealed to him in that brief moment of illumination (Snyder, personal
communication, September 28, 1976). In the words of the official report,
moreover, the results "proved to be far better than had been hoped
[Smyth, 1945, p. 182]."

That the solution was instantly grasped as a whole is especially noteworthy in this case because the process that it represented possessed a
complex temporal as well as spatial structure: Under specially controlled
variations of temperature, concentric sleeves of the constituent metals were
caused, by their own different coefficients of expansion, to come together
in the proper sequence and pressure and later to separate, leaving the
desired bonded composite core. That a process drawn out in time in this
way should be pictured, as Snyder emphasized, *instantaneously* suggests a

possible abstract connection with Watt's "indicator diagram," in which, too, dynamic changes in temperature, pressure, and spatial configuration are captured in a static picture. It also reminds one of the famous passage in a letter attributed to *Mozart* in which the composer speaks not only of musical themes spontaneously arising within him but also of the point when, according to one translation of his words,

> the whole, though it be long, stands almost complete and finished in my mind, so that I can survey it, like a fine picture or a beautiful statue, at a glance. Nor do I hear in my imagination the parts successively, but I hear them, as it were, all at once (*gleich alles zusammen*). What a delight this is I cannot tell! All this inventing, this producing, takes place in a pleasing, lively dream [Mozart, in Ghiselin, 1952, p. 45].

James D. Watson.   A twentieth-century development with perhaps the profoundest implications for the future of man was the "cracking" of the genetic code. Since the discovery of the three-dimensional double helical structure of DNA, for which Watson and Crick shared the Nobel Prize, represented in large part the solution of a complex geometrical problem, it would be surprising if spatial visualization did not play a significant role. In fact, according to Watson's account of the discovery, it was achieved by adopting a methodology previously exploited with great success by another Nobel Laureate, *Linus Pauling:* Instead of proceeding deductively or trying to infer the underlying structure by "staring at X-ray pictures, the essential trick . . . was to ask which atoms like to sit next to each other. In place of pencil and paper, the main working tools were a set of molecular models superficially resembling the toys of preschool children [Watson, 1968, p. 38]."

Watson makes clear that visualization played a role both in his own thought processes and those of his collaborator, *Francis Crick.* As he writes in one place, "For over two hours I happily lay awake with pairs of adenine residues whirling in front of my closed eyes [p. 118]" and, in another, "I wandered into the lab to see Francis, unquestionably early, flipping the cardboard base pairs about an imaginary line [p. 128]." Moreover, as in other cases we have considered, the realizations of crucial structural relationships was typically quite precipitate: "Suddenly I realized the potentially profound implications of a DNA structure in which . . . each adenine residue would form two hydrogen bonds to an adenine residue related to it by a 180-degree rotation [p. 116]"; and, at the later and most critical juncture of all, "Suddenly I became aware that an adenine–thymine pair held together by two hydrogen bonds was identical in shape to a guanine–cytosine pair held together by at least two hydrogen bonds [p. 123]." In view of the structural complexity of the shapes involved (see Watson, 1968, p. 119), it seems reasonable to suppose that the processes leading to this sudden awareness were more holistic and analogical than atomistic and logical (cf., Cooper & Shepard, 1978).

Friedrich A. Kekulé. The theory of chemical bonds and molecular structure, which was subsequently to be brought to its present elegant state of elucidation by Pauling and others and which has formed the foundations for Watson and Crick's discovery of the molecular structure of the genetic code, owes much of its earliest development to the highly visual thinking of the German chemist Kekulé. From time to time, over a period of 7, or 8 years Kekulé, during idle reveries, experienced images of what he took to be atoms dancing before his eyes. Then, as he was returning by bus through the deserted streets "one fine summer evening," he perceived how atoms join to form molecules. His own description of the incident has been translated as follows:

> I fell into a reverie, and lo! the atoms were gambolling before my eyes. Whenever, hitherto, these diminutive beings had appeared to me, they had always been in motion; but up to that time, I had never been able to discern the nature of their motion. Now, however, I saw how, frequently, two smaller atoms united to form a pair; how a larger one embraced two smaller ones; how still larger ones kept hold of three or even four of the smaller; whilst the whole kept whirling in a giddy dance. I saw how the larger ones formed a chain. . . . I spent part of the night putting on paper at least sketches of these dream forms [Findlay, 1948, p. 42].

Later, after years of trying to discover the molecular conformation of benzene, Kekulé made the signal discovery of its hexagonal ringlike structure, and thus revolutionized organic chemistry, through a dream image of a snake swallowing its tail. While dozing in a chair before the fire one afternoon in 1865 he again found that, as he put it,

> the atoms were juggling before my eyes . . . my mind's eye, sharpened by repeated sights of a similar kind, could now distinguish larger structures of different forms and in long chains, many of them close together; everything was moving in a snake-like and twisting manner. Suddenly, what was this? One of the snakes got hold of its own tail and the whole structure was mockingly twisting in front of my eyes. As if struck by lightning, I awoke. . . . [In a report of his discovery in 1890, Kekulé concluded]: Let us learn to dream gentlemen, and then we may perhaps find the truth [MacKenzie, 1965, p. 135]." [4]

[4] A translation of words by F. A. Kekulé from *Dreams and Dreaming* by Norman MacKenzie, © 1965 by Aldus Books, London.

Kekulé is not alone in making a fundamental discovery through dream imagery. Like Newton and Cardan much earlier (Lombroso, 1901, p. 21), a majority of mathematicians responding to a questionnaire by Howard Fehr reportedly believed that they had at one time or another solved problems in their dreams (Krippner & Hughes, 1970). Moreover, the solutions to a number of concrete scientific and technological problems that allegedly first emerged in dreams appear to have emerged in an essentially visual form. Among those mentioned by Krippner and Hughes are *Elias Howe's* dream that, because he had not yet perfected his invention of the sewing machine, he was being attacked by spears with holes through the points—which led to the crucial step in his invention of drilling the "eye" near the point of the needle rather than at the other end where it had previously always been; *Louis Agassiz's* thrice repeated dream of the appearance of a fossilized fish—which finally revealed how to extract the fossil from the slab of stone on which he had been working; and *James Watt's* recurrent dream of being showered with solid pellets—which led to his discovery of a much simpler method of manufacturing lead shot by splashing molten lead through the air so that the droplets of themselves cooled and solidified into the desired spherules. Even more remarkable is the case, recounted by MacKenzie (1965, p. 135), in which an elaborate dream finally provided the geometrical clue that the Assyrian scholar *H. V. Hilprecht* had been needing in order to decipher the cuneiform characters on two small fragments of agate thought to have been finger rings. This was the clue that the fragments were not finger rings at all, but two of three pieces of a single votive cylinder—a fact that Hilprecht later confirmed when, as a result of his dream, he tried for the first time to fit the pieces together. And a plastic surgeon recently told me that sometimes, when confronted with a particularly difficult case, he discovers how a skin graft can best be translated, rotated, folded, and temporarily joined from one part of the patient's body to another by trying out various alternatives in a dream.

Creative imagery is not confined to the visual modality. In the case of composers, including Mozart, Schumann, Saint-Saëns, and d'Indy (Krippner & Hughes, 1970), Tartini (MacKenzie, 1965, p. 126), and the contemporary Rosalyn Tureck (Kozinn, 1977, p. 38), who have reported that some of their original musical ideas first came to them spontaneously in dreams, an important component of the imagery appears to have been auditory. This does not however preclude a significant role of spatial intuition—whether visual, kinesthetic, or more abstract and metaphorical. The connection with space is revealed, at the abstract level, in the underlying tendency (formalized in musical notation) to represent pitch in terms of spatial height and time in terms of a left-to-right progression; and, at the concrete kinesthetic level, in the common urge to move in synchrony with a musical beat. In my own experience, when my recreational activity of keyboard improvisation spontaneously intrudes into my dreams, the auditory component of the sound of the piano or organ, and the visual and tactual–kinesthetic components of the spatially extended keyboard all seem to be essential parts of the integrated experience, just as they are when I play while fully awake. In either case, incidentally, my mental picture of the keyboard's spatial structure is just as compelling when I experience the keyboard with eyes closed or lights out as when I experience literally "seeing" it.

I also find that in dreams in which I am practicing or executing a motor skill, such as a figure-skating jump (Shepard, 1968, p. 288), the kinesthetic components are central to the experience and, clearly, are spatial in character. In the local ice rink, I was delighted to see posted an article that someone had clipped from *The New York Times* during the Winter of 1966 about a 17-year-old figure skater, *Margo "Taffy" Pergament* (the 1963 National Novice titlewinner), who developed a new jump in a dream. In the new maneuver, since called "The Taffy," she spins out of her jump to land forward on the inside edge of her takeoff skate. She said, "When I woke up, I wrote it down on the cover of my math book." Likewise, the golf champion Jack Nicklaus reported that, while practicing swings in a dream, he discovered what had been wrong with the way he had been holding his club and, as a result, his game improved by 10 points literally overnight (Dement, 1972, p. 101). A different kind of spatial problem that was solved in a dream of a primarily tactual–kinesthetic nature is reported by Ann Faraday (1972). According to her, it was during his sleep that a gynecologist "discovered how to tie a surgical knot deep in the pelvis with his left hand [p. 303]."

Nonverbal and therefore unrecorded visual images, as much as the recorded words themselves, seem to have played a prominent role in the most famous of all dream creations: *Samuel Taylor Coleridge's* "Kubla Khan." For not only did the poem come already formed, while Coleridge slept in his chair after taking two grains of opium prescribed for "a slight indisposition," but, in Coleridge's own words, "all the images rose up before him as *things* with a parallel production of the correspondent expressions, without any sensation or consciousness of effort [Coleridge, in Ghiselin, 1952, p. 85]." In any case, as we shall see, it has since been claimed that a mental image, in addition to inspiring a piece of writing, may even dictate its grammatical form.

Joan Didion. In many of the cases reviewed so far, the final form in which the inspirational image was concretely externalized was itself of the structurally isomorphic spatial character of a steam engine, and electric motor, or a diagram of the benzene ring. And the spatial isomorphism is even more obvious in some cases (to be considered) in which a work of graphic art was directly inspired by a dream image or waking vision. However, there may be other cases in which the end product, though initially inspired by a visual image, is not either explicitly or implicitly spatial in character—cases, for example, in which what starts out as a private image is externalized in the purely verbal form of a poem or story.

A most enlightening description of this phenomenon has been furnished by the contemporary American writer Joan Didion. In the published version of her Regents' lecture given at the University of California at Berkeley, Didion (1976) informs us, "I began 'Play It as It Lays' just as I have begun each of my novels, with no notion of 'character' or 'plot' or even 'incident,' [but, instead, certain] pictures in my mind. . . ." [5] Illustrating the concreteness of such mental "pictures," she describes a memory image of a briefly visited airport in Panama, which played a "coalescing" role throughout the writing of her latest novel, *A Book of Common Prayer,* as follows:

> I can still feel the hot air when I step off the plane, can see the heat already rising off the tarmac at 6 a.m. . . . I can feel the asphalt stick to my sandals. I remember the big tail of the Pan American plane floating motionless down at the end of the tarmac. I remember the sound of the slot machine in the waiting room . . . [and later,] the pastel concrete walls would rust and stain and the swamp off the runway would be littered with the fuselages of cannabalized Fairchild F-227's and the water would need boiling [Didion, 1976, p. 98].

Of greatest interest, however, is her account of how the structure of the image "dictates" the syntax of the writing:

> To shift the structure of a sentence alters the meaning of that sentence, as definitely and inflexibly as the position of a camera alters the meaning of the object photographed. . . . The arrangement of the words matters, and the arrangement you want can be found in the picture in your mind. . . . The picture dictates whether this will be a sentence with or without clauses, a sentence that ends hard or a dying-fall sentence, long or short, active or passive. The picture tells you how to arrange the words and the arrangement of the words tell you, or tells me, what's going on in the picture. *Nota bene:*
>
>> It tells you.
>> You don't tell it.   [Didion, 1976, pp. 2; 98].

In a recent interview *Judith Guest,* whose unusually successful first novel *Ordinary People* has been making best-seller lists across the country,

[5] This and the following quotes from Didion, 1976 are © 1976 by The New York Times Company. Reprinted by permission.

makes some strikingly similar remarks. She reports that her novel began as a "mental image" of a boy sitting on a stone bench in the garden of a mental hospital. "I wanted to write about him," she says, "to find out who he was" and, in the process, he became the central character of the story. One of the most appealing of the other characters, the psychiatrist, also came to Guest as a mental image—this time in a dream. "I saw him in the dream—exactly what he looked like, everything. Even some of his conversation in the book came verbatim from my dreams." Much as had Didion, Guest concludes "Subjects choose me. I didn't have much choice [Friedman, 1977, p. 3]."

Sculptors and Architects. The cases assembled to this point constitute only a sample of those thinkers who by introspective report as well as by objective performance have provided evidence that nonverbal processes in general and processes of visual imagery in particular sometimes play a decisive role in the origin of exceptionally creative achievements. Of course problems of geometry, theoretical physics, engineering design, and molecular structure, which figured so prominently in these cases, may place an especially heavy burden on visualization and spatial intuition. Other endeavors that may also share this property—such as those of architecture, sculpture, choreography, and gymnastics—I have not explicitly discussed because I am less familiar with specific cases. Possibly this is in part because especially creative people in these fields may tend to be so thoroughly nonverbal or "right-brained" that nothing could be more inimical to their whole approach than to try to articulate it in words (cf., the earlier mentioned case of the sculptor Rodin). Nevertheless we so have it from *Henry Moore* that a sculptor, not surprisingly, must be an expert in visualizing three-dimensional form (Samuels & Samuels, 1975, p. 254). More specifically, the modern American sculptor *James Surls* has described how the image for one of his pieces came to him while he was lying on a couch, listening to music. Before fixing the image in his mind concretely enough to say he was going to build it (out of logs with chain saw and power drills), "he manipulated the image around in his mind. He saw it tumbling and rolling, took an arm off, put an arm on, . . . [Samuels & Samuels, 1975, p. 261]." And, not insignificantly, perhaps the most innovative of modern designers and architects, *Buckminster Fuller,* has subtitled his magnum opus "Explorations in the Geometry of Thinking" (Fuller, 1975).

Mnemonists and Chess Masters. There can in any case be little doubt that, even in purely intellectual endeavors, some of the more esoteric varieties require unusual capacities for spatial visualization. One thinks, here, of the performances of mnemonists and eidetic subjects (Luria, 1968; Stromeyer & Psotka, 1970) and, especially, of blindfold chess masters (see DeGroot, 1965). *George Koltanowski* (1955) for example, in playing 30 games of chess simultaneously, won 20, lost none, and was the following day able completely to reconstruct all but 2 of the games from memory. The nonverbal nature of these feats of blindfold chess is attested by other demonstrations, such as one in which a performance of this kind by Pills-bury was not hampered when, during the course of the games, he was required to memorize and to repeat back, both forward and backward, long lists of uncommon words (Mott-Smith, 1958). Recently Koltanowski has been demonstrating his powers of spatial visualization in another striking way. He first studies for 3 or 4 minutes the eight-by-eight grid of a chess board in each square of which someone has written one of 64 ran-domly chosen words. Then, after turning away from the board, he pro-ceeds to "read off" the words corresponding to a knight's tour starting with any audience-designated square.

Geometers. Within the field of mathematics, the various branches of geometry might be expected to call upon especially well-developed powers of spatial visualization. Consider, for example, such problems of differen-tial geometry as the problem of the classification of the "elementary catastrophes" solved by René Thom (1975), or the problem of the explicit construction of a continuous deformation for turning a sphere inside out, first proved to be possible by Stephen Smale (see Phillips, 1966). In both cases advanced methods of computer graphics are being used in order to facilitate the visualization of these extraordinarily convoluted structures by the less spatially perspicacious (see Godwin, 1972; Max & Clifford, 1975; Woodcock & Poston, 1974). It is, incidentally, an intriguing fact that the French mathematician, *Bernard Morin,* who originally conceived the particular method of eversion of the sphere chosen for computer ani-mation by Max and Clifford (1975), is himself blind!

Another branch of geometry that, perhaps even more clearly, seems to require a rather special kind of spatial visualization is that concerning structures in spaces of four or more dimensions. It appears to be the case, anyway, that many of the most original discoveries in this particular branch were made by isolated individuals quite outside the mathematical mainstream who, by dint of some powerful spatial intuition of their own, were able to establish facts and relationships that had eluded the most advanced mathematicians using more standard, formal methods.

In his book on regular polytopes, Coxeter (1948) has included relevant biographical information about some of these higher-dimensional geo-meters as follows: *John Flinders Petrie,* who discovered the properties of the skew polyhedra and polygons bearing his name, manifested an early ability "in periods of intense concentration [to] answer questions about complicated four-dimensional figures by 'visualizing' them [p. 31]." (He may have come by this ability through his father, the great British Egyptologist Sir Flinders Petrie, who, according to Galton (1883), performed addition by mentally setting one scale against another on an imaginary slide rule and then reading off the sum with his mind's eye.) His set of drawings of stellated icosahedra also reveal a considerable talent for drafting. *Thorold Gosset,* upon finding that he had no clients after taking a degree in law, "amused himself by trying to find out what regular [and, then, 'semiregular'] figures might exist in *n* dimensions." However, because the mathematician who reviewed the manuscript in which he reported his novel findings found his methods too "intuitive" and his generalizations too "fanciful," only the "barest outline" was published and Gosset, being a modest man, returned to his career as a lawyer, leaving his geometrical results to be rediscovered by other, later researchers (p. 164). *Ludwig Schläfli* completed his pioneering work on four-dimensional polytopes at a time when the great mathematicians Cayley, Grassmann, and Möbius "were the only other people who had ever conceived the possibility of geometry in more than three dimensions." And Schläfli's work "was so little appreciated in his time that only two fragments of it were accepted for publication [p. 142]." Interestingly from our standpoint, Coxeter notes that Schläfli "never managed to speak German properly." Finally, *Alicia Boole Stott,* the middle of five daughters of the renowned inventor of the algebra of logic, George Boole, must have developed her singular "power of geometrical visualization" quite on her own, since her father died when she was only 4 and circumstances thereafter precluded any "education in the ordinary sense." In any case a set of wooden cubes brought into the house by a family friend, though proving a bore to her sisters, "inspired Alice (at the age of about eighteen) to an extraordinarily intimate grasp of four-dimensional geometry." Having never learned analytic geometry, she determined by purely synthetic methods the sections of the four-dimensional polytopes—well before the mathematician Schoute published descriptions of a subset of these which he had determined by more orthodox methods (p. 258).

Designers of Particle Accelerators.   Within the science of physics, it is not just the orbits, fields, and waves of the physical phenomena themselves that place heavy demands on our spatial intuition. Geometric visualization is at least as crucial in the design of the machines used to study these phenomena. In 1930 *Ernest O. Lawrence* conceived the idea of the cyclotron, which opened the door to the modern era of high-energy particle accelerators and gained him the Nobel Prize, on reading a report of an experiment (by Wideröe) in which charged particles moving in resonance with a radiofrequency electric field emerged with twice the energy. Lawrence pictured how, by placing the whole apparatus within a strong magnetic field, the path of the charged particles would be curved into a circular spiral, enabling the particles to be subjected to a further accelerating kick with the completion of each successively larger orbit, in resonance with the alternating electric field (Livingston, 1969, p. 13).

Just as in the case of four-dimensional geometry, contributions in high-energy physics, too, can come from outside the mainstream of the field. The most remarkable case in point is the invention of the alternating gradient synchrotron which came about in the following curious way: In 1952 a team of top accelerator physicists, engineers, and mathematicians working toward the design of a new-generation (10 GeV) accelerator at the Brookhaven laboratory attempted to improve on the efficiency of the magnets used in the preceding synchrotron. In an effort to reduce the effects of asymmetric saturation of the yokes of the magnets inherent in their C-shaped configurations, a new design arose in which every other yoke was oppositely oriented. A mathematical analysis then yielded the unexpected discovery that the weak alternations in the gradients of the field that resulted from this change—far from making the orbits of the particles less stable, as had been feared—actually made the orbits more stable and tightly confined. Indeed, further analyses revealed that, by properly shaping the poles of the magnets (into steeply inclined rectangular hyperbolas) and thus maximizing the contrasts between the successive positive and negative gradients, the transverse orbital oscillations could be minimized, making possible in turn (a) a smaller vacuum chamber, (b) smaller magnets, (c) a much larger radius of curvature of the entire machine and, hence, (d) acceleration of the particles to much higher energies. The geometrical basis of this breakthrough, which resulted in machines whose performance surpassed even the favorable predictions, is evident in the numerous complex diagrams that accompany the published reports (see Livingston, 1966, Chapter IV).

Then, about a year after the initial reports by this prestigious American team reached the scientific community with much fanfare, a remarkable fact came to light: Buried in a "crackpot file" at the Lawrence Radiation Laboratory of the University of California was a letter, received there well before the Brookhaven team had even initiated its study, in which a *Nicholas Christofilos* set forth the entire concept and design of such an alternating gradient synchrotron which he had developed entirely on his own in his spare time while employed as an elevator engineer in Athens, Greece (Livingston, 1966, p. 269; 1969, p. 69; Omar Snyder, personal communication, April 5, 1977). The fact that the importance of the development described in Christofilos' letter was not recognized by the American physicists until after such a machine had been independently worked out in full detail in this country points, once again, to the limitations of verbal encoding.

Some Factors That May Be Associated with the Development of Exceptional Powers of Imagery

In reviewing what information we have about the childhoods of many of the cases we have considered, I have been struck by the recurrence of certain suggestive patterns. Putting together a kind of composite caricature, we might say that the genetic potential for visual–spatial creativity of a high order seems especially likely to be revealed and/or fostered in a child (*a*) who is kept home from school during the early school years and, perhaps, is relatively isolated from age mates as well, (*b*) who is, if anything, slower than average in language development, (*c*) who is furnished with and becomes unusually engrossed in playing with concrete physical objects, mechanical models, geometrical puzzles or, simply, wooden cubes. In addition, the inspiration to press relentlessly and concertedly toward the highest achievements that such a creativity makes possible may require the stimulus or model provided by a previous great thinker of a similar turn of mind. Thus Einstein may require his Maxwell and Maxwell his Faraday, Watt may require his Newcomen, Watson and Crick their Pauling, and so on. At the same time, some of the factors that contribute to this kind of creativity may also carry with them an increased predisposition not only toward some degree of dyslexia (as we have already noted) but also toward the sorts of mental breakdowns, aberrations, or even hallucinations that at one time or another afflicted several of the scientists we have mentioned, including Newton, Faraday, Cardan, Pascal, and Tesla (see Hunt & Draper, 1964, pp. 32, 195; Koestler, 1964, p. 171; Lombroso, 1901).

Of course there may be quite different kinds of creative thinking that do not depend upon concrete mental imagery. Even according to Galton's (1883) survey, many scientists of his day did not believe that visual imagery played a prominent role in their processes of thought. And, although self-reports of imagery are difficult to evaluate, they generally do correlate to some extent with objective performance on tasks requiring complex spatial memory or manipulation (e.g., Gur & Hilgard, 1975; Marks, 1973; Paivio, 1971; Richardson, 1969; Shepard, 1975, p. 97; Snyder, 1972). Instances of nonvisual and nonspatial thinking may have been underrepresented in my selection of examples in which the nature of the problem, whether concretely physical or abstractly geometrical, seems to favor spatial visualization as a mode of problem solving. Nevertheless in other, less geometrical branches of science too (and even, as we have seen, in creative writing) there have always been those who might have said, as did that great proponent of introspectionism in psychology, *E. B. Titchener,* "My mind, in its ordinary operations, is a fairly complete picture gallery,—not of finished paintings, but of impressionist notes [Titchener, 1926; see Arnheim, 1969, p. 107]."

Some Reasons for the Special Effectiveness of Mental Imagery

The effectiveness of nonverbal processes of mental imagery and spatial visualization in the kinds of creative works just reviewed can perhaps be explained, at least in part, by reference to the following interrelated aspects of such processes: their private and therefore not socially, conventionally, or institutionally controlled nature; their richly concrete and isomorphic structure; their engagement of highly developed, innate mechanisms of spatial intuition; and their direct emotional impact.

To amplify a bit on the first of these aspects, it seems reasonable that the most novel ideas and radical departures from traditional ways of thinking are not likely to arise within the very system of verbal communication that is the primary vehicle for maintaining and perpetuating established ideas and entrenched traditions. Rather, the challenges to such a system are likely to come from outside the system itself—perhaps particularly from the idiosyncratic probings of a few unique individuals who, for reasons of a congenital predilection for visual–spatial over verbal thinking, often together with a degree of early isolation from the standard socialization afforded by the peer group and/or formal schooling, are less constrained by tradition.

Second, the richness of concrete visual imagery, together with its structurally "isomorphic" relation to the external objects, events, or processes that it represents (Cooper & Shepard, 1978; Shepard, 1975; Shepard & Podgorny, 1978; Shepard & Chipman, 1970; Sloman, 1971) may well permit the noticing of significant details and relationships that are not adequately preserved in a purely verbal formulation. As Galton (1883) well put it, "A visual image is the most perfect form of mental representation wherever the shape, position, and relations of objects in space are concerned [p. 113]." Thus Watson's sudden and crucial realization that adenine–thymine and guanine–cytosine pairs form identically shaped overall configurations could hardly have come about as a result of processes of purely verbal deduction; but it is an example of exactly the kind of thing that my students and I have found can be done with considerable speed and accuracy by "mental rotation" (Cooper, 1975; Cooper & Shepard, 1978; Metzler & Shepard, 1974; Shepard & Metzler, 1971).

Third (and intimately connected with the immediately preceding, second aspect), the spatial character of visual images makes them directly accessible to powerful competencies for spatial intuition and manipulation that have developed during the eons of evolution of our prehuman ancestors in a three-dimensional world—long before the first appearance of any sort of linguistic competency. The ability to carry out mental rotations is presumably illustrative of one such competency (see Shepard, 1975, pp. 112–116). As another example consider that, because of the very great rate of exponential expansion of possible branches of the proof trees, it has been suggested that even the elementary theorems of plane geometry would be largely inaccessible in the absence of the heuristics of spatial intuition possessed by the average high school student (Marvin Minsky, personal communication, July 1958; see also, Shepard, 1964b, p. 59).

And fourth, vivid mental images, because they provide psychologically more effective substitutes than do purely verbal encodings for the corresponding external objects and events, have a greater tendency to engage the affective and motivational systems. This is undoubtedly why powerful emotions of fear, anger, and desire tend to be more strongly determined by the vividness with which one concretely pictures the relevant object or event (a plane crash or a terminal illness, in the case of fear) than by the probability that one abstractly assigns to that event by verbal reasoning. This is also why many current methods of behavior modification (systematic desensitization, implosion, etc.) make such heavy use of imagery to extinguish fears, overcome phobias, etc. Likewise, the scientist or inventor who vividly envisions the problems, paradoxes, and possibilities implicit in a situation (whether a steam engine, a rotating magnetic field, a helical molecule, or an observer traveling at the speed of light), may thereby possess a more insistent inner incentive for continuing to struggle with those problems or paradoxes, and to pursue those possibilities.

Related to several of these aspects is the further possible factor, noted in connection with Einstein, Maxwell, and Watson, that the search for invariances and symmetries, which has proved so productive in theoretical physics and molecular biology, may be traceable to the responsiveness to structural symmetry that seems to have reached an unequaled degree of development in the visual system. The preoccupation with structural symmetry as such, as in the cases of the geometers of the four-dimensional polytopes, may seem to be too esoteric to be of any broad significance. However we should remember that four-dimensional geometry is basic to the special theory of relativity and that the tensor calculus, which seemed equally esoteric and remote from significant application when it was originally invented by the mathematicians Ricci and Levi-Città, turned out to provide exactly the tools that Einstein later needed to characterize the gravitational curvature of the four-dimensional space–time continuum in his general theory of relativity. Moreover, the regular polygons, polyhedra, tesselations, and honeycombs of the pure geometers contain, as a subset, the symmetrical structures that are currently proving so handy in the representation of the relationships among the subatomic particles—as in the meson octet or the baryon decuplet within the quantum-number space of "isospin" and "hypercharge" (Capra, 1975, pp. 253–254; and, for more general discussions of the role of symmetry in science and art, Boardman, O'Connor, & Young, 1973; Critchlow, 1976; Shubnikov & Koptsik, 1974; Weyl, 1952).

Clearly, many of the greatest conceptual advances of modern science—including electromagnetic theory, special and general relativity, the theories of atomic structure and of subatomic particles, and the discovery of the molecular structure of DNA have a strongly geometrical component. Consider, also, the appeal of pictorial representations such as the Minkowski diagrams for the space–time manifold in special relativity, the Feynman diagrams for quantum electrodynamics, or the "crossing" diagrams of Heisenberg's quantum-mechanical S-matrix formalism for particle interactions. The appeal of such diagrams is, in part, that the underlying physical invariances are preserved geometrically under those pictorial mental transformations, such as rotation or reflection, that come most naturally to the human mind (compare, Capra, 1975, p. 271; Cooper & Shepard, 1978).

In this connection, a contemporary mathematician and Stanford colleague, Stefan Bergman, has proposed a technique for facilitating the visualization of four-dimensional structures by presenting spatially ordered three-dimensional sections successively in time (Bergman, 1950; and personal communication; and, for recent interactive computer-graphical implementations of this sort of idea, see Friedman & Tukey, 1974, "PRIM-9"; Sagan, 1977, p. 213). Particularly in view of the fact that, since the time of that thinker of unsurpassed vision with whom we started, Albert Einstein, spatio–temporal processes have been represented as static four-dimensional configurations, "*en block,*" I am led to raise the following highly speculative question: Might there be anything in common between an ability, like that demonstrated so remarkably by John Petrie or by Alice Stott, to imagine the structure or sections of four-dimensional objects; and the curious phenomenon, reported by Snyder and by Mozart, in which a complex temporal pattern is experienced, so to speak, all at once? In *The Tao of Physics,* Capra (1975) points out that "many of the Eastern teachers emphasize that thought must take place in time, but that vision can transcend it [p. 186]," and cites Lama Anagarika Govinda who said that "vision [in this special sense] is bound up with a space of higher dimension, and is therefore timeless [Govinda, 1974, p. 116]." In a recent letter amplifying on his own experience of sudden illumination, Omar Snyder has emphasized its four-dimensional character. He argues that the difficulty in externalization and communication of such an insight is the vast expansion in time required to unpack its four-dimensional structure into three-dimensional space (in the form of a model operating over time) or the even vaster expansion to unpack it in the form of one-dimensional language (Snyder, personal communication, April 5, 1977).

TOWARD THE SYSTEMATIC STUDY OF MENTAL IMAGES THROUGH GRAPHIC TECHNIQUES OF EXTERNALIZATION

Because of their private, inaccessible nature, mental images and related nonverbal processes have been relatively little studied by cognitive psychologists. Yet, as our review of a number of salient cases suggests, it is just these sorts of processes that appear to have played a crucial role in a number of the most fruitful creations of human thought. Indeed some of the theories and inventions that have most transformed scientific understanding, technology, and, hence, our everyday way of life seem to represent concrete, if metaphorical, "externalizations" of certain originally purely mental images. These considerations suggest two things:

1. Mental imagery may very well be a matter of great practical and theoretical importance and, accordingly, we should reopen the question of whether there might not after all be some way to bring it under scientific study.
2. It may be possible to devise more objective, precisely controlled, and less metaphorical techniques of "externalization" that would permit at least the beginnings of such a scientific study.

We might thus go some way toward redressing the imbalance to which one commentator pointed when he said "Much contemporary psychology is occupied with investigating the question of: How do we represent within us the world outside? The other question: How do we represent outside us 'the World' we create within? has been almost totally neglected . . . [Cohen, 1960, p. 515]." In fact the program of research in which I have been engaged during the last few years has been motivated by the notion that we cannot make very much progress toward answering either of these two questions in isolation from the other. Before turning to some of the attempts that have been made to achieve faithful external reconstructions of mental images, I need to distinguish between some of the different varieties of such images.

Some Different Types of Mental Images

Perceptual Images. The one type of image whose existence would be denied by the fewest—perhaps only by those subscribing to some version of the philosophical position of direct realism (cf., Gibson, 1966; Ryle, 1949)—is the internal perceptual representation that is directly elicited by sensory stimulation resulting from the corresponding external object. In this case, however, the problem of externalization of the internal representation does not usually arise since the causative object is itself the external counterpart of the inner image. Still, the fact that the externally elicited images are nonetheless images needs to be explicitly acknowledged here because, subjectively, such images seem to shade off continuously into purely internally generated images some types of which (as in dreams and hallucinations) may even be indiscriminable from those of veridical perception.

Entoptic Images. In accordance with Müller's 1826 doctrine of the "specific energies of nerves" (see Herrnstein & Boring, 1966, p. 26), neural activity originating in the visual sensory system is experienced in the visual modality regardless of whether that activity resulted in the normal way, from focused projection of light through the lens onto the retina, or in any of a variety of abnormal ways—from diffuse transmission of light through the sclerotic wall, from reflection, diffraction, or obstruction of light within the eye, or, even in the absence of any light, from mechanical, electrical, or chemical stimulation of the retina or of the optic nerve. In order to be experienced as visual images, of course, the effects of any of these normal or abnormal, optical or nonoptical types of stimulation must propagate up to the visual cortex of the brain. However, so long as the experienced phenomena are caused by processes that originate within the eye but that differ from those mediating normal visual perception, one speaks of "entoptic" phenomena (Moses, 1975; Myers, 1903, p. 225; Tyler, in press).

The entoptic phenomena that are most likely to be of some relevance to our general topic are those that occur spontaneously. Even under normal conditions, anyone who attends to such subjective visual phenomena particularly with eyes closed or in total darkness becomes aware of the incessantly shifting and seemingly meaningless play of subtle lights, colors, textures, and patterns that is sometimes referred to as the "intrinsic light of the retina." It presumably corresponds to the background level of neural activity in the visual system that continues even in the complete absence of optical excitation. Because of its subtlety and lack of meaningful or memorable organization and because of its independence of external events and, hence, lack of relevance for survival, this subjective visual play is largely disregarded and may have little significant influence on creative thinking. However, possibly as a result of generally heightened neural irritability, chemical imbalances, drugs, fever, disease, or genetic predisposition, such spontaneous visual phenomena sometimes become quite salient and may be further elaborated, at higher levels of the nervous system, into more organized visions or hallucinations in some creative individuals— compare, for example, phenomena described by Tesla (1919, p. 745; see Hunt & Draper, 1964, p. 184), Cardan (Lombroso, 1901, p. 74), Kekulé (Koestler, 1964, p. 170), and Bergson (1958, p. 22). In any case, these phenomena may be at least symptomatic of something significant about the visual system as a whole in such individuals.

Solely on the basis of spontaneous visual phenomena, of course, one cannot establish with certainty whether the phenomena originated within the eye itself and, so, are truly entoptic or whether they originated higher in the nervous system. In order to bring such phenomena under a degree of experimental control, we must resort to direct mechanical, electrical, or optical excitation, in which case we can be reasonably sure of the peripheral locus of their origin. Perhaps the simplest and most familiar of such deliberately induced entoptic phenomena are (*a*) the fleeting lights and visual patterns produced by transitory mechanical pressure on the eyeball itself (as by pressing through the skin at the side of the closed eye by one's own finger); (*b*) the "phosphenes" induced by electrical stimulation of the eye and, thus, of the neural network of the retina; and (*c*) the various sorts of positive and negative afterimages precipitated by a brief, intense flash of light. The externalization of the subjective images produced in such ways might provide another source of evidence concerning the nature of retinal mechanisms and, more importantly for our purpose here, might help us to distinguish spontaneous visual phenomena that have a retinal origin from those that originate within some more central station of the nervous system.

Entencephalic Images. The types of images of greatest relevance to our topic, are, presumably, the more complex and meaningful ones that arise spontaneously within the brain. Following Myers (1903, p. 225), I refer to these as "entencephalic" images. Because of their anatomical locus within the vastly more complex and less accessible brain itself, the physiological mechanisms underlying such images are as yet less well understood than those originating within the eye. Phenomenally, moreover, such images are very complex and diverse. Principally, they include memory images, imagination images, hypnagogic and hypnopompic images (experienced during the process of falling asleep or awakening, respectively), dream images, and (usually under the influence of drugs, sleep deprivation, sensory isolation, or pathological conditions) more or less full-blown hallucinations.

Sometimes the single term "hypnagogic" is used, generically, to refer to the transitional state between sleep and wakefulness, regardless of the direction of the transition. The images experienced in such a state often share, with dream images, the concrete vividness of perceptual images. But they typically differ from dream images in the following respects: Insight is retained that the images are purely subjective; and the images are fleeting and disconnected rather than part of the sort of organized, self-involving, and ongoing drama typical of dreams. Sometimes hypnagogic imagery seems to arise as a perseveration of long-continued or repeated perceptual imagery; as when, after a wearying day of driving, one finally retires at a motel only to find oneself still negotiating that winding road; or when, after compulsively digging weeds out of the lawn on a long summer evening, one's passage into sleep is disturbed by the sudden visual appearance—like the blossoming flashes of fireworks—of huge, ugly blotches of crabgrass. More typically, there is no obvious connection between preceding waking experience and the ensuing hypnagogic images, which may be of faces, landscapes, and sometimes (as we shall see) highly regular geometrical patterns. Since creative ideas and solutions have often been said to emerge during the transition between sleep and wakefulness, we should give careful consideration to the nature of hynagogic imagery.

Some writers reserve the word "hallucination" for instances in which there is an accompanying delusion that the hallucinated object or event actually exists or is taking place in the external world. Others, however, use the term, more generally, for any experience that has all the subjective *perceptual* qualities (of vividness, richness, and concreteness) of a normal perceptual image even when the "insight" is retained that the image is purely hallucinatory—that is, purely a product of one's own mind. There may, in fact, be a more or less continuous gradation of intensity and concreteness between the vaguest and most schematic images of imagination and the most vivid and compelling hallucinations. It is often difficult to determine, from anecdotal reports, exactly where an experienced image falls along such a continuum.

In any case, it is characteristic of most entencephalic images, in contrast to purely entoptic phenomena, that they have a more meaningful or object-like quality, and have the appearance of being "out there." Even when the meaningfulness of an image is uncertain, the appearance of the image as located in external space independent of voluntary eye movements furnishes in practice one of the surest signs that the image is not to be attributed solely to retinal processes. Thus my father, upon awakening during a fever, recently had the visual experience of a surface covered with marks resembling hieroglyphics which he at first thought might have arisen as some sort of an afterimage. However as soon as he moved either his head or his eyes he found that the image remained fixed in space, indicating that it did not have its origin within the eyes (O. Cutler Shepard, personal communication, May 1977).

To invoke a very old distinction in psychology, the relation between entencephalic and entoptic images is somewhat analogous to the relation between perception and sensation. It is not surprising therefore that entencephalic imagery, in all the forms just listed, seems to have played a more significant role than purely entoptic imagery in the cases of creative thinking that we have reviewed. Again, however, there may be some significant intermediate cases in which relatively meaningful imagery results from the entencephalic elaboration of what first originated entoptically. And, as we shall note, some entencephalic phenomena associated with particular conditions such as migraine or fever, though spatially patterned, are subjectively less meaningful and seemingly more akin to entoptic phenomena. Presumably such phenomena arise in parts of the cortex devoted to relatively earlier stages of perceptual processing.

Previous Attempts to Externalize Specific Mental Images through Graphical Reconstruction

In our laboratory studies of visual imagery, my students and I have been exploring diverse methods of externalization, including the related methods of constrained reconstruction and selection from parametric arrays (see, for example, Shepard & Cermak, 1973; Shepard, in press a, b), and of response to spatially localized probes (Podgorny & Shepard, in press; Robins & Shepard, 1977; Shepard & Podgorny, 1978). However, because all these methods require that something be known in advance about the time, place, and general nature of the object or visual pattern to be imaged, they are not directly applicable to the case of greatest interest here; namely, that in which an image of potentially creative significance arises quite spontaneously and unpredictably in a reverie, dream, or hypnagogic state. For this reason, I shall refrain from discussing these laboratory methods of externalization or the studies that have used them, except to mention two points: These studies do provide evidence that purely mental images retrieved from memory or generated in imagination can be quite equivalent, functionally, to externally supported perceptual images (Shepard, in press b; Shepard & Podgorny, 1978). They also add to the evidence that we have secured by other methods (Cooper & Shepard, 1978) that, during an imagined rotation—of the sort reported by Watson or Tesla, for example—there is a very specific and well-defined sense in which the rotation, though purely mental, is nevertheless a real rotation (Robins & Shepard, 1977).

Here I confine consideration to the most natural and obvious method for the externalization of a mental image and, apparently, the only feasible one in the case of an image that arises spontaneously. I mean the method in which the person who experienced the image attempts to capture it, concretely, in a more permanent, external form through drawing, painting, sculpture, or even still photography (e.g., Tress, 1973) or motion pictures (see Dunning, 1977, concerning Robert Altman's currently much discussed film "Three Women" which was reportedly based on a dream). Since my interest here is in the externalized product as a "window" to the original image rather than as work of art in itself, moreover, I wish to focus principally on works that appear to have attempted a relatively faithful reconstruction of the image as experienced, rather than on works that merely found their initial inspiration in some vision, dream, or other image.

In view of criticisms that are often leveled against the "picture metaphor" for visual imagery (see, for example, Pylyshyn, 1973), I hasten to explain, here, that I am regarding a drawing or painting of a visual image as an "externalization" of that image in a rather special sense only. I do not at all mean that the internal image is, in any literal sense, itself a concrete sort of picture. According to my own, more abstract notions of the "isomorphism" between internal representations and their external objects (Shepard, 1975; Shepard & Chipman, 1970; Shepard & Podgorny, 1978), such a drawing or painting is an externalization of the internal image only in the sense that, when it is externally presented to a viewer (whether the one who originally experienced the image or someone else), it produces a perceptual experience that recreates to a high degree of approximation the subjective visual–spatial qualities of the original mental image. I shall amplify on the difficult philosophical and methodological aspects of this view on another occasion (Shepard, in press b). For now, I note only that, to speak of "externalization" in this sense, we do not need to make any specification concerning the neurophysiological processes that underlie such imaging—we merely suppose that, whatever they are, they have important components in common, whether a given object or scene is experienced in perception, memory, imagination, dream, or hallucination. Although it does require some artistic talent and, often, tedious labor, such unconstrained graphical reconstruction can, under favorable conditions, lead to extremely rich and detailed externalizations in this sense and, as we shall see later in the case of memory images, the accuracy of the externalization can be quite directly evaluated.

MacKenzie's (1965) unusually well-illustrated book on dreaming contains reproductions of a number of graphic reconstructions of images from dreams, visions, hynagogic states, and hallucinations. Especially noteworthy are a painting of a "prodromic" dream of cosmic disaster by the ailing sixteenth-century German artist Albrecht Dürer called "Dream of the Falling Waters" (p. 64); one of the remarkable engravings from the series *Le Carceri d'invenzione* by the eighteenth-century Italian artist Piranesi depicting dark and cavernous interiors of vast, rough-hewn gothic halls that appeared to him in the delirium-induced visions of a high fever (p. 130); and a painting, in color, by a nineteenth-century author of a book on dreams, Marquis d'Hervey, depicting six of his own hypnagogic images (p. 109).

A variety of drawings and paintings have also been published that depict hallucinations, visions, and perceptual distortions occurring as a result of psychotic states and neurologic disease (Baldwin, 1962, pp. 78–79; Feinberg, 1962, pp. 68–69; Horowitz, 1970; Plokker, 1964, pp. 117–118, 146), hallucinogenic drugs (MacKenzie, 1965, pp. 130, 302; Maclay & Guttman, 1941; Michaux, 1963), and sensory isolation (Shurley, 1962, p. 155). Indeed, the singularly wild and radiant quality of Raphael's "San Sisto Madonna and Child" lends some credence to the claim (e.g., by Myers, 1903, p. 227) that it was painted from a vision rather than from a physically present model.

Of special interest, in view of the significant role that the search for symmetries seems to have played in some of the most profound scientific discoveries, are the beautifully symmetric mandalas that Tantric artists are reported to base directly on visions arising in a state of deep meditation (Samuels & Samuels, 1975, p. 257). The vivid visual patterns that Herschel (1867, p. 409) experienced under chloroform were also the circular ones with a high degree of mandala-like central symmetry. Jung (1972) presents a number of elegant color reproductions of similar mandalas that some of his patients have experienced in waking images and dreams; and the ornate, repeating, and symmetrical designs sometimes produced in psychotic states have some of the same properties (see, e.g., MacKenzie, 1965, pp. 180, 281, 285; Plokker, 1964, pp. 87, 95, 96). That the visual system has a natural tendency toward such symmetrical structures is indicated, even more directly, by the fact that subjects who are presented with nothing more than a homogeneous circle of light flashing at approximately the alpha rhythm of the brain often experience elaborate, spatially symmetric patterns closely resembling such mandalas. Subjects' own drawings of some of these mandala-like patterns are presented in Small and Anderson (1976, p. 33).[6]

Among the subjective images that have been externalized for more explicitly formulated scientific purposes are the momentary monocular visual field as reconstructed by the nineteenth-century physicist Ernst Mach (see Mach, 1959; Gibson, 1950, p. 28); various entoptic phenomena caused by mechanical pressures (Moses, 1975, p. 553; Tyler, in press) or by higher-order aberrations of the eye (Howland & Howland, 1976, cover photograph); the creeping serrated arcs of the "fortification illusion" experienced during the onset of migraine attacks (Richards, 1971; Sacks, 1973); the imagination images of Rev. George Henslow studied by Galton (1883, p. 159 & Plate IV); the various memory images reconstructed in experiments by, for example, Bartlett (1932), Cooper (1973, p. 76), Downs and Stea (1977, p. 169), and Linde and Labov (1975); and the mental images arising in the recipient in attempts to investigate telepathy using pictorial materials (Hardy, Harvey, & Koestler, 1973; Sinclair, 1962; Targ & Puthoff, 1977). Also of possible relevance are the drawings of familiar objects by patients who have been blind until adulthood (Gregory, 1973, pp. 198–199), who have suffered brain damage (Heaton, 1968, p. 127), or who have had the two hemispheres surgically disconnected to control severe epilepsy (Gazzaniga, Bogen, & Sperry, 1965, p. 228). However, whether the peculiarities of such drawings reflect anomalies in the images of such patients or in the generative schemata necessary for the externalization of such images through drawing may sometimes be difficult to determine.

More directly related to the acts of creation considered earlier are the quite explicit efforts of scientists or engineers to capture by sketches or drawings the fleeting visual images that may provide creative ideas or solutions to difficult problems. A striking example is Kekulé's already-noted attempt to sketch the dancing chains of atoms that appeared to him in his visual reveries and that contributed materially to his development of the theory of molecular structure. McKim (1972), in his profusely illustrated book *Experiences in Visual Thinking,* furnishes many examples, especially from engineering and industrial design. In a promising attempt to study visual imagery in problem solving and scientific creativity more systematically, Krueger (1976) has had scientists and engineers make quick sketches of what they were visualizing during the process of problem solving. Such a technique might contribute a much needed visual–spatial "protocol" to the purely verbal one on which Newell and Simon (1971) have based their influential studies of problem solving.

[6] Recently brought to my attention are reports, going beyond those mentioned on pages 166–167, in which subjective visual experiences of regular spatial patterns are elicited by unstructured electrical or optical stimulation. (See Oster, 1966; Young *et al.,* 1975; and earlier papers cited in these.)

Reconstructions of Some Highly Regular Spontaneous Images

In addition to the earlier-mentioned efforts that my students and I have been making to study mental imagery under controlled laboratory conditions, I have for many years attempted to externalize particularly salient, interesting, or memorable images that have, from time to time, occurred to me spontaneously—particularly during dreams or hypnagogic states, but also as a result of apparently entoptic excitations. Just as with most people who have described entencephalic images, most of my hypnagogic and dream images have been of more or less realistic or perceptually unremarkable landscapes, rooms, people, animals, faces and so on (cf., Herschel, 1867 p. 403). However, from time to time I, like Herschel, have experienced vivid visual images of a different sort characterized by a striking degree of geometrical regularity and symmetry.

Most of the reconstructions I present here are of this repeating, symmetrical, and often two-dimensional type. This is for five interrelated reasons. First, because of their high degree of regularity and redundancy, such images can be remembered and subsequently reproduced with much greater ease and assurance of accuracy than can complex three-dimensional scenes not possessing any obvious elements of repetition or symmetry. Second, such highly regular, geometrical patterns are inherently interesting in that their spontaneous appearance suggests the aesthetic play of intelligent though unconscious mechanisms in a way that is not suggested by more naturalistic scenes that appear to be but minor variations or simple compositions of memory images from ordinary waking life. Third, imagined spatial arrays not unlike these repeating patterns seem to have played a role in the development of some significant scientific models, such as Maxwell's infinite cylinder-and-ball model of the electromagnetic field. Fourth, such spatially repeating patterns may be in some way related to a lattice-like cytoarchitecture that has been neuroanatomically identified in the visual cortex (Colonnier, 1964; see also Richards, 1971; Trehub, 1977). And fifth, repetition or symmetry have often been noted previously in the images that spontaneously appear (and in the drawings that are made) under altered states of consciousness. Thus, in hypnagogic states or as a result of hallucinogenic drugs, sensory isolation, sleep deprivation, or other abnormal conditions, subjects often speak of visual experiences of periodic, latticework, fretwork, arabesque, tesselated, or web-like patterns, or of otherwise symmetrical or mandala-like structures (Cohen & Gordon 1949, p. 102; Klüver, 1966, p. 66; Malitz, Wilkins, & Esecover, 1962, p. 57; Small & Anderson, 1976).

Now Herschel (1867) claimed that his geometrically regular images could not be explained in terms of any regularity of structure in the retina or the optic nerve, and Myers (1903, p. 88) likewise claimed that "Goethe's well-known phantasmal flower was clearly no mere representation of retinal structure." Nevertheless, one reason for undertaking a close examination of the characteristics of entoptic images is just that, through such an examination, we may secure a firmer empirical basis for judging exactly what sorts of images might be attributable to retinal structures. Accordingly, before presenting the highly regular and geometrical images that I have reconstructed from dreams and hypnagogic states, I first present my reconstructions of some types of visual phenomena that, because they are precipitated by mechanical pressure on my eye or because they appear to move with my eyes, I have taken to be of entoptic origin.

Reconstructions of Entoptic Images. In Plate I,[7] I present six reconstructions that I have attempted of some of the more recurrent, memorable, readily reconstructed, or possibly significant types of entoptic images that I have experienced. I have had to experiment with a variety of combinations of optical, graphic, and photographic techniques in my efforts to approximate the experienced images as I remember them. (And, strictly speaking, all of these reconstructions are based, at best, on memory images of the original, more fleeting entoptic images.) Because they are necessarily static, these reconstructions fail to capture the everchanging and, often, rapidly moving, flickering, vibrating, or boiling appearance of the entoptic phenomena themselves. A closer approximation to an adequate externalization would probably require vastly more expensive and tedious cinematographic techniques. Since, however, my principal purpose in illustrating entoptic images here is to provide a basis with which to compare entencephalic images of a generally less volatile character, I hope these "frozen" reconstructions will suffice.

Panels A and B illustrate two of a number of guises in which an image has appeared to me since childhood, while awake but with closed eyes. Although the ring occasionally shifts in color to a complementary purple, it almost always appears as a yellow against a darker violet or brown background. Its color and shape have always reminded me of a pineapple ring. I have found no way to bring up the image voluntarily but, when it does spontaneously appear, it often persists for seconds or even minutes, gradually changing, fading in and out, or reversing in color in the manner of an afterimage (though as far as I can determine, it is not an afterimage of any external stimulus). Sometimes there is a blurred border or halo of golden brown or complementary purple around the inside and outside edges. Sometimes, too, the ring disintegrates by the gradual incursion of "bubbles" or holes forming around the edge and working inward. Often a portion of the ring disappears leaving a shape

[7] Plates I–IV can be found following page 176.

like a "C" with rounded ends, as indicated in Panel A; and sometimes the hole, which varies somewhat in relative size, fills in entirely, leaving a complete circular, irregular, or occasionally flattened or "D"-shaped disk. The reconstructions illustrated in Panels A and B were based on sketches that I made on the morning of October 9, 1977 of particularly intense images of this type that occurred just after running, immediately upon arising. (So there may be some circulatory component in their causation.) By blinking first one eye and then the other, I was able to "project" the image of each eye onto a piece of paper and, by tracing each outline with eyes fixed, to achieve an externalization of both images with considerable accuracy. Only the right-eye image formed a complete ring on this occasion (Panel B), the left-eye image formed a "C"-shaped part of the ring (Panel A) that was exactly superimposed over the corresponding lower portion of the right-eye image (as is indicated in Panel C). As always, both images moved with my eyes, but the hole in the ring in both images was centered about the point of fixation. On the basis of a very approximate estimate of the distance of my eyes from the paper, I calculate that on this occasion, as on other occasions, the overall diameter of the ring subtended a visual angle of roughly 20°. It seems to differ from Perkinje's "fiery ring," which may be caused by mechanical stress of the optic nerve (C. W. Tyler, personal communication, May 26, 1977; cf., Tyler, in press).

Panel D is a reconstruction illustrative of just one of a much more heterogeneous class of entoptic images that are difficult to characterize in any general way. The apparently endless variety, complexity, meaninglessness and, especially, the transiency of most such images discourages attempts at reconstruction. But the resemblance of some to recent, pointillist variants of abstract painting that I have seen lends credence to the claims of some contemporary artists that they have been influenced by patterns discerned in the "intrinsic lights" of their own retinas.

Panels E and F, finally, present images of a quite different type with perhaps more current scientific relevance. I classify these also as entoptic because I have experienced them only following the release of mechanical pressure applied to the eyeballs. Patterns of this sort seem to be particularly volatile and short-lived. When such a pattern appears, it does so quite suddenly, whereupon the striated regions seem to migrate about while the striations within each region vibrate or alternate rapidly. Then, before I have a chance to attempt any systematic observation, it is all over. What lasting conception I have of the appearance of such a display I have only been able to build up gradually from observations of similar images occurring over a period of years. The colors generally range between a light amber or cream for the light bars and a deep brown for the dark bars. Most regions seem to consist of alternating dark and light bars, with a well-defined orientation and spatial frequency characteristic of each region, and with horizontal and vertical orientations perhaps the most common. Some regions, however, seem to contain flickering patterns other than simple parallel striations such, for example, as square or triangular arrays of light or dark dots, orthogonally crossed striations, checkerboards, and, possibly, other more symmetrical or mandala-like local patterns. I need many more observations to try to pin down exactly what sorts of local patterns occur and to determine whether, as it sometimes seems, there is some larger-scale symmetry relating the local patterns in different regions.

The striations, about which I no longer have any doubt, are of considerable interest in themselves. They may correspond to the spatial frequency analyzers that, according to current beliefs of a number of sensory neurophysiologists (Blakemore & Campbell, 1969; Campbell, 1974; Pollen, Lee, & Taylor, 1971), play an important role in the early stages of visual processing. Whether such spatial frequency mechanisms are actually located in the retina, or whether they are being excited in the brain, in my case as a result of neural signals resulting from mechanical stimulation of the retina, is not clear. However a cortical location is suggested by some similarities between these flickering striated images and the striated patterns of the "fortification illusions," which sometimes precede migraine attacks. These latter phenomena have been described and sketched by a number of scientists, starting over a century ago with the British astronomer royal George Biddell Airy and his medically trained son Hubert Airy, and including the noted, more recent neurophysiologists Karl Lashley and Warren McCullock (Richards, 1971; Sacks, 1973). On the basis of these reports and more detailed drawings produced by his wife during the onsets of her own migraine attacks, Whitman Richards (1971, p. 91) presented an illustration that has some striking similarities to the patterns illustrated in Panels E and F of my Plate I, even though I had not seen his article until it was called to my attention after I had completed those panels. According to Richards, moreover, the visual phenomena of opthalmic migraine are characterized by an oscillating reversal of brightness of the bars at about five cycles per second yielding the sort of "boiling or rolling motion" very much as I have just described (Richards, 1971, p. 90).

Now, although I have suggested that retinal processes probably play little if any role in creative imagination, the phenomena we are considering now seem to exhibit more structure than most entoptic phenomena and, as we have just seen, are very likely not confined to the retina. There are in fact some suggestive similarities between the visual manifestations of migraine, as described by Richards and by Sacks, and some of the visual phenomena reported by Tesla and by Herschel (1867), who himself referred to the advancing pattern he observed as resembling "the drawing of a fortification [p. 406]." In both cases, patterns of closely spaced parallel lines or bars slowly passed across the visual field leaving behind, in Tesla's case, what he described as "a ground of rather unpleasant and inert gray [1919, p. 745]." This gray region, within which the typical migraine sufferer is temporarily blind, gave way in Tesla's case "to a billowing sea of clouds seemingly trying to mould themselves in living shapes." That this whole process is linked in some way to his extraordinary powers of visualization is suggested by his further remark: "It is curious that I cannot project a form into this gray until the second phase is relaxed [1919, p. 745]." Finally, in view of the important roles apparently played by the visualizations of electric and magnetic fields by Faraday, Maxwell, and Tesla, it may not be irrelevant just to take note of Richards's remark that the successive arcs of the fortification illusion "resembles a map of an electric field [Richards, 1971, p. 90]."

Reconstructions of Hypnagogic Images. In Plate II I present the six highly regular hypnagogic images that I have experienced, during the last 7 years, with enough clarity to permit detailed reconstruction. These are designated from A to F in the chronological order in which they occurred, starting with the image portrayed in Panel A which involuntarily appeared before me in the process of awakening on the morning of December 27, 1970, fully formed and with such exceptional vividness and clarity that the event inspired me immediately to get up and produce a sketch and to resolve to attempt the detailed reconstruction of it and of any subsequent images of this type that might appear thereafter. The images in Panels B, C, D, E, and F then followed in 1971, 1972, 1974, 1976, and 1977, respectively. During recent years, apparently, these highly geometrical images have been appearing to me, under circumstances in which they are remembered anyway, at a rate of a little under one per year. Most of these are, strictly speaking, hypnopompic images occurring, as did A, in the process of awakening. I do not know whether they less often occur while I am falling asleep or whether they are simply less likely to be remembered when they do occur then. Panels B and E, like A, occurred in the early morning, C and F during the night, and D while awakening from an afternoon nap. In every case I was able to make a sketch of the pattern immediately upon gaining full wakefulness; that is, within minutes of experiencing the image, during which delay I endeavored to maintain my memory image of the experienced pattern.

These hypnagogic images differed radically from entoptic images, such as those illustrated in Plate I. Instead of being blurred, irregular, constantly changing, and constrained to move with my eyes; they were always sharply defined, highly regular, and both long-lasting and stationary in such a way that I could successively attend to different parts without the pattern itself appearing to move. Indeed several of these hypnagogic images had a pristine, sharply etched quality that I doubt could ever be matched by the ordinary perception of any external stimulus (let alone by my imperfect reconstructions). Also, in contrast to the entoptic images, many of which were so fleeting and subtle that they would probably have been entirely ignored if I had not intentionally focused my attention on them, most of the images in Plate II hit me with great force, wholly commanding my attention. (The intensity that can be reached by my hypnagogic images is indicated by two nongeometrical images that appeared to me in April and December of 1970—one of the blue-violet flash of a welder's arc and one of the glare of reflected sunlight on a body of water—in which I experienced the kind of ocular pain that, in the case of intense external illumination, I presume to result from the spasmodic contractions of the pupillary reflex.)

All of these images except C and E appeared in color. The diamond-shaped panels in A were a shimmering amber separated by what resembled bevelled strips of gleaming gold or brass. [A number of those who have written about their mental images have likewise emphasized the "dazzling" (Herschel, 1867, p. 409; Sacks, 1973, p. 79) or "shimmering" (Didion, 1976, pp. 2; 98) quality of especially significant images.] I was aware of a boundary to the repeating pattern only in the case of B, where the total set of duplicated objects composed a free-form shape approximately as shown. In the other cases the repeating patterns seemed to be space-filling, though in the case of the pattern E it was as if I were so close to the pattern that I was principally aware of little more than the region corresponding to one of the large triangles and its immediately surrounding neighbors.

Three general observations of a geometrical nature are suggested by this limited sample of periodic hypnagogic images: First, they all seem to be viewed as if on a plane normal to the line of sight. Second, within that plane, they all seem to be nonarbitrarily oriented with respect to vertical and horizontal. And, third, as a set they clearly include all three of the possible regular tesselations of the plane (see Coxeter, 1948, p. 59); namely, the square or rhombic (as in A, D, and F), the hexagonal (as in B), and the triangular (as in E). There are, furthermore, some noteworthy correspondences between some of these patterns and some of those described by Herschel (1867) and others (Siegel, 1977)—even though I had completed my own reconstructions before coming across Herschel's paper. In particular, the pattern reproduced in A apparently resembles what Herschel experienced in "the great majority of instances"—that is, a rhombic latticework with "the larger axes of the rhombs being vertical." And subconfigurations in B certainly correspond to Herschel's experience, on one occasion, of a "circular hoop, surrounded with a set of other circles of the same size, exterior tangents to the central circle and to each other [Herschel, 1867, pp. 408, 410]."

Reconstructions of Memory Images. A question naturally arises at this point as to the accuracy of the reconstructions in Plate II. This question is difficult to answer in any objective way, since I cannot, of course, produce the original subjective images for direct comparison. I have, however, attempted the next best thing. My research assistant, Mary Koto, sent copies of the more interesting of these reconstructions (namely, those shown in Panels A, B, D, and E) to a graphic artist friend of hers in Southern California (whom I have as yet not met), Jerry Kano, with the request to produce a repeating design of a similar sort. Actually the artist prepared two, one in color and one in black and white. These were then delivered to my wife in sealed envelopes with the instruction to open one envelope as I was just awakening, on each of two successive mornings, and to allow me to view each picture for just 4 seconds before replacing the picture in the envelope. I then proceeded, as in the case of my hynagogic images, to attempt to sketch quickly and then reconstruct fully what I remembered of each picture. The 4-second exposure was based on my conservative, if crude, estimate of the typical duration of my reconstructed hypnagogic images; and the presentation on just awakening was intended to approximate, as nearly as possible, the hynopompic state and general circumstances under which those images typically appeared. The results of these tests, which were carried out in the early mornings of September 18 and 19, 1976, are presented in Plate III.

The original black-and-white design presented on September 18 is exhibited in Panel A, and my reconstruction of it, following the 4-second exposure, is shown in Panel B. Although this design is relatively simple, the reconstruction does seem to capture most of its structure. The principal discrepancies are some differences in the proportions of the circles and the rotation by 45° of the small black squares at their centers.

More typical of the repeating patterns experienced in my hypnagogic images is the colored design displayed to me on the following morning and reproduced here in Panel C. [Indeed this pattern seems to have elements in common with two images spontaneously experienced by Herschel (1867, pp. 409–410) in which, in one, "the whole visual area was covered with separate circles, each having within it a four-sided pattern of concave circular arcs" and in which, in the other, "the intersections of the circles with each other" contained "lozenge-shaped forms."] My final reconstruction, based on my memory image after the 4-second exposure, is shown in Panel D. There were some discrepancies in both color and spacing. The dark, desaturated blue–green of the outer, larger sectors of the circular lobes verged more toward blue in the original but more toward green in my reconstruction; while the lighter, desaturated yellow–orange of the inner, smaller sectors verged more toward yellow in the original but more toward orange in my reconstruction. And the rows of the four-lobed forms are more widely separated in my reconstruction than in the original. [During the detailed reconstruction, a closer spacing, exactly like that of the original, looked more correct to me (Panel E) but, instead of relying on my intuitive response of recognition at that point, I unfortunately chose to stick with the wider spacing indicated in my initial sketch (Panel F).] Apart from these two discrepancies, the major features of the pattern seem again to have been successfully reconstructed. The results of these tests suggest, then, that the externalizations of my spontaneous hypnagogic images, reproduced in Plate II, may also be reasonably faithful.

Reconstructions of Visual Dream Images. In Plate IV I present a sample of just six of the numerous reconstructions I have attempted of dream images that I still remembered vividly enough to sketch immediately upon awakening. For purposes of comparison with the hypnagogic images of Plate II, I have selected for this particular sample those images in which geometrical regularity is especially prominent. And these dream images in fact occurred in the early mornings over the same period of years, 1970 to 1977, as those hypnagogic images. However, because the transition to a state of full wakefulness seems to be greater from dreaming sleep than from the hypnopompic state between sleep and wakefulness, I am less certain of the fidelity of some of the details of some of these reconstructions than I am of those displayed in Plate II. I am however quite confident that I have faithfully externalized the general appearance and overall feel of each scene and in some cases, as I shall note, I have reason to believe that even the details have been quite accurately captured.

The images in Panels A and B of Plate IV are reconstructions of two out of several geometrical white-on-black pictures that I was successively looking at in the first of the dreams represented here. The two shown are from a series of pictures that seemed to portray a cratered moon in varying degrees of geometrical abstraction, ranging from some like B, that clearly resembled the moon we know, to some like C, that were extremely abstract, symmetrical, and, in fact, resembled some of Buckminster Fuller's "geodesic domes." Among the pictures there also were some that showed similarly abstract geometrical two-dimensional latticelike structures that, however, were flat and space-filling in the manner of the hypnagogic. Unfortunately, upon awakening, these were not as clearly remembered and, although I attempted some reconstructions of these too, I was never satisfied that I had come sufficiently close to the patterns of the original images. In all of these images the white lines were so perfect, dimensionless, and sharply etched against the black background that no crude physical reconstructions could do justice to the experience. Nevertheless the extraordinary sense of exhilaration and awe that these images inspired in my dream motivated me to make the attempt for the few that I best remembered after awakening.

The image of the peculiar web depicted in Panel C appeared in a dream in the early morning of January 3, 1977, a few months after I had photographed an unusually perfect spider web backlit against a dark background by the early morning sun. More significantly, the dream occurred during a period in which I had been struggling with photographic techniques for reconstructing the schematically similar striated images in Panels E and F of Plate I. I have no doubt that this dream image represented a concrete integration of the perceptual qualities of the wispy threads of the real web that I had earlier photographed glistening against a dark background, and the schematic structure of the striated patterns that I was at the time striving to duplicate in the laboratory. (Incidentally, it was also in a dream—on the night of September 27, 1971—that I first realized how I might best simulate the constantly shifting and vibrating appearance of entoptic images of that particular type by certain techniques of computer animation developed by Knowlton and Schwartz at the Bell Telephone Laboratories.)

Panel D shows the most recently experienced dream image reproduced here. In this dream, from the early morning of February 3, 1977, I was looking out through a rectangular window onto what I took to be some sort of tile roof of an unusually sculptured geometrical pattern. I was so struck with the visual appearance of this deeply sculptured terra-cotta roof with its geometrical lines and highlights and shadows under the crystal-clear deep blue sky that I studied it carefully for quite some time before awakening. As a result, I vividly remembered the structure in such detail that, in this case, I am quite confident that the sketch that I made immediately after awakening is fully as accurate as those based on the hypnagogic and memory images reconstructed in Plates II and III.

The two scenes portrayed in Panels E and F are, like those in Panels B and C, from a single dream. In this 1972 dream I seemed to have been transported into the future where I was being given some sort of architectural tour. I was shown many strange and wonderful things, but the two that I remembered clearly enough to try to reconstruct upon awakening were the buildings featured in these two panels. My guides assured me that the curious, organic conformation of the building in Panel C was dictated by the function carried on within that building (though what that function was my guides neglected to say). The oddly twisted building in Panel D was also quite well remembered, though I am not sure of the precise relationship between this building and others, such as the domed building to the right. In this dream, too, I was very much aware of colors—particularly the deep blue of the sky and the gleaming white of some of the buildings.

This sample of the most geometrically regular of my reconstructed dream images (Plate IV) and the above-presented sample of my similarly geometrical hynagogic images (Plate II) are both too small and haphazard to support any firm generalizations. Still, comparison between these two sets of reconstructions does suggest three closely related ways in which geometrically regular images arising in dreams tend to differ from those arising in hypnagogic or hypnopompic states. First, each of the images reconstructed in Plate IV occurred within the context of an ongoing episode with some degree of coherence and continuity in which I found myself engaged as a more-or-less active participant (for E and F I was on an architectural tour, for D I was gazing out a window, and for A and B I was intently looking through a set of pictures); whereas each of the images reconstructed in Plate II suddenly appeared and later vanished, in isolation from any meaningful context. Second, the repeating patterns in the dream images always seemed to constitute or to be a part of some meaningful (and usually bounded and three-dimensional) object such as a spider web, a roof, or the side of a building; whereas the repeating patterns in the hypnagogic images were more often completely abstract, space-filling designs. (Although the geometrical dream image reconstructed in Panel B of Plate IV is quite abstract, it differs from the hynagogic images in being taken in the dream as a print or photograph and, also, as a pictorial representation of a three-dimensional object—namely, a cratered moon.) And third, variations in depth are more often a prominent part of the dream images. Thus, although the "roof" in Panel D of Plate IV approximates a two-dimensional plane, it differs from the patterns reconstructed in Plate II both in being viewed as tipped back in depth and, also, as being deeply sculptured.

The dream images and the hypnagogic images alike often seemed to differ from ordinary perceptual images—not in being more tenuous, ill-defined, or hazy (as one might expect from the absence of externally driven sensory support)—but, rather, in being more vivid, sharply etched, and luminously colored. It is as if the central processes representative of higher-level properties such as rectilinearity, circularity, or absence of width in the case of lines, or such as spectral purity in the case of colors could be fully activated without the degrading influence of lower-level sensory input, which is necessarily determined by the finite width, flaws and impurities of actual physical lines or colors, especially as conveyed

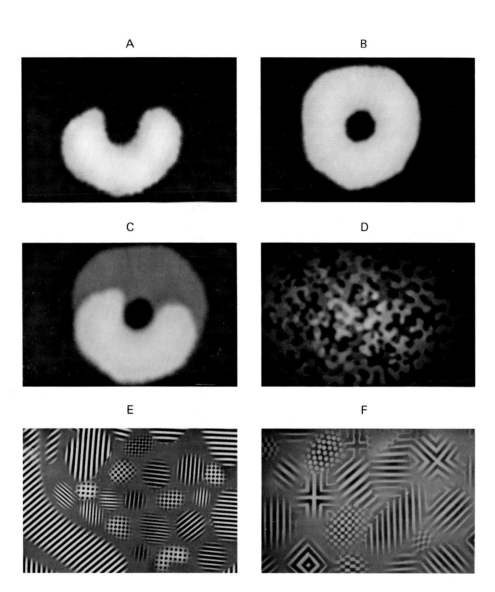

PLATE I. Entoptic images reconstructed by R. N. Shepard.

A   B

C   D

E   F

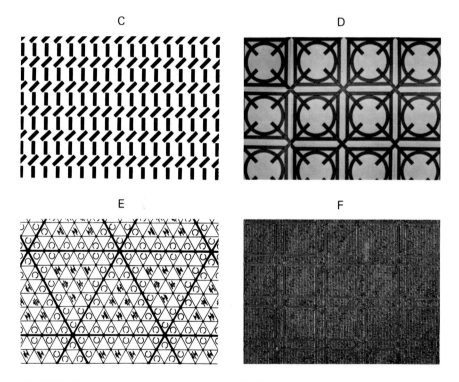

PLATE II.   Hypnopompic images reconstructed by R. N. Shepard.

A

B

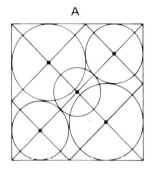
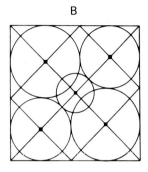

C

D

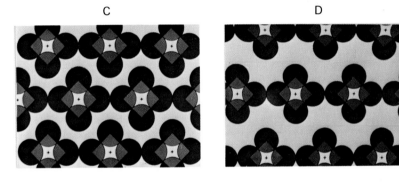

E

F

Sept 19, 1976
4 sec.

PLATE III. Memory images reconstructed by R. N. Shepard.
(A and C are the original test stimuli, B, D, E, and F are the reconstructions.)

A

B

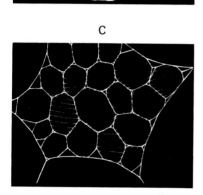

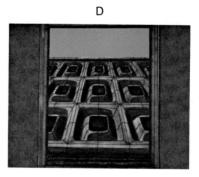

C

D

E

F

PLATE IV.   Dream images reconstructed by R. N. Shepard.

through the imperfect optics and finite retinal grain of the eye. Further support for such a view comes from evidence that Cooper and I have obtained which suggests that some color-blind subjects are able to form mental images of colors (red and green) that are much more vivid than any perceptual images that they experience as a result of the physical presentation of those colors (Shepard & Cooper, 1975).

Herschel, too, spoke of the strikingly "lively and conspicuous" and "exceedingly delicate" character of the lines of the "beautiful and perfectly regular and symmetrical" images that he experienced under chloroform (Herschel, 1867, pp. 409–410). As befits the originator of the concepts of the positive and negative image in photography, he noted that the lines were "sometimes dark on a lighter background, and sometimes the reverse." (Compare my own images reproduced in Plates II and IV.) In some instances, moreover, he found these lines to resemble "the delicate coloured fringes formed along the shadows of objects by very minute pencils of light [Herschel, 1867, pp. 408–410]." The fact that, under the influence of hallucinogenic drugs, even perceptual images are sometimes reported to exhibit some of these characteristics suggests that such drugs may shift the balance of control of the internal process away from the concrete details of the sensory input and toward the purer, if less reality-oriented, organizing principles inherent in the brain itself.

Reconstructions of Auditory Dream Images. Although our principal concern here has been with visual imagery; auditory and, in particular, musical imagery can exhibit many of the same properties of spontaneous emergence, highly developed structural or even "spatial" regularities and symmetries. Certainly a fugue, with its architectonic repetitions, transpositions, inversions, and sometimes diminutions, augmentations, and retrogressions is almost geometrical in quality. I have already noted the claim by a number of composers that musical ideas have involuntarily emerged in their dreams, but I do not know of any very detailed accounts of such spontaneous origins by the composers themselves. (See, however, the remarkable case of the musical medium Rosemary Brown, 1975; Philips record PHS 900–256, *A Musical Séance*.) Nevertheless, similar phenomena that have occurred in my own dreams have pointed to two striking respects in which musical imagery parallels the visual imagery just described.

The first is the compellingly rich and perceptual or hallucinatory character of the imagery when it occurs in the dream or hypnagogic state, as opposed to the waking state. The contrast was most dramatically demonstrated to me one night when I fell asleep thinking of Bach's *Toccata in F major*. While still awake, the piece was going through my head, but this is a very different thing from actually hearing the music.

Then at a certain point, I apparently crossed over into a kind of dream state and suddenly heard the pipe organ, in all the richness and majesty of reality, thundering forth with such force that I awoke with a start. It is as if the concrete perceptual system, when released from external sensory control by the onset of sleep, was captured and entrained by the ongoing, more abstract internal representational processes.

The second, related aspect is the psychedelic, seemingly even more-perfect-than-real quality that the auditory imagery, like visual imagery, sometimes takes on while dreaming. Thus, on the night of January 24, 1972 I dreamed that I had awakened to see, in the semidarkness, a large light-gray rectangular cabinet sitting on a low table beside the bed. The side of the cabinet facing me consisted of a geometrical array of eight square, funnel-shaped portals. I had just concluded that the cabinet must be some new kind of super-fidelity speaker system when extraordinarily quiet and crisp clicks and chirps began to emerge. There followed the sound of a baritone saxophone softly playing jazz in a manner reminiscent of Gerry Mulligan, as if right next to the bed, and with a sound that seemed so much more real than reality itself that the sound of any actual instrument would have to be described as "muddy" by comparison. Each click of key, each peculiarly breathy, husky tone and deep "squawk-like" transient unique to the saxophone registered itself with crystal clarity. Then, as I lay there listening in a state of total relaxation and bliss, a second sax joined the first in an almost unbearably exquisite syncopated counterpoint. Similarly, during a nap on the afternoon of May 13, 1972, I was again transported into a rapturous psychedelic state, but this time more of bitter-sweet longing than of ecstatic bliss, by the similarly more-perfect-than-real sound, very close by, of a harmonica, soon joined by a second and then by a clarinet, in the most unutterably soulful and plaintive music—reminiscent of nothing so much as the haunting adagio movement of the first *Brandenberg Concerto* played, perhaps, at half its usual speed. A quite different, but equally powerful mood, this time of mystery, grandeur, and awe, pervaded a much earlier dream of wandering through a deserted nightscape in which there rose to great heights, here and there, the isolated, fragile, and geometrical polished red stone ruins of great gothic towers, while the night sky reverberated with the thunderous organ toccota from Boëllman's *Suite Gothique*.

The most interesting case is that in which the music seems both complex and beautiful and yet, upon awakening, is not recognized as anything I remember having heard before. I am then intrigued by the question of whether my unconscious mind has indeed constructed a complex structure *de novo* or whether it has simply retrieved a long-dormant memory. Often it becomes quite impossible to answer this question because my lack of fluency in musical notation prevents me from writing down more than a fragment before my memory for the rest has largely evaporated. (On at least two occasions, the entire piece was lost because, having gone on to dream that I had awakened and painstakingly written the whole thing down, I continued sleeping, secure in the knowledge that I no longer needed to make any effort to hold it in memory!) In a few instances, however, I have been able to reconstruct enough upon awakening to capture, in addition to the theme itself, more than a trivial part of the harmonic or contrapuntal structure.

I include two illustrative examples here. The first is a Bach-like fugue that greatly moved me in a dream early in the morning of September 21, 1966. It was still so vivid in my mind upon awakening that, by rushing to the piano, I was able to reconstruct the subject, which in the dream was introduced by a cello, with virtually complete certainty though my grasp of the countersubject was by then somewhat tenuous. The exposition, up through the introduction of the third voice, which is about all I was able to reconstruct with any confidence, is shown in Figure 8.1A. The second example is illustrative of the reconstruction of harmonic rather than contrapuntal complexity. This was piano music that I heard with incredible

A. Reconstructed beginning of fugue heard in a dream

FIGURE 8.1. My partial reconstructions of music heard in two dreams. (Part B is on overleaf.)

B. Reconstructed piano music heard in a dream

FIGURE 8.1.   Continued.

clarity in a dream early in the morning of January 2, 1970. Again, by hastening to the piano upon awakening, I was able to reconstruct the first six measures with great confidence, and another half-dozen or so measures with steadily increasing uncertainty. The result is exhibited in Figure 8.1B. Perhaps some musicologically inclined reader will be able to recognize a similarity of one of these two fragments to some previously existing piece, which I may once have heard and subsequently lost to conscious recall. Naturally I would be most interested in learning of any such coincidence.

CONCLUDING   REMARKS

Concerning the Perceptual Richness of the Original Images

Of course the reconstructions exhibited in Plates III and IV and Figure 8.1 are not directly based on the dream or hynagogic images themselves. Necessarily they are based only on the memory image remaining, after a transition in state of consciousness, from the original dream or hynagogic state. For this reason, sceptics can always argue that the memory image is not a purely passive trace of the original image and that much of the richness and structure externalized here may be a construction of the process of memory or imagination arising, perhaps, during the transition into wakefulness and never really present in anything like such fullness in the original image. In response, I would make the following points: First, the main concern here is with the externalization of subjective images manifesting some creative aspects; the particular state of consciousness within which these creative images arise is of only secondary importance. Second, whatever that state of consciousness may have been, it is noteworthy that the images *seem* to have emerged quite spontaneously, without any consciousness of voluntary planning or effort. Third, once they have thus spontaneously arisen and stabilized in the form of memory images, it appears from tests such as those illustrated in Plate III that the external reconstructions may be relatively faithful to those internal images. And fourth (despite Malcolm, 1959), I simply find implausible the claim that I should awaken with a vivid, rich, and compelling memory of a dream image unless that memory did derive from a preceding dream image that was itself of comparable vividness and richness.

On the night of August 29, 1971 I in fact had a dream concerning this very issue. I dreamed that I had awakened and was thinking about the dream I had just had. I went on to dream that I got up, dressed, and was driving down the street on an exceptionally brilliant day. As I drove along, I took special note of the blueness of the sky, the various shades of green of the leaves of the trees along the sides of the road and, especially, the crisp, rich articulation of the leaves and branches of the trees, and of the sidewalks and buildings behind the trees as these flowed past the car and, also, of my own hands on the steering wheel immediately in front of me. At this point I exclaimed to myself "Yes, the sceptics are right; no dream could ever approach the perceptual richness of waking experience such as I am having now!" And then I woke up.

Concerning the Role of Such Images in Creative Thought

Looking back over the sorts of periodic and symmetric structures that have unexpectedly sprung full-blown before my astonished mind in hynagogic images (Plate II) and in dreams (Plate IV and Figure 8.1), I cannot better express what intrigues me about such spontaneous images than to quote Sir John Herschel's remarks about his own involuntarily experienced and highly regular visual images:

> Now the question at once presents itself—what are these Geometrical Spectres? and how, and in what department of the bodily or mental economy do they originate? . . . If it be true that the conception of a regular geometrical pattern implies the exercise of thought and intelligence, it would almost seem that in such cases as those above adduced we have evidence of a *thought*, an intelligence, working within our own organisation distinct from that of our own personality [—or "working," as we might now tend to say, within a system inaccessible to our own conscious introspection. Herschel went on to suggest that] in a matter so entirely abstract, so completely devoid of any moral or emotional bearing, as the production of a geometrical figure, we, as it were, seize upon [a creative and directive] principle in the very act, and in the performance of its office [Herschel, 1867, p. 418].

Perhaps, then, it is no accident that a number of creative insights in science have taken the form of a regular, repeating, or symmetrical pattern in space. Suggestive examples include Tesla's image of the circular rotation of Faraday's symmetrical magnetic field; Kekulé's, Pauling's, Watson's, or Crick's images of twisted or helically repeating patterns of atoms in space; and, most clearly of all, Maxwell's space-filling cylinder-and-ball model of the electromagnetic field (illustrated in Newman, 1955, p. 63). This particular model has a direct correspondence to the regular hexagonal tesselation of the plane that has emerged in spontaneous images (see Panel B of Plate II) and may even be related to underlying neuroanatomical structures (Richards, 1971, pp. 93–94). If, moreover, an identifiable cytoarchitecture does underlie what Herschel (1867, p. 412) aptly called this "kaleidoscopic power" of the brain, then attempts to discover and to represent the neuroanatomical basis of this kaleidoscopic power will in turn call for the full application of that very power. In one very preliminary effort to design spatially distributed neural networks capable of carrying out some of the kinds of mental rotations and translations that my associates and I have been studying (see Cooper & Shepard, 1978), Trehub (1977) has recently presented visually appealing schematic diagrams of regular two-dimensional networks that suggest that the ultimate result, in addition to its scientific interest, may have an aesthetic value as well.

In any case, if the visual–spatial regions of the brain have an inherent tendency toward such kaleidoscopic productions, it is not entirely surprising that so many thinkers have remarked on the tendency of creative ideas or long-sought solutions to emerge when the verbal–analytical regions are relatively quiet—just upon awakening (Helmholtz, Hadamard), during reveries verging, perhaps, into hypnagogic states (Watt, Kekulé, Tesla), or even during full-fledged dreams (Watt, Kekulé, Hilprecht). Certainly many of the more original of my own ideas have taken sudden and essentially complete, though unverbalized, form in a hypnopompic state preceding full awakening. And, although at this point I feel, with Herschel (1867), that "I ought perhaps to apologize [p. 413]" for going on at such length about my own personal experiences, they are the experiences that I know best. Moreover, as Herschel explained, it is only in this way that each individual can contribute to the "stock of facts accumulating" about such inherently subjective phenomena and their possible role in creative thought. So, asking for a final indulgence, I close by briefly mentioning a few of the better documented and more easily cited examples of my own research ideas that first arose in the process of awakening from sleep.

These are: the conception (at 5:45 a.m. on October 10, 1968) of a program of research on schemata and their formation using two-dimensional lattice-like arrays of Fourier-synthesized free forms, the first calibrational study of which was published some 5 years later (Shepard & Cermak, 1973); the conception (at about 6:00 a.m. on November 16, 1968) of a program of research on mental rotation using computer-generated perspective views of three-dimensional objects, the first study of which was published about 2 years later (Shepard & Metzler, 1971); the conception (during the early morning of June 1, 1971) of the model and basic structure of the computer algorithm underlying additive, nonhierarchical cluster analysis, the first published reports of which appeared over 4 years later (Shepard, 1974, p. 414; Shepard & Arabie, 1975); and the much earlier conception of the first method of nonmetric multidimensional scaling, the first successful demonstration of which was achieved less than a year later on March 17, 1961 and the first published report of which appeared a little over a year after that (Shepard, 1962). I believe that it was the first thing in the morning, also, when the possibility of my auditory illusion in which computer-synthesized tones appear to ascend endlessly in pitch (Shepard, 1964a; and Decca record DL 710180, *The Voice of the Computer*) first occurred to me as a geometrical consequence of the possibility of collapsing an endless helix into a circle, but this (like the just-preceding case) took place before I started recording the exact dates and circumstances of such illuminations. I do however know in vivid detail that upon awakening on the very morning of making the final revisions of this concluding section (June 13, 1977), I suddenly "saw" how the principal properties of the major musical scales follow from the representation of musical tones not only in a double helical structure resembling that discovered for DNA by Watson and Crick (and, also, that embodied in the twisted "dream building" of Plate IV) but also, and equivalently, in a space-filling rhombic lattice not unlike those spontaneously experienced by Herschel and by many others, including myself (especially as in Panels A, C, and F of Plate II).

That in all of these sudden illuminations my ideas took shape in a primarily visual–spatial form without, as far as I can introspect, any verbal intervention is in accordance with what has always been my preferred mode of thinking. As described more fully in a recent biographical statement (*American Psychologist,* January 1977, pp. 62–65), many of my happiest hours have since childhood been spent absorbed in drawing, in tinkering, or in exercises of purely mental visualization. My continuing interest in the possibility of externalizing mental images has in fact been motivated by my long-standing recognition of the importance of spatial visualization in my own processes of thought.

ACKNOWLEDGMENTS

I had the benefit of help, suggestions, and comments by several friends and colleagues, including Christa Hansen, Benton Jamison, Jerry Kano, Mary Koto, Tomasa Ramirez, and Omar Snyder.

REFERENCES

Arnheim, R. *Visual thinking.* Berkeley: Univ. of California Press, 1969.

Ashvaghosha. *The awakening of faith* (D. T. Suzuki, trans.). Chicago: Open Court, 1900.

Baldwin, M. Hallucinations in neurologic syndromes. In L. J. West (Ed.), *Hallucinations.* New York: Grune & Stratton, 1962.

Bartlett, F. C. *Remembering: A study in experimental and social psychology.* Cambridge: Cambridge Univ. Press, 1932.

Bergman, S. On visualization of domains in the theory of functions of two complex variables. *Proceedings of the International Congress of Mathematicians,* 1950, *1,* 363–373.

Bergson, H. *The world of dreams.* New York: Philosophical Library, 1958.

Beveridge, W. I. B. *The art of scientific investigation* (3rd ed.). New York: Vintage, 1957.

Blakemore, C., & Campbell, F. W. On the existence in the human visual system of neurons selectively sensitive to the orientation and size of retinal images. *Journal of Physiology,* 1969, *203,* 237–260.

Boardman, A. D., O'Connor, D. E., & Young, P. A. *Symmetry and its applications in science.* New York: Wiley, 1973.

Brown, R. *Immortals at my side.* Chicago: Regnery, 1975.

Campbell, F. W. The transmission of spatial information through the visual system. In F. O. Schmitt & F. G. Warden (Eds.), *The neurosciences: Third study program.* Cambridge, Massachusetts: M.I.T. Press, 1974.

Cannon, W. B. *The way of an investigator.* New York: Norton, 1945.

Capra, F. *The tao of physics.* Boulder, Colorado: Shambhala, 1975.

Cohen, J. Psychology as the mirror of man. *Proceedings of the Sixteenth International Congress of Psychology.* Amsterdam: North-Holland, 1962. Pp. 515–516.

Cohen, J., & Gordon, D. A. The Prevost–Fechner–Benham subjective colors. *Psychological Bulletin,* 1949, *46,* 97–136.

Colonnier, M. The tangential organization of the visual cortex. *Journal of Anatomy* (London), 1964, *98,* 327–344.

Cooper, L. A. Internal representation and transformation of random shapes: A chronometric analysis. Unpublished doctoral dissertation, Stanford University, 1973.

Cooper, L. A. Mental transformation of random two-dimensional shapes. *Cognitive Psychology,* 1975, *7,* 20–43.

Cooper, L. A., & Shepard, R. N. Transformations on representations of objects in space. In E. C. Carterette & M. P. Friedman (Eds.), *Handbook of perception.* Volume VIII. *Space and object perception.* New York: Academic Press, 1978.

Coxeter, H. S. M. *Regular polytopes.* London: Methuen, 1948; third edition, Dover Publications, Inc., 1973.

Critchlow, K. *Islamic patterns: An analytical and cosmological approach.* New York: Schocken, 1976.

Davidson, S. A visit with Joan Didion. *The New York Times Book Review,* April 3, 1977. Pp. 1; 35–38.

DeGroot, A. D. *Thought and choice in chess.* The Hague: Mouton, 1965.

Dement, W. C. *Some must watch while some must sleep.* (The Portable Stanford.) Stanford, California: Stanford Alumni Association, 1972.

Didion, J. Why I write. *The New York Times Book Review,* December 5, 1976. Pp. 2; 98–99.

Downs, R. M., & Stea, D. *Maps in minds: Reflections on cognitive mapping.* New York: Harper & Row, 1977.

Dunning, J. The man who painted Robert Altman's '3 Women.' *The New York Times,* April 24, 1977, Sunday Section D, p. 19.

Faraday, A. *Dream power.* New York: Coward, McCann & Geoghegan, 1972.

Feinberg, I. A comparison of the visual hallucinations in schizophrenia with those induced by mescaline and LSD-25. In L. J. West (Ed.), *Hallucinations.* New York: Grune & Stratton, 1962.

Ferguson, E. S. The mind's eye: Nonverbal thought in technology. *Science,* 1977, *197,* 827–836.

Findlay, A. *A hundred years of chemistry* (2nd ed.). London: Duckworth, 1948.

Friedman, J. H., & Tukey, J. W. A projection pursuit algorithm for exploratory data analysis. *IEEE Transactions on Computers,* 1974, *C–23,* 881–890.

Friedman, M. Every author's perfect dream comes true. *San Francisco Sunday Examiner & Chronicle,* August 7, 1977, p. 3 of Scene.

Fuller, R. B. (in collaboration with E. J. Applewhite). *Synergetics: Explorations in the geometry of thinking.* New York: Macmillan, 1975.

Galton, F. *Inquiries into human faculty and its development.* London: Macmillan, 1883.

Gazzaniga, M. S., Bogen, J. E., & Sperry, R. W. Observations on visual perception after disconnexion of the cerebral hemispheres in man. *Brain,* 1965, *88,* 221–236.

Ghiselin, B. *The creative process.* New York: New American Library, 1952.

Gibson, J. J. *The perception of the visual world.* Boston: Houghton-Mifflin, 1950.

Gibson, J. J. *The senses considered as perceptual systems.* Boston: Houghton-Mifflin, 1966.

Godwin, A. N. Three-dimensional pictures for Thom's parabolic umbilic. *Institut des Hautes Études Scientifiques. Publications Mathématiques,* 1972, *40,* 117–138.

Govinda, L. A. *Foundations of Tibetan mysticism.* New York: Samuel Weiser, 1974.

Gregory, R. L. *Eye and brain: The psychology of seeing* (2nd ed.). New York: McGraw-Hill, 1973.

Gregory, R. L., Wallace, J. G., & Campbell, F. W. Change in the size and shape of visual after-images observed in complete darkness during changes of position in space. *Quarterly Journal of Experimental Psychology,* 1959, *11,* 54–56.

Gur, R. C., & Hilgard, E. R. Visual imagery and the discrimination of differences between altered pictures simultaneously and successively presented. *British Journal of Psychology,* 1975, *66,* 341–345.

Hadamard, J. *The psychology of invention in the mathematical field.* Princeton, New Jersey: Princeton Univ. Press, 1945.

Hardy, A., Harvey, A., & Koestler, A. *The challenge of chance.* New York: Random House, 1973.

Heaton, J. M. *The eye: Phenomenology and psychology of function and disorder.* London: Tavistock, 1968.

Heisenberg, W. *Physics and philosophy.* New York: Harper, 1958.

Herrnstein, R. J., & Boring, E. G. *A source book in the history of psychology.* Cambridge, Massachusetts: Harvard Univ. Press, 1966.

Herschel, Sir J. F. W. *Familiar lectures on scientific subjects.* London: Strahan, 1867.

Holton, G. On trying to understand scientific genius. *American Scholar,* 1972, *41,* 95–110.

Horowitz, M. J. *Image formation and cognition.* New York: Appleton, 1970.

Howland, B., & Howland, H. C. Subjective measurement of higher-order aberrations of the eye. *Science,* 1976, *193,* 580–582 (and cover photograph).

Hunt, I., Draper, W. W. *Lightning in his hand: The life story of Nikola Tesla.* Denver, Colorado: Sage, 1964.

Hutchinson, E. *How to think creatively.* New York: Abingdon-Cokesbury, 1949.

Jung, C. G. *Mandal symbolism* (R. F. C. Hull, trans.). Princeton, New Jersey: Princeton Univ. Press, 1972.

Kendall, J. *Michael Faraday, man of simplicity.* London: Faber and Faber, 1955.

Klüver, H. *Mescal and mechanisms of hallucinations.* Chicago: Univ. of Chicago Press, 1966.

Koenigsberger, L. *Hermann von Helmholtz* (F. A. Welby, trans.). New York: Dover, 1965.

Koestler, A. *The act of creation.* New York: Macmillan, 1964.

Koltanowski, G. *Adventures of a chess master* (M. Finkelstein, Ed.). New York: McKay, 1955.

Kozinn, A. Rosalyn Tureck's 40-year search for Bach. *The New York Times,* October 9, 1977, Art and Leisure, Section 2, p. 19.

Krippner, S., & Hughes, W. Genius at work zzz. *Psychology Today,* June 1970, pp. 40–43.

Krueger, T. H. *Visual imagery in problem solving and scientific creativity.* Derby, Connecticut: Seal Press, 1976.

Linde, C., & Labov, W. Spatial networks as a site for the study of language and thought. *Language,* 1975, *51,* 924–939.

Livingston, M. S. (Ed.) *The development of high-energy accelerators.* New York: Dover, 1966.

Livingston, M. S. *Particle accelerators: A brief history.* Cambridge, Massachusetts: Harvard Univ. Press, 1969.

Lombroso, C. *The man of genius.* New York: Scribner's, 1901.

Luria, A. R. *The mind of a mnemonist.* New York: Basic Books, 1968.

Mach, E. *The analysis of sensation* (C. M. Williams, trans.). New York: Dover, 1959, (Originally published, 1886.)

Maclay, W. S., & Guttman, E. Mescaline hallucinations in artists. *Archives of Neurology and Psychiatry,* Chicago, 1941, *45,* 130–137.

MacKenzie, N. *Dreams and dreaming.* London: Aldus Books, 1965.

Malcolm, N. *Dreaming.* London: Routledge & Kegan Paul, 1959.

Malitz, S., Wilkins, B., & Esecover, H. A comparison of drug-induced hallucinations with those seen in spontaneously occurring psychoses. In L. J. West (Ed.), *Hallucinations.* New York: Grune & Stratton, 1962.

Marks, D. F. Visual imagery differences in the recall of pictures. *British Journal of Psychology*, 1973, *64*, 17-24.

Maugh, T. H. The EAE model: A tentative connection to multiple sclerosis. (Research news) *Science*, 1977, *195*, 969–971.

Max, N. L., & Clifford, W. H., Jr. Computer animation of the sphere eversion. *Computer Graphics*, 1975, *9*, 32–39.

Maxwell, J. C. *A treatise on electricity and magnetism* (2nd ed.). Oxford: Clarendon, 1873.

McKim, R. H. *Experiences in visual thinking*. Monterey, California: Brooks/Cole, 1972.

Metz, W. D. Midwest computer architect struggles with speed of light. *Science*, 1978, *99*, 404–409.

Metzler, J., & Shepard, R. N. Transformational studies of the internal representation of three-dimensional objects. In R. Solso (Ed.), *Theories in cognitive psychology: The Loyola Symposium*. Potomac, Maryland: Lawrence Erlbaum, 1974.

Michaux, H. *Miserable miracle* (L. Varese, trans.). San Francisco: City Lights Books, 1963.

Moses, R. A. Entoptic and allied phenomena. In R. A. Moses (Ed.), *Adler's physiology of the eye* (6th ed.). Saint Louis: Mosby, 1975.

Mott-Smith, G. Chess. In *Collier's Encyclopedia* (Vol. 5). New York: Collier, 1958. Pp. 92–99.

Myers, F. W. H. *Human personality and its survival of bodily death* (Vol. I). New York: Longmans, Green, 1903.

Newell, A., & Simon, H. A. *Human problem solving*. Englewood Cliffs, New Jersey: Prentice-Hall, 1971.

Newman, J. R. James Clerk Maxwell. *Scientific American*, 1955, *192*(6), 58–71.

O'Neill, J. J. *Prodigal genius: The life of Nikola Tesla*. New York: Ives Washburn, 1944.

Oster, G. Phosphenes. *Art International*, 1966, *10* (5), 36–46.

Paivio, A. *Imagery and verbal processes*. New York: Holt, 1971.

Patten, B. M. Visually mediated thinking: A report of the case of Albert Einstein. *Journal of Learning Disabilities*, 1973, *6*, 415–420.

Phillips, A. Turning a surface inside out. *Scientific American*, 1966, *214*(5), 112–120.

Planck, M. *Where is science going?* (J. Murphy, trans.). London: Allen & Unwin, 1933.

Platt, W., & Baker, R. A. The relationship of the scientific "hunch" to research. *Journal of Chemical Education*, 1931, *8*, 1969–2002.

Plokker, J. H. *Artistic self-expression in mental disease*. London: Charles Skilton, 1964.

Podgorny, P., & Shepard, R. N. Functional representations common to visual perception and imagination. *Journal of Experimental Psychology: Human Perception and Performance*, in press.

Pollen, D. H., Lee, J. R., & Taylor, J. H. How does the striate cortex begin the reconstruction of the visual world? *Science*, 1971, *173*, 74–77.

Pylyshyn, Z. What the mind's eye tells the mind's brain: A critique of mental imagery. *Psychological Bulletin*, 1973, *80*, 1–24.

Richards, W. The fortification illusions of migraines. *Scientific American*, 1971, *224*(5), 88–96.

Richardson, A. *Mental imagery.* New York: Springer, 1969.

Robins, C., & Shepard, R. N. Spatio-temporal probing of apparent rotational movement. *Perception & Psychophysics,* 1977, *22,* 12–18.

Ryle, G. *The concept of mind.* London: Hutchinson's University Library, 1949.

Sacks, O. *Migraine: The evolution of a common disorder.* Berkeley: Univ. of California Press, 1973.

Sagan, C. *The dragons of Eden: Speculations on the evolution of human intelligence.* New York: Random House, 1977.

Samuels, M., & Samuels, N. *Seeing with the mind's eye.* New York: Random House, 1975.

Shepard, R. N. The analysis of proximities: Multidimensional scaling with an unknown distance function. I & II. *Psychometrika,* 1962, *27,* 125–140; 219–246.

Shepard, R. N. Circularity in judgments of relative pitch. *Journal of the Acoustical Society of America,* 1964, *36,* 2346–2353. (a)

Shepard, R. N. Computers and thought: A review of the book edited by E. Feigenbaum & J. Feldman. *Behavioral Science,* 1964, *9,* 57–65. (b)

Shepard, R. N. Cognitive psychology: A review of the book by Ulric Neisser. *American Journal of Psychology,* 1968, *81,* 285–289.

Shepard, R. N. Representation of structure in similarity data: Problems and prospects. *Psychometrika,* 1974, *39,* 373–421.

Shepard, R. N. Form, formation, and transformation of internal representations. In R. Solso (Ed.), *Information processing and cognition: The Loyola Symposium.* Hillsdale, New Jersey: Lawrence Erlbaum, 1975.

Shepard, R. N. The mental image. *American Psychologist,* in press. (a)

Shepard, R. N. Reconstruction of witnesses' experiences of anomalous phenomena. In R. F. Haines (Ed.), *UFO phenomena and the behavioral scientist.* Metuchen, New Jersey: The Scarecrow Press, in press. (b)

Shepard, R. N., & Arabie, P. Additive cluster analysis of similarity data. In *Theory, methods and applications of multidimensional scaling and related techniques,* Proceedings of the U.S.–Japan Seminar, University of California, San Diego, August 20–24, 1975.

Shepard, R. N., & Cermak, G. W. Perceptual-cognitive explorations of a toroidal set of free-form stimuli. *Cognitive Psychology,* 1973, *4,* 351–377.

Shepard, R. N., & Chipman, S. Second-order isomorphism of internal representations: Shapes of states. *Cognitive Psychology,* 1970, *1,* 1–17.

Shepard, R. N., & Cooper, L. A. Representation of colors in normal, blind, and color blind subjects. Paper presented at the joint meeting of the American Psychological Association and the Psychometric Society in Chicago, September 2, 1975.

Shepard, R. N., & Metzler, J. Mental rotation of three-dimensional objects. *Science,* 1971, *171,* 701–703.

Shepard, R. N., & Podgorny, P. Cognitive processes that resemble perceptual processes. In W. K. Estes (Ed.), *Handbook of learning and cognitive processes.* Hillsdale, New Jersey: Lawrence Erlbaum, 1978.

Shubnikov, A. V., & Koptsik, V. A. *Symmetry in science and art* (G. D. Archard, trans.). New York: Plenum, 1974.

Shurley, J. T. Mental imagery in profound experimental sensory isolation. In L. J. West (Ed.), *Hallucinations.* New York: Grune & Stratton, 1962.

Siegel, R. K. Hallucinations. *Scientific American,* 1977, *237*(4), 132–140.

Sinclair, U. *Mental radio.* Springfield, Illinois: Charles C. Thomas, 1962.

Sloman, A. Interactions between philosophy and artificial intelligence: The role of intuition and non-logical reasoning in intelligence. *Artificial Intelligence,* 1971, *2,* 209–225.

Small, E. S., & Anderson, J. What's in a flicker film? *Communication Monographs,* 1976, *43,* 29–34.

Smyth, H. DeW. *Atomic energy for military purposes: The official report on the development of the atomic bomb.* Princeton, N.J.: Princeton Univ. Press, 1945.

Snyder, C. R. C. *Individual differences in imagery and thought.* Unpublished doctoral dissertation, University of Oregon, 1972.

Sullivan, W. The Einstein papers: Childhood showed a gift for the abstract. *The New York Times,* March 27, 1972, p. 1.

Stromeyer, C. F., & Psotka, J. The detailed texture of eidetic images. *Nature,* 1970, *225,* 346–349.

Targ, R., & Puthoff, H. *Mind-reach: Scientists look at psychic ability.* New York: Delacorte Press, 1977.

Tesla, N. My inventions. *Electrical Experimenter,* February 1919. Pp. 696–747.

Tesla, N. *Nikola Tesla: Lectures, patents, articles.* Beograd: Nikola Tesla Museum, 1956.

Thom, R. *Structural stability and morphogenesis* (D. H. Fowler, trans.). Reading, Massachusetts: W. A. Benjamin, 1975.

Thompson, L. J. Language disabilities in men of eminence. *Journal of Learning Disabilities,* 1971, *4,* 34–45.

Thurston, R. H. *A history of the growth of the steam-engine.* New York: Appleton, 1878.

Titchener, E. B. *Lectures on the experimental psychology of the thought-processes.* New York: Macmillan, 1926.

Trehub, A. Neuronal models for cognitive processes: Networks for learning, perception, and imagination. *Journal of Theoretical Biology,* 1977, *65,* 141–169.

Tress, A. *The dream collector* (with text by J. Minahan). New York: Avon, 1973.

Tyler, C. W. Some new entoptic phenomena. *Vision Research,* in press.

Tyndall, J. *Faraday as a discoverer.* London: Longmans, Green, 1868.

Warren, R. M., & Warren, R. P. *Helmholtz on perception: Its physiology and development.* New York: Wiley, 1968.

Watson, J. D. *The double helix.* New York: New American Library, 1968.

Wertheimer, M. *Productive thinking.* New York: Harper, 1945.

Weyl, H. *Symmetry.* Princeton, New Jersey: Princeton Univ. Press, 1952.

Woodcock, A. E. R., & Poston, T. A geometrical study of the elementary catastrophes. *Lecture notes in mathematics,* Vol. 373. New York: Springer-Verlag, 1974.

Young, R. S. L. et al. Subjective patterns elicited by light flicker. *Vision Research,* 1975, *15,* 1291–1293.

9

Visual Trinity: An Overview

BIKKAR S. RANDHAWA
University of Saskatchewan
Saskatoon, Saskatchewan, Canada

"Retrospect and Prospect of Visual Learning, Thinking, and Communication from an Interdisciplinary Perspective" was the theme of the conference from which this volume was born. Linking visual learning, thinking, and communication in the theme was intentional. When planning the conference, we made a tacit assumption that while the act of visual learning provides visual knowledge to the learner, at the same time it also provides opportunities for visual thinking—reorganizing, restructuring, and interrelating prior knowledge—and for visual communication, some new knowledge to communicate. The basic questions that emerge are whether it is possible to learn without communicating and/or thinking, to think without learning and communicating, and to communicate without thinking and/or learning. I chose to answer these questions in the negative and will show why it is reasonable and sensible to regard these processes the way I and others do.

In providing justification for my answer, I will first attempt to survey some of the theoretical perspectives that bear on this issue. This aspect of the chapter will deal with the visual trinity as a unified and integrated field of study and research. Next, I consider the theoretical consistencies in the papers presented at the conference and their potential for stimulating edu-

Visual Learning, Thinking,
and Communication

cational and instructional applications. Finally some emerging issues will be outlined, and an attempt will be made to suggest specific guidelines for research and practice. To deal comprehensively with each of these topics is beyond the scope of this chapter. I hope, however, that the ideas presented here will stimulate all who read this volume to seek closure for themselves to some of the important issues outlined here. Only after much additional effort may it be possible to prepare in a coherent volume a comprehensive and exhaustive treatment of visual learning, thinking, and communication. I hope that we will not have long to wait.

INDEPENDENT OR JOINT STUDY OF VISUAL LEARNING, THINKING, AND COMMUNICATION

Certain assumptions about the nature of the human organism and the epistemology of knowledge have led researchers with exclusive behavioristic or cognitivistic orientations to treat learning, thinking, and communication as independent areas of investigation. Some of the assumptions about the human organism that may have led to such treatment are

1. An organism deals with the environment (tasks) in predictable and predetermined fashion.
2. The change in the organism as a result of certain environmental encounters is predictable and predetermined.
3. A particular environmental encounter impinges or affects only a certain functional process.
4. An organism can be manipulated in such a way as to invoke only a certain mental operation.
5. The organism handles similar future environmental encounters in exactly the same way.

Research paradigms based on assumptions such as these do provide data that permit the rejection or acceptance of the scientific hypothesis under investigation, but may not afford an understanding of the processes underlying the principle inherent in the hypothesis. Piaget (1976) underscores the importance of explanation of scientific phenomena through investigations that have unity despite the diversity of their perspective. "To explain a psychologic reaction or a cognitive mechanism (at all levels, including that of scientific thought) is not simply to describe them, but to comprehend the processes by which they were formed; failing that, one can but note results without grasping their meaning [Piaget, 1976, p. vi]."

Epistemological assumptions that favor dealing with learning, thinking, and communication separately may stem from considering *knowledge* as a copy of reality, from the more refined conceptions of "functional copy"

(Hull's behaviorism), or from logical positivism that attempts at reducing scientific knowledge exclusively to physical experience and to language. Specifically, Piaget and Inhelder (1976) state that

> If we look for common factors in these diverse approaches we find a central idea: the function of cognitive mechanisms is to submit to reality, copying its features as closely as possible, so that they may produce a reproduction which differs as little as possible from external reality. This idea of empiricism implies that reality can be reduced to its observable features and that knowledge must limit itself to transcribing these features.
>
> . . . Such a conception of knowledge meets with three fundamenal diffi-culties. Biologists have shown that the relationship between an organism and its environment (at a certain level of scientific study this dichotomy is in itself an abstraction) is one of constant interaction. The view that the organism sub-mits passively to the influence of its environment has become untenable. How then can man, as a *"knower,"* be simply a faithful recorder of outside events. Second place, among the fields of human knowledge and endeavor, mathematics, for one, clearly escapes from the constraints of outer reality. This discipline deals essentially with unobservable features, and with cognitive construction in the literal sense of the word. Thirdly, as man acts upon and modifies reality, he obtains, by transforming his world, a deeper understanding than reproduc-tions or copies of reality could ever provide. Furthermore, cognitive activity can be shown to have structural properties: certain broad structures underlie the thought processes at different levels of development [pp. 24–25].

Though Piaget and his associates have never explicitly dealt with learning, thinking, and communication as interrelated mental processes, their dis-cussion of cognitive development of the organism seems to regard such processes as inseparable. More direct evidence of the relationship of learn-ing and thinking can be had from Piaget's illustrative examples of adapta-tion and equilibration. The role of communication (covert and overt) is implied in most of the work of Piaget and his associates.

Let us pursue this matter a bit further and examine how fractionation of human behaviors may have started. I think it may be a typical phenomenon of the Industrial Revolution. After the Industrial Revolution the human organism came to be seen as exhibiting the characteristics of a machine. Early machines—even machines of the not too distant past—were typically an assembly of components. The components in these machines did not bear a dynamic relationship to each other. They were simple to handle. Relationships among the components were generally linear and sequential. Similarly, the human organism was seen as behaving in componential fashion such that when a human organism was learning something it was just doing that and not much else of any consequence. If the organism was engaged in a thinking act, that was all the organism was supposed to be doing and this thinking behavior was not seen as bearing any con-sequential effect on any learning and/or communication behavior one might observe subsequently. This sort of human model made the human science easy to study, but one may raise questions about whether or not it really contributed to an increasing understanding of the complex nature of the human organism despite all the research from a number of disciplines.

The componential treatment of things, entities, and humans transcends our social organizations and institutions. Even the academic disciplines are componentially divided, and, in many instances, the lines of division are blurred and their academic missions are overlapping. Still, separate strands exist and continue to flourish. Lately, however, it has been realized that complex social, organizational, technical, and ecological problems require interdisciplinary (wholistic) efforts for sensible solutions. Broudy (1970, 1972) has been a persistent advocate of the importance, even the necessity, of interdisciplinary work if solutions are to be found for the problems of a complex technological society. But interdisciplinary efforts have been beset with problems. Narrow disciplinary concentration seems to have made many of our scientists what they were never intended by nature to be— nondynamic and nonadaptive systems. Petrie (1976) has emphasized the importance of the factors of idea dominance, psychological characteristics of the participants, and institutional setting if interdisciplinary efforts are to succeed in the face of disciplinary myopia. The interdisciplinary arrangement for an important idea (problem) would put the various componential expertise in a dynamic interaction. The necessity of sharing one another's cognitive maps (the whole paradigmatic and perceptual apparatus) cannot be overemphasized if an interdisciplinary enquiry is to succeed (Kuhn, 1962).

But what would be the consequence of interdisciplinary participation on the scientists involved? Besides several other related effects, the scientists would undergo significant changes in their learning, thinking, and communication processes. Truly interdisciplinary encounters would add to the knowledge base (learning), which in turn would alter the thought mechanisms, which in turn would significantly change the communication pattern of the participants. Investigative unity would emerge in the sense that interdisciplinary participation would encourage the study of variables that are ordinarily ignored in unidisciplinary investigations. Such interdisciplinary investigations may not require what Glass (1976) refers to as secondary and meta analysis in order that these studies be integrated. As a result, both the investigators and their studies may not be the victims of supercilious scorn and insufficient respect as many of us and our studies in education and the social sciences are.

To gain new insights into the nature of the phenomena involved in visual learning, thinking, and communication it will be necessary to integrate the information that already exists in a myriad of studies from a number of scholarly fields. However, the integration of information from unrelated and uncoordinated studies done in small parcels for the sake of simplicity and experimental convenience is bound to be complicated. Undoubtedly, principles and conditions of learning, say, have much in common with principles and conditions of thinking and communication.

Thomson (1959), while emphasizing the importance of language in learning, thinking and communication, admits there are intricate relationships involved. He writes that

> all the capacities, skills, dispositions, and insights which constitute thought—are largely a function of . . . *perception, learning, motivation,* and *abstraction.* Nevertheless, without language . . . few skills could originate and develop . . . Most higher-level thought is dependent on language and is largely a matter of using language intelligently in relation to whatever one is considering, *but not all thought is of this kind* [pp. 180–181; emphasis added].

Again, the interdependence of learning, thinking, and communication, regardless of the medium, is evident from the fact that identical discoveries and inventions have frequently been made almost simultaneously and independently by different individuals. For example, Leibnitz and Newton came up with the calculus and Darwin and Wallace with the theory of evolution of species independently and almost simultaneously. Personal accounts of Henri Poincaré, Stephen Spender, and others reported in Ghiselin (1952) supported the fact that they needed training and other favorable assistance in their work. Skills and techniques were acquired and practiced. Interaction with other people provided great geniuses stimulation and direction (Chomsky 1970; Penfield, 1970). Several other recent great thinkers admit the influence of other people and the role of past experience (Rosner & Abt, 1970).

The papers presented at the conference and reported in this volume provide a basis for interaction with several theoretical and empirical perspectives that bear directly on the problems of visual learning, thinking, and communication. In the following sections these papers are discussed in order to examine their theoretical consistencies, to sharpen the focus, and to raise issues and problems that require further study.

THE VISUAL TRINITY AND VISION
IN BIOSOCIAL EVOLUTION

In their chapters in this volume Hewes and Wescott present convincing evidence that from an evolutionary perspective the visual system has exercised almost undisputed primacy in surveying and recording the information for humans to process. Hewes (Chapter 1, this volume), in particular, supports the notion that visual communication preceded speech and that "a very large part of the labeling that characterizes all languages involves visible attributes [p. 7]." However, he seems to reflect a linguistic (verbal) bias in stating that "the advent of language contributed to the growth of human conceptual thinking [p. 7]." Hewes has chosen his wording carefully. In holding out only the *possibility* that the advent of language added incrementally to the acquisition of conceptual behavior, does he also admit thereby that conceptual thinking can take place without the verbal language? I hope so. If he does not, then when he says "we remain primarily visual in our thinking [p. 1]" he contradicts not only himself but also several others (Arnheim, 1969; McKim, 1972).

Wescott (Chapter 2, this volume) suggests a main reason for the controversy that remains over the relative importance of the auditory and visual components of human communication, assumed to be "overwhelmingly audiovisual." He argues that it is due to both the relative strengths of the sensory channels involved for transmission and the nature of the communication involved. From a consideration of communication effectiveness, two aspects become very important, the message content, and mode of transmission (coding). We just do not utter a message. There is more to a message generation than that which is communicated. Besides physiological properties of the human sensory system, cognitive aspects are an important consideration. Unless a human communication system is considered from both ontogenetic and phylogenetic perspectives our thinking and understanding of the human communication network may not improve. Hewes and Wescott have contributed considerably in their respective chapters in this regard. Communication is both a learned and a creative act. Humans usually *know* more than they are able to communicate. Methods that can open up communication bottlenecks may help us understand better the higher mental processes, including imagery and internal representation.

Hewes refers to the investigation of "mental maps" and asserts that other sensory inputs besides the visual are involved in their formation. However, he does not develop the argument as to how the information from a variety of sources is "worked in". I think he touches on a very important concept—integration—but leaves it at that, as he does the possibility of studying the mental maps of individuals and groups. Also important to consider is what constitutes a mental map. How, for instance, does a mental map differ from the notion of a "cognitive map" (Tolman, 1932), or a cognitive strategy, and what is the nature of internal representation of mental maps? I am not sure whether Hewes is using the term *mental maps* in a strictly metaphoric sense or whether he is referring to it in the context of psychological investigations of internal representations of external events (Shepard, Chapter 8, this volume).

Hewes considers the concept "visual literacy" superfluous if it refers simply to the general human condition. However, he admits "visual literacy" on a continuum of *competence* ranging from restricted to highest. What constitutes competence in Hewes's terms is not clear. Unless attributes defining competence are described clearly the measurement of visual literacy on a continuum is nothing but arbitrary. It seems to me that the question is hedged rather than answered. I am tempted to suggest that visual literacy may be operationalized in terms of visual learning, thinking, and communication. In doing so, I recognize the difficulty of finding appropriate measures for doing this at this time. However, it is a lesser problem than that of the global concept—visual literacy—which evokes all kinds of predispositional associations.

Although both Hewes and Wescott endorse and appreciate the instructional value of visualization of experiences, Wescott draws a distinction between the visual language and the language of vision. He discusses the language of vision from the perspective of cross-cultural differences in color terms and from the "use of visual metaphor in intellectual discourses [p. 27]." However, the visual language is discussed, I think, in the context of the American Sign Language and visual instruction. In my opinion, nonverbal languages have generally been designated in terms of the medium of articulation, as for example, language of film and language of art, and the underlying organizational principles involved have been derived from the formal verbal languages. Also, cultural determinism of the visual languages have stripped them of the universal structural invariance of visual phenomena. It will be valuable to know the similarities and differences between the structural properties of verbal and visual languages. Does the myth of linguistic determinism, that is, the Whorfian hypothesis, pervade our understanding and thinking of visual languages?

THE MEANING IN VISUALS

Where is the "meaning"—in people or in communication itself? I think the meaning is in both the people and the message. The notion that people innately possess linguistic structures—potential to create and understand sentences—has been around since Chomsky proposed the theory of structural linguistics. Hochberg and Brooks (1962) provided some initial and analogous evidence on the ability of a young child to recognize pictures, even if the child had never been exposed to pictures. A message, a communication, or an environment has a meaning in and of itself (Becker, Chapter 3, this volume).

The chapter by Becker certainly provides a fresh and invigorating perspective on research in visual communication, and there is not much that I disagree with in it. However, I will attempt to sharpen the focus and embed the emphasis in an alternative framework which, I am sure, will provide convergent and divergent viewpoints on the issue of comprehension, interpretation, and understanding of visual communication as well as on the research paradigm.

As Becker contends, it is important in any inquiry to ask the right kinds of questions. But, this issue is not as simple as it looks. It has deep epistemological implications for science and the nature of inquiry. The kinds of questions an investigator asks is a reflection of the particular paradigm he has adopted for his investigation (Kuhn, 1962). A question that is significant and important for one investigator with a specific paradigm may or may not at all intrigue another who uses a different paradigm. But, Becker's concern, I think, is within one paradigm—empiricism. Within a particular paradigm who is to judge what is the right question? At times we must wait to find out whether a certain study, which is acclaimed to be significant or useless at the time, really meets the test of history. We already have ample evidence in science, art, and literature that some of the most creative contributors were not recognized or accepted by their respective elite groups until long after their deaths. Sometimes we ignore an important and significant question or study because of our investigative biases and/or paradigmatic conflicts. Usually, a radical approach within a particular paradigm of research meets with just about as much opposition from those working within the paradigm as from people with a different paradigm. And this includes the kinds of questions that are addressed in a specific study.

Furthermore, I do not think we would be satisfied if our search stopped at the right question. It is not easy to answer whether we have the right question, but I have seen so often in research, especially with graduate theses and dissertations, that a significant and important question is modified so that it can be handled using the available methodological and analytical sophistication. So, the type of questions asked in research are a function of the paradigm of investigation and the degrees of freedom it permits the investigator to answer that question. Also, the type of question asked is a joint function of the perception an investigator has and the research paradigm's answerability. Training researchers to ask the right questions would depend upon the paradigm to which they have been made faithful and the degree of their concomitant research and cognate area abilities and skills. It seems to me that this line of argument leads to two conclusions:

1. The worth of a question is a relative matter and depends on who is asked to judge its worth or relevance.
2. It is just as important to consider the right paradigm as the right question if the right question is to yield a worthwhile answer.

Becker's conceptualization of the process of communication through the communication mosaic consisting of sources of information (message), information increments provided by the various sources of a message, elapsed time, and other related message sets is certainly enlightening and complex. I presume it to be an initial formulation in an effort to deal with the construction and development of meaning as a result of an organismic interaction with the message. This formulation is quite similar to that of Hunt and Sullivan's (1974) model of dynamic interaction of an organism with its environment. The kernel of this particular model is that with its interaction with the environment, the organism changes while at the same time bringing about some change in the environment. So, as is evident from Becker's model, Hunt and Sullivan's formulation would predict that the saliency of various message sources for an individual's information increment is a function of the extent and kind of that individual's interaction with the message. But, how do we study the construction of meaning from such a concept? Do we have methodological and analytical techniques to answer the "right questions" originating from this formulation? I think some kinds of questions, not necessarily the right kinds, can be handled using the existing empirical methods after a simplification of the proposed model. In fact, a number of research issues identified in Becker's paper are results of eliminating the dynamics of perpetual interaction of the organism with the message. The model seems to reduce to a static state if we ask the type of questions identified. How do we resolve this paradox?

I concur with Becker in emphasizing the need for macroscopic research but only if macroscopic investigations are cast in some dynamic interactive model. I am a bit disappointed that I did not find many issues or questions raised in the chapter that, in my judgment, necessarily lend themselves to realistic macroscopic study. Perhaps it is a reflection of his acknowledged socialization with academia that Becker is bound to precise and microscopic research. Certainly, unequivocal results and sensible interpretation of data are the goal of any research. But these goals are easier to achieve in precise, laboratory, and microscopic investigations—although we are not enamored of their generalizability to real-life situations.

Another issue I think is important to mention is that the "message" in

Becker's chapter is assumed to be given. We have not considered the message generator, especially in film, television, pictures, or paintings. It is important to determine how the professional message-maker structures and organizes the message for meaning extraction. How do their particular message sets affect the information increments from various sources along a time continuum? Do we, as individuals, typically try to portray the roles we perceive as message receivers and message generators? How does interactive communication feedback alter the information saliency of various sources of messages?

Becker's chapter is cast in such an exciting framework that it should stimulate much research and discussion. I believe the issues he has identified are serious and should be pursued with enthusiasm and through unconventional methods of investigation. I share his willingness to applaude a vague answer to a fundamental, important, and relevant question. Let us hope that some new ground will be explored before too long.

PRAGMATICS AND IMAGINATION

Education as an art can be considered from two perspectives: the rational and scientific and the philosophical and intuitive. Not many educational practices that are based on the former can be identified. The educational system, informal or formal, has existed since before the dawn of history. So far as we can tell from history, the second perspective—philosophical and intuitive—has dictated educational practices, and still does to a large extent. Philosophical differences have, on occasion, warranted the division of educational responsibility into a number of distinct organizational units. Even within the same organizational unit, however, it is not infrequent to find a variety of philosophical and intuitive perspectives guiding various educators. McKim's approach (Chapter 4, this volume) originates, it appears to me, from a firm commitment to and belief in imagination and from a conviction that it can be cultivated by training through polysensory stimulation and associated activities.

Regardless of the perspective on which a particular educational practice is based, it has sometimes been necessary to ask the question: What is its worth—is it doing what it is supposed to be doing for the students? I think McKim has informal data which assure him that his experiential approach for training in imagination, imagery, and visual (creative) thinking is worth its salt—he has been using it since 1962. We know of several other individuals who are providing training in creative thinking and imagery using some sort of sensory experiences as the basis. We also know that there are a number of skeptics who would like some convincing data to demonstrate the value of such an experiential approach. It is also likely that even if data were available, some of those skeptics would never change their minds. But still, it is important to provide some basic evidence, so that if this kind of educational experience is really valuable, it may be accepted and tried by others. Obviously, some additional capital outlay is needed for implementing sensory training programs. If positive evaluation data can be provided they will enable those interested and convinced to justify their capital requests.

PSYCHOPHYSIOLOGICAL CONSIDERATIONS

Mulholland's chapter is concerned primarily with the study of visuals in relation to "visual attention" as measured by the EEG program of "alpha suppression." Admittedly "EEG can reveal large-scale gradations of cortical processes related to attention [p. 79]," but what specific cortical processes are involved in the "looking behavior" or "paying attention"? Can the EEG program distinguish between someone looking at the specific stimulus elements and just looking at irrelevant visual elements? Is alpha suppression related to the specific cognitive mechanisms that are concerned with visual learning, thinking, and communication? So far, the research has been nonspecific with regard to the concerns of these questions. Measurement of attentional behaviors, directly or indirectly, without regard to the specific internal mental operations or explicit behavioral indicators may not be useful for either theoretical or practical pedagogical considerations.

In fact, Mulholland (Chapter 5, this volume) admits that biofeedback research with attentional applications is at a very early stage of development. Much further research is needed before any firm claims can be made about the utility of "visual attention" as operationalized in Mulholland's chapter.

The feedback method described is sensitive to visual stimuli, but why is it not sensitive to auditory stimuli? If, in fact, alpha suppression indicates cognitive processing through the related cortical processes, should it not be sensitive to any task that demands cognitive activity? Curiously, Mulholland makes a distinction between a "person" and "brain" and says, "Actually the whole *person,* not just the brain," receives and interprets the display cognitively and emotionally, and decides whether or not to play the feedback game [p. 82]." I am not sure what central role the "person" plays in the feedback loop other than through the brain function. After all, alpha waves are picked up from the scalp, and it is assumed that these waves are affected by the cortical activities associated with visual stimulation. Does emotionality reside outside the brain regions of a person? How is the emotional factor accounted for in the attentional indicator, alpha suppression? Further research bearing on these issues and much greater understanding of what is going on is necessary before this novel and exciting strategy for studying visual attention can be adopted generally. I hope Mulholland and other biofeedback scientists pursue this area a bit further before applied researchers get involved. Once the theory and technique are refined a bit, perhaps it may be possible to assess the specific instructional value of visuals via alpha suppression.

IS PICTORIAL COMPREHENSION ANALOGOUS TO READING A FALLACY?

Pictorial comprehension is an important and relevant concern in the context of visual learning, thinking, and communication. It is especially necessary to consider pictorial comprehension from a developmental perspective. Obviously such a consideration of the topic permits the understanding of the process of comprehension of the picture relative to the critical periods in development and to the course of cognitive development. In Chapter 6, Sigel considers pictorial comprehension developmentally under two basic themes. First, the external world is comprehended through an active engagement and the construction of mental representations. Second, the cognitive mechanisms serve as both a filter and a moderator of behavior. However, Sigel deals with several aspects of the themes and does not always achieve an integration. For instance, picture is first defined as "any two-dimensional representation [p. 94]," but later there is a multi-dimensional classification of picture types along an open-ended continuum. Similarly, "comprehension" is carefully distinguished from "recognition" (in terms of reading literature) but later is referred to in ambiguous terms such as "understanding" and "meaning extraction" without any explicit mention of the behavioral attributes involved so that the original distinction is fully realized and clarified. He gives instances of what comprehension is not instead of what comprehension is. In fact what is more serious is that in the latter sections of the Chapter the distinction between recognition and comprehension tends to erode when he begins to use expressions such as "recognizing and/or comprehending [p. 100]."

Sigel asserts but does not prove that "comprehension of written language and pictures involves comparable cognitive processes [p. 95]." If, as he admits, competence in different rule systems is necessary for the comprehension of material in different symbolic modes, then it is not certain that comparable cognitive mechanisms underlie the processing of these rule systems. Moreover, the weight of the evidence to date in cerebral asymmetry suggests that different brain regions are involved in processing verbal and pictorial information (Bogen, 1969; Sperry, 1973). Is Sigel's observation regarding the awareness of an organism that "objects and/or events can be represented in some alternative media or mode [p. 95]" in itself sufficient for him to conclude that it is engaged in comparable cognitive processes during comprehension of pictures or of written language? I do not think so. If the specific rule systems of various media dictate differential cognitive processing depending on the nature of the comprehension task, then the comparability of the cognitive processes in comprehending pictures and words is highly unlikely. The nature of the comprehension tasks in terms of media type and the response mode had been shown to be the result of various transformations (Randhawa, 1972, 1973). The specific transformations require specific cognitive structures. These cognitive structures are determined by a dynamic interaction of the experiential and developmental determinants (Ausubel, 1965; Piaget, 1950).

Sigel's theory of picture comprehension is couched in the Piagetian notion of "conservation" of physical properties. Specifically, this theory is presented in terms of "conservation of meaning" where meaning refers to the "definition of a case whereby an instance is identified, labeled and/or in some other way differentiated from other particulars [p. 106]." The child achieves the conservation of meaning through interaction with the world, and this accomplishment guarantees *object constancy*. I am not sure whether picture comprehension, according to Sigel, is a function of meaning conservation regardless of the medium of representation or whether picture comprehension is in itself meaning conservation. It seems that the former position is more tenable. With the latter position, pictorial comprehension tends to become a stable phenomenon such that engagements of the child with the world subsequent to a meaning conservation epoch do not affect the level of comprehension.

Definitions and theory need to be tightened in this important area of study and research. Sigel has made a remarkable contribution in exposing the area and showing how it is related to the work of others in art, cognition, and development psychology. I hope we proceed fervently and enthusiastically in exploring the mysteries of pictorial comprehension.

IMAGERY AND DUAL CODING

The phenomenon of imagery was ignored for a long time because it was not considered as an appropriate psychological problem (Paivio, 1970). However, since the early 1960s, Paivio, his students, and others have established this area of investigation as an acceptable psychological concern. Still, despite very vigorous research activity, theory seems to lag behind empirical evidence. For instance, as Palermo (1970) pointed out,

> There does not seem to be anything in Paivio's theorizing which suggests why images should be particularly good "pegs" upon which to hang or from which to retrieve material that has in some way been related to them. The simple conceptual-peg hypothesis, however, does have the virtue of accounting for a large portion of the findings [p. 416].

Similarly, dual-coding theory accounts for many empirical results, but there are some results which are not fully explained by this theory. It does support the global observation that two memory traces are better than one; however, what specific contributions the individual verbal or visual system make to a particular task we do not know. For instance, Paivio's interpretation of the Paivio and Csapo (1969) results does not directly follow parsimoniously from the dual-coding hypothesis. The test trials for both the pictures and words presented at fast and slow rates required the subjects to name the items in sequential order or regardless of the order. One wonders if naming response does not require a verbal transformation and imposes a verbal code demand. It will be of significant interest to investigate the sequential reconstruction for pictures and words given the discrete items in their own modality to be arranged in the order in which they were presented. Paivio's conclusion in Chapter 7 that "verbal and nonverbal systems differ in their capacity to store information concerning temporal order [p. 116]," though reasonable, does not seem convincing on the basis of the experimental evidence.

The "symbolic distance effect" obtained in several of Paivio's experiments involving a variety of representations of visual knowledge is exciting and offers a number of practical educational implications. For instance, most perceptual and affective properties are represented in the visual knowledge through the concrete referential system of objects possessing those properties. In order to impart instruction on referential properties a direct experiential engagement of the learner seems to be indicated since "visual knowledge is indeed linked to modality-specific perceptual memory processes [p. 123, this volume]." Although this is an old educational principle, it is often disregarded in many educational settings. This principle should be even more relevant as educators are required to deal with learners with more varied environmental histories.

If it is true that "at all levels, memorability is directly related to the pictureability or image arousing value of the materials [p. 123]" then educational researchers should investigate the pictureability of specific instructional contents for learners of different characteristics. What are some of the strategies and techniques for making instructional content with variable degrees of pictureability salient for the learners? How can a variety of mnemonics be appropriate for learning tasks with different cognitive demands? The imagery results of Paivio and others point to several other applied and theoretical research questions that should be investigated. This area offers exciting possibilities for visual learning, thinking, and communicating.

WHAT IS THE FORM OF HIGHLY ORIGINAL IDEAS AND HOW CAN THEY BE EXTERNALIZED?

Those who know Roger Shepard only from his remarkable contributions to the literature in experimental psychology and mathematical models will be surprised and at the same time impressed by his chapter in this volume (Chapter 8). I am sure it has required great courage to support a position that rests largely on documentary and testimonial evidence. Such a position may not be palatable to those who have an objective scientific disposition and who would prefer conclusive evidence based on rigorous and replicative investigations rather than speculative case histories. However, Shepard's work has already contributed tremendously toward making the study of psychology an objective and rational science as witnessed by his receiving one of the APA Outstanding Scientific Contributions Awards for 1976. And the evidence of systematic efforts to provide an experimental methodology for studying the role of spatial visualization and mental imagery in creative contributions in the sciences, engineering, music, art, and literature provided by his chapter promises equally important contributions in the future.

Shepard's chapter points to an interesting, but at the same time puzzling fact: Many of the great geniuses were not very successful in their early schooling and their behavior patterns were rather odd. For instance, a number of them manifested language disabilities suggestive of dyslexia. As he says,

> It is tempting to conjecture that Einstein's early and often solitary preoccupation within a relatively private visual–spatial domain, in preference to the socially and institutionally controlled verbal domain, set the stage for his latter roles in the developments that have transformed twentieth-century physics; namely, those of quantum theory and the special and general theories of relativity [p. 135, this volume].

However, we need to be careful in reading Shepard's chapter, for we might be led to think that verbal abilities are not involved at all in creative and original work. This viewpoint is the other extreme to the position that higher conceptual thought mechanisms operate only through language skills and abilities. Shepard's point is that solutions in concrete images often come suddenly to people at moments when they are not in active pursuit of solutions to the problems on which they have been working. He does not document the hard work or dedicated engagement that may have preceded the sudden "illumination." Others have documented the absolute necessity for the "dreamer" of original ideas to have a thorough background and sophistication in the discipline involved (for example, see Rosner & Abt, 1970). Ideas do not come to barren minds.

On the basis of a composite pattern of the childhoods of many of the creative individuals, Shepard concludes that

> the genetic potential for visual–spatial creativity of a high order seems especially likely to be revealed and/or fostered in a child (a) who is kept home from school during the early school years and, perhaps, is relatively isolated from age mates as well, (b) who is, if anything, slower than average in language development, (c) who is furnished with and becomes unusually engrossed in playing with concrete physical objects, mechanical models, geometrical puzzles or, simply, wooden cubes. In addition, the inspiration to press relentlessly and concertedly toward the highest achievements that such a creativity makes possible may require the stimulus or model provided by a previous great thinker of a similar turn of mind [p. 155].

Again, however, it is important not to interpret the description as implying a program for fostering creativity in children generally. Obviously, not all homes would provide the "ideal" situation that was available to the cases reviewed by Shepard; and it is unlikely that isolating children will generally encourage creativity. Also, I would think that at least some of the great geniuses found, in formal schooling, stimulation, encouragement, and models that perhaps would not have been available elsewhere. The self-reports may not have reflected adequately the impact of schooling. Some of the schools and a few of the teachers surely had significant influence in the development of many creative individuals (Rosner & Abt, 1970; Thomson, 1959).

We do not know from the available reports (Shepard, this volume) whether the relatively slow language development of creative individuals was due to the same etiological factors that led to early isolation. If some etiological variables were indeed involved, then the language development ought to be considered in that perspective. Under the present circumstances, it would appear unwise to ignore and/or suppress early language development in hopes of nourishing creative potential. Certainly we do not presently have any method of identifying future geniuses. Under the circumstances, it seems advisable to provide as stimulating an environment for our children as our resources permit. Whether the great geniuses are born or made is a debatable, but related, issue that I will not go into here.

The third aspect of Shepard's analysis in Chapter 8 is that genetic potential for visual–spatial creativity of a high order is revealed and/or fostered in a child who is provided with and shows unusual occupation with concrete physical objects, mechanical models, etc. Although this expectation seems reasonable, I wonder whether the developed and prosperous countries that usually provide such opportunities to youngsters have significantly higher incidences of contributors to unique discoveries in mathematics, physics, chemistry, etc.

Regardless of the issues that have been raised thus far, it seems clear from Shepard's chapter that internal mental imagery provided the basis for many original scientific theories. Furthermore, some creative works of art may have got their initial inspiration in some vision, dream, or other image. Graphic techniques of externalization toward the systematic study of mental images are the focus of the second section of Shepard's chapter.

Mental images involved in creative productions seem to be of *private, concrete, complex,* at times *unconventional* and *inaccessible* nature. Shepard has indicated that although many contemporary psychological investigations are concerned with the study of internal representation of external events, the investigation of how the internal imagery is represented outside us is almost completely ignored. I concur with Shepard "that we cannot make very much progress toward answering either of these questions in isolation from the other [p. 159]."

Shepard and his students have done highly original and influential work dealing with the problem of internal representation of the external world. Also, their investigations have probed the concomitant cognitive mechanisms involved in the "isomorphic" internal representational processes. But, how their early and ongoing work can be related or directly applied to the study of externalization of "subjective and private" mental images—those which comprise the source of uniquely original creations—is not quite evident from Shepard's chapter. We recognize that the method of unconstrained reconstruction that has been so often used in many previous investigations of dreams, visions, hallucinations, and entencephalic images is "the most natural and obvious method for the externalization of a mental image and, apparently, the only feasible one in the case of an image that arises spontaneously [p. 164]." However, Shepard has pointed out that the method of unconstrained reconstruction has several serious limitations. The alternative methods, constrained reconstruction, selection from parametric array, and response to spatially localized probe, while they overcome some of the limitations of the method of unconstrained reconstruction are not directly applicable to the study of spontaneous images of the sort that are of greatest interest in connection with creative thinking. (R. Shepard, personal communication, April, 1977). So, it appears that we still have some time to wait before objective and scientific investigations of creative imagery will shed new insights into the mechanisms of creative processes. Shepard's work reported in this volume and the expectation that he, his students, and others will carry it on provides some hope.

EMERGING ISSUES

The basic issue around which the conference was convened and to which the presenters were asked to address themselves was that of the role of the visual and the figural in learning, thinking, and communication. As can be discerned from the chapters, the authors have taken varied perspectives on the issue and have pointed out a number of problems that need further study and research. In my discussion thus far I have tried to highlight certain of these in the context of each chapter. In this concluding section I will attempt to identify what I consider the important emerging issues and to suggest how they might be investigated.

Visual skills, it seems, develop with experience and practice. Research in the verbal domain shows that the effect of practice and experience is not monotonic for all skills; rather it depends upon the specific skill being practiced and on the particular cognitive variables present in the context (e.g., Underwood & Shaughnessy, 1975). Experiments in visual acuity, luminal thresholds, and visual discrimination have demonstrated, to some extent, corresponding effects of experience and practice in the visual domain (Gibson, 1969; Neisser, 1967). It remains an intriguing problem for educational researchers to extend the laboratory research and to determine the effects of training in and the influence of these visual skills on academically relevant behaviors. One way to do this is to use a multidimensional and multivariate approach such that the independent variables are themselves multidimensional and the dependent variables are represented as interdependent multivariate vectors. Only in such macroscopic experiments can it be possible to determine the effect of training on visual skills and the concomitant influence of visual abilities on other academic tasks. Studies of single variables in unidimensional independent classifications, though easier to carry out, are not likely to be useful for understanding complex educational applications. Educational situations are not simplistic univariate analogs but are rather interdependent and complex *multilogs*.

The complexity of educational research is further accentuated by the factors of individual differences of learners and instructors. The nature of individual variability on a variety of abilities involved in the formulation of visual learning, thinking, and communication requires systematic study and research so that both it and its implications for educational practice are understood. One perplexing problem in the entire specter of the visual trinity is the problem of how to measure the involved abilities. In the tests already available, recognition is the most typical format in which responses are elicited. The manner in which a response is generated, and thus the cognitive strategy an individual employs, is not assessable using the recognition format. Also, the assessment of visual communication, I think, would certainly not be possible with recognition tests. Some sort of production response involving a rearrangement of visual sequence or utilizing new visual elements would appear to be required to provide valid assessment of visual communication abilities. This argument must not be construed as contradicting my conceptualization of the visual trinity as interdependent processes. The point is, rather, that a single response mode may not be adequate for the assessment of the diversity of visual skills and abilities that exist.

Several paired-associate or free-recall studies have demonstrated that pictures are learned better than words at normal rates of stimulus presentation (Levin, 1976). On the other hand, Paivio and Csapo (1969, 1971) have found that pictures are serially recalled more poorly than words when the presentation rate is too fast for verbal labeling to occur. Another exception to the general superiority of pictures over words was observed in experiments dealing with the acquisition and utilization of concepts and/or semantic categories (e.g., Katz & Paivio, 1975; Runquist & Hutt, 1961). Runquist and Hutt (1961) suggested that the immensity of unique perceptual cues associated with pictures impedes the formation or retrieval of broader, more abstractly defined concepts and results in "conceptual blindness." They supported this notion in their study, where the word-over-picture effect was diminished when pictures were used which perceptually highlighted the intended concept. If the larger number of perceptual cues available in pictures act as demonstrated in the Runquist and Hutt (1961) study, then how can the premise that pictures concretize the concepts or materials to be learned be justified? I think pictures have the potential of making the materials to be learned both *concrete* and *abstract*. Learner characteristics, task demands, and pictorial integrity interact, and the future research should be directed to reveal the variety of these interactions. Another related area of investigation which begs for answers is the attributional saliency of pictures for a variety of learning tasks and a number of learner types. Several practical research questions remain as to where, when, and why imagery and internal representation of the visual would act as organizational strategies.

We can say at this juncture that a good theoretical and applied beginning has been made in the area of visual learning, thinking, and communication. Many issues remain unresolved. However, interest in this area is high. Future advances would depend, to a large extent, upon the systematic pursuit of research, development, and evaluation in an interdisciplinary perspective. Let us hope that those who are interested in this area are not disappointed with the future outcomes!

ACKNOWLEDGMENT

I am indebted to my colleague, William Coffman, for many valuable comments and suggestions during the preparation of this chapter. For all the flaws that remain I bear full responsibility.

REFERENCES

Arnheim, R. *Visual thinking.* Berkeley: Univ. of California Press, 1969.

Ausubel, D. P. The influence of experience on the development of intelligence. In M. J. Aschner & C. E. Bisch (Eds.), *Productive thinking in education.* Washington, D.C.: National Education Association, 1965. Pp. 45–62.

Bogen, J. E. The other side of the brain II. An appositional mind. *Bulletin of the Los Angeles Neurological Society,* 1969, *34,* 135–162.

Broudy, H. S. On knowing with. In H. S. Broudy (Ed.), *Proceedings of the philosophy of education society: Studies in philosophy and education.* Edwardsville, Illinois: Southern Illinois Univ., 1970. Pp. 89–103.

Broudy, H. S. *The real world of the public schools.* New York: Harcourt, 1972.

Chomsky, N. Interview with N. Chomsky. In S. Rosner & L. E. Abt (Eds.), *The creative experience.* New York: Grossman, 1970.

Ghiselin, B. *The creative process.* Berkeley: Univ. of California Press, 1952.

Gibson, E. J. *Principles of perceptual learning and development.* New York: Appleton, 1969.

Glass, G. V. Primary, secondary, and meta-analysis of research. *Educational Researcher,* 1976, *5*(10), 3–8.

Hochberg, J., & Brooks, V. Pictorial recognition as an unlearned ability: A study of one child's performance. *American Journal of Psychology,* 1962, *75,* 624–628.

Hunt, D. E., & Sullivan, E. V. *Between psychology and education.* Hinsdale, Illinois: Dryden Press, 1974.

Katz, A. N., & Paivio, A. Imagery variables in concept identification. *Journal of Verbal Learning and Verbal Behavior,* 1975, *14,* 284–293.

Kuhn, T. S. *Structure of scientific revolutions.* Chicago: Univ. of Chicago Press, 1962.

Levin, J. R. What have we learned about maximizing what children learn? In J. R. Levin & W. Allen (Eds.), *Cognitive learning in children: Theories and strategies.* New York: Academic Press, 1976.

McKim, R. H. *Experiences in visual thinking*. Monterey, California: Brooks/Cole, 1972

Neisser, U. *Cognitive psychology*. New York: Appleton, 1967.

Paivio, A. On the functional significance of imagery. *Psychological Bulletin*, 1970, *73*, 385–392.

Paivio, A., & Csapo, K. Concrete image and verbal memory codes. *Journal of Experimental Psychology*, 1969, *80*, 279–285.

Paivio, A., & Csapo, K. Short-term sequential memory for pictures and words. *Psychonomic Science*, 1971, *24*, 50–51.

Palermo, D. Imagery in children's learning: Discussion. *Psychological Bulletin*, 1970, *73*, 415–421.

Penfield, W. Interview with W. Penfield. In S. Rosner & L. E. Abt. (Eds.), *The creative experience*. New York: Grossman, 1970.

Petrie, H. G. Do you see what I see? The epistemology of interdisciplinary inquiry. *Educational Researcher*, 1976, *5*(2), 9–15.

Piaget, J. *The psychology of intelligence*. New York: Harcourt, 1950.

Piaget, J. Foreword. In B. Inhelder & H. H. Chipman (Eds.), *Piaget and his school: A reader in developmental psychology*. New York: Springer-Verlag, 1976.

Piaget, J., & Inhelder, B. The gaps in empiricism. In B. Inhelder & H. H. Chipman (Eds.), *Piaget and his school: A reader in developmental psychology*. New York: Springer-Verlag, 1976. Pp. 24–35.

Randhawa, B. S. Nonverbal information storage in children and developmental information processing channel capacity. *Journal of Experimental Child Psychology*, 1972, *13*, 58–70.

Randhawa, B. S. Perceptual information processing of different visual stimuli by eight-year-old children. *Journal of Experimental Child Psychology*, 1973, *16*, 55–62.

Rosner, S., & Abt, L. E. *The creative experience*. New York: Grossman, 1970.

Runquist, W. N., & Hutt, V. H. Verbal concept learning in high school students with pictorial and verbal representation of stimuli. *Journal of Educational Psychology*, 1961, *52*, 108–111

Sperry, R. W. Lateral specialization of cerebral function in the surgically separated hemispheres. In F. J. McGuigan (Ed.), *The psychophysiology of thinking*. New York: Academic Press, 1973

Thomson, R. *The psychology of thinking*. Baltimore, Maryland: Penguin Books, 1959.

Tolman, E. C. *Purposive behavior in animals and men*. New York: Appleton, 1932.

Underwood, B. J., & Shaughnessy, J. J. *Experimentation in psychology*. New York: Wiley, 1975.

Name Index

Numbers in italics refer to the pages on which the complete references are listed.

Subject Index